Global Civil Society

For many commentators, global civil society is revolutionising our approach to global politics as new non-state-based and border-free expressions of political community challenge territorial sovereignty as the exclusive basis for political community and identity. This challenge 'from below' to the nation-state system is increasingly seen as promising nothing less than a reconstruction, or re-imagination, of world politics itself. Whether in terms of the democratisation of the institutions of global governance, the spread of human rights across the world, or the emergence of a global citizenry in a world-wide public sphere, global civil society is understood by many to provide the agency necessary to these hoped-for transformations.

Global Civil Society asks whether global civil society is such a qualitatively new phenomenon after all; whether the transformation of the states' system is actually within its reach; and what some of its drawbacks might be. The authors explore and critically evaluate a variety of perspectives: the cosmopolitan vision; the view of global civil society as transnational movements advocating a growing moralisation of world politics; and more sceptical views, advancing new possibilities for understanding the role of non-state actors in global politics.

This book brings together for the first time the whole range of established and alternative voices on global civil society, both congratulatory and critical, to set a marker for the state of the debate about global civil society today. This book will be invaluable for students and researchers in the fields of International Politics, Democratisation and Civil Society.

Gideon Baker is a lecturer in Political Theory at the University of Salford. He is the author of *Civil Society and Democratic Theory: Alternative Voices* (also published by Routledge). **David Chandler** is a senior lecturer in International Relations at The Centre for the Study of Democracy, The University of Westminster. He is the author of *Constructing Global Civil Society: Morality and Power in International Relations*; *From Kosovo to Kabul: Human Rights and International Intervention*; and *Bosnia: Faking Democracy after Dayton*.

Routledge advances in international relations and global politics

1 **Foreign Policy and Discourse Analysis**
France, Britain and Europe
Henrik Larsen

2 **Agency, Structure and International Politics**
From ontology to empirical enquiry
Gil Friedman and Harvey Starr

3 **The Political Economy of Regional Co-operation in the Middle East**
Ali Carkoglu, Mine Eder and Kemal Kirisci

4 **Peace Maintenance**
The evolution of international political authority
Jarat Chopra

5 **International Relations and Historical Sociology**
Breaking down boundaries
Stephen Hobden

6 **Equivalence in Comparative Politics**
Edited by Jan W. van Deth

7 **The Politics of Central Banks**
Robert Elgie and Helen Thompson

8 **Politics and Globalisation**
Knowledge, ethics and agency
Martin Shaw

9 **History and International Relations**
Thomas W. Smith

10 **Idealism and Realism in International Relations**
Robert M. A. Crawford

11 **National and International Conflicts, 1945–1995**
New empirical and theoretical approaches
Frank Pfetsch and Christoph Rohloff

12 **Party Systems and Voter Alignments Revisited**
Edited by Lauri Karvonen and Stein Kuhnle

13 **Ethics, Justice and International Relations**
Constructing an international community
Peter Sutch

14 **Capturing Globalization**
Edited by James H. Mittelman and Norani Othman

15 **Uncertain Europe**
Building a new European security order?
Edited by Martin A. Smith and Graham Timmins

16 **Power, Postcolonialism and International Relations**
Reading race, gender and class
Edited by Geeta Chowdhry and Sheila Nair

17 **Constituting Human Rights**
Global civil society and the society of democratic states
Mervyn Frost

18 **US Economic Statecraft for Survival 1933–1991**
Of sanctions, embargoes and economic warfare
Alan P. Dobson

19 **The EU and NATO Enlargement**
Richard McAllister and Roland Dannreuther

20 **Spatializing International Politics**
Analysing activism on the Internet
Jayne Rodgers

21 **Ethnonationalism in the Contemporary World**
Walker Connor and the study of Nationalism
Edited by Daniele Conversi

22 **Meaning and International Relations**
Edited by Peter Mandaville and Andrew Williams

23 **Political Loyalty and the Nation-State**
Edited by Michael Waller and Andrew Linklater

24 **Russian Foreign Policy and the CIS**
Theories, debates and actions
Nicole J. Jackson

25 **Asia and Europe**
Development and different dimensions of ASEM
Yeo Lay Hwee

26 **Global Instability and Strategic Crisis**
Neville Brown

27 **Africa in International Politics**
External involvement on the Continent
Edited by Ian Taylor and Paul Williams

28 **Global Governmentality**
Governing international spaces
Edited by Wendy Larner and William Walters

29 **Political Learning and Citizenship Education Under Conflict**
The political socialization of Israeli and Palestinian youngsters
Orit Ichilov

30 **Gender and Civil Society**
Transcending boundaries
Edited by Jude Howell and Diane Mulligan

31 **State Crises, Globalisation and National Movements in North-East Africa**
Edited by Asafa Jalata

32 **Global Civil Society**
Contested futures
Edited by Gideon Baker and David Chandler

Global Civil Society

Contested futures

**Edited by Gideon Baker and
David Chandler**

 Routledge
Taylor & Francis Group

LONDON AND NEW YORK

First published 2005
by Routledge
2 Park Square, Milton Park, Abingdon, Oxon OX14 4RN

Simultaneously published in the USA and Canada
by Routledge
270 Madison Ave, New York, NY 10016

Routledge is an imprint of the Taylor & Francis Group

© 2005 Gideon Baker and David Chandler for selection and editorial matter; individual contributors for their contribution

Typeset in Times by Wearset Ltd, Boldon, Tyne and Wear
Printed and bound in Great Britain by MPG Books Ltd, Bodmin

British Library Cataloguing in Publication Data
A catalogue record for this book is available from the British Library

Library of Congress Cataloging in Publication Data
A catalog record for this book has been requested

ISBN 0–415–35480–3

Contents

Notes on contributors   ix

**Introduction: global civil society and the future of world
politics**   1
GIDEON BAKER AND DAVID CHANDLER

PART 1
Global civil society – contesting current trends   15

1 **Global civil society: analytical category or normative concept?**   17
   ALEJANDRO COLÁS

2 **Cosmocracy and global civil society**   34
   JOHN KEANE

3 **The demoralised subject of global civil society**   52
   VANESSA PUPAVAC

4 **The changing role of global civil society**   69
   RICHARD FALK

5 **Contextualising the 'anti-capitalism' movement in global civil
   society**   85
   JAMES HEARTFIELD

PART 2
Global civil society – contesting future possibilities   101

6 **The idea of global civil society**   103
   MARY KALDOR

7   **Saying global civil society with rights**   114
    GIDEON BAKER

8   **Global civil society: thinking politics and progress**   130
    KIMBERLY HUTCHINGS

9   **Constructing global civil society**   149
    DAVID CHANDLER

10 **Global civil society and global governmentality: resistance,
    reform or resignation?**   171
    RONNIE D. LIPSCHUTZ

11 **Global civil society as politics of faith**   186
    VOLKER HEINS

    Index   202

Contributors

Gideon Baker is a lecturer in Political Theory at the University of Salford. He is the author of *Civil Society and Democratic Theory: Alternative Voices* (2002). His publications on global civil society include the widely cited 'Problems in the Theorisation of Global Civil Society' (*Political Studies*, 2002). His work has also appeared in *Critical Review of International Social and Political Philosophy*, *Journal of Political Ideologies*, *Democratization*, *Contemporary Politics* and *Space and Polity*. He is currently writing a book on New Theories of Democracy.

David Chandler is a senior lecturer in International Relations at The Centre for the Study of Democracy, The University of Westminster. He is the author of *Constructing Global Civil Society: Morality and Power in International Relations* (2004); *From Kosovo to Kabul: Human Rights and International Intervention* (2002); and *Bosnia: Faking Democracy after Dayton* (2000). He is also editor of *Rethinking Human Rights: Critical Approaches to International Politics* (2002) and of numerous journal articles on IR, human rights, cosmopolitan citizenship, humanitarian intervention, democratisation, peace-building and the Balkan protectorates.

Alejandro Colás is a lecturer in International Relations in the School of Politics and Sociology at Birkbeck, University of London. He is author of *International Civil Society: Social Movements in World Politics* (2002) and is currently writing a book on Empire for the Polity Press Key Concepts series. His main interests lie in IR theory; social movements in IR; historical sociology and the international politics of the Maghreb region. His work has appeared in *Millennium*, *Global Society* and the *Journal of North African Studies*. He is a member of the editorial board of *Historical Materialism*.

Richard Falk is Albert G. Milbank Professor of International Law and Practice, Emeritus Visiting Professor, Global Studies, University of California, Santa Barbara (2001–04); and Chair of the Board, Nuclear Age Peace Foundation. His recent research has focused on various aspects of international relations, with an emphasis on the role of international law and institutions. His most recent books are *The Great Terror War* (2003), *Religion and Humane Global Governance* (2002), and *Human Rights Horizons* (2001).

James Heartfield teaches economics on the University of Delaware's London programme, and wrote *The 'Death of the Subject' Explained* (2002).

Volker Heins is a fellow at the Carr Center for Human Rights Policy at Harvard University and a senior researcher at the Institute for Social Research in Frankfurt, Germany. Recent publications include: 'Globalisierung und soziales Leid', in A. Honneth (ed.), *Befreiung aus der Mündigkeit. Paradoxien des gegenwärtigen Kapitalismus* (2002); 'Modernity and life politics: conceptualizing the biodiversity crisis', *Political Geography* (2002) (with Michael Flitner); 'Germany's New War: 11 September and Its Aftermath in German Quality Newspapers', *German Politics* (2002); 'How to Meet the First Public Obligation: Contending Discourses in Humanitarian Organizations', Research Report, Carr Center for Human Rights Policy, Harvard University (2004); 'Civil Society's Barbarisms', *European Journal of Social Theory* (forthcoming). He is currently doing research on human rights cultures in France, Germany and the US.

Kimberly Hutchings is a reader in International Relations at the London School of Economics. She is the author of: *Kant, Critique and Politics* (1996); *International Political Theory: Re-thinking Ethics in a Global Era* (1999); *Hegel and Feminist Philosophy* (2003); and co-editor, with Roland Dannreuther, of *Cosmopolitan Citizenship* (1999). She is a founder editor of the journal *Contemporary Political Theory* and currently Associate Editor of the *European Journal of International Relations*. Her interests range across the fields of continental and feminist philosophy, international ethics and international political theory.

Mary Kaldor is Professor in Global Governance and Programme Director of the Centre for the Study of Global Governance, The London School of Economics. She is author of *Global Civil Society: An Answer to War* (2003), a co-editor of the influential *Global Civil Society Yearbook*, and the author of numerous articles and book chapters on global civil society and democratisation.

John Keane is Professor of Politics at The University of Westminster. In 1989, he founded The Centre for the Study of Democracy there. Among his many books are *The Media and Democracy* (1991); *Democracy and Civil Society* (1988; 1998); *Reflections on Violence* (1996); *Civil Society: Old Images, New Visions* (1998); *Tom Paine: A Political Life* (1995); and *Václav Havel: A Political Tragedy in Six Acts* (1999).

His most recent work is *Global Civil Society?* (2003). He is currently writing a full-scale history of democracy – the first for over a century.

Ronnie D. Lipschutz is Professor of Politics and Associate Director of the Center for Global, International and Regional Studies at the University of California, Santa Cruz. His primary areas of research and teaching include international politics, global environmental affairs, US foreign policy, globalisation, international regulation, and film, fiction and politics. His most recent books include *Global Environmental Politics: Power, Perspectives and Practice* (2004); *After Authority – War, Peace and Global Politics in the 21st Century* (2000); and *Cold War Fantasies – Film, Fiction and Foreign Policy* (2001).

Vanessa Pupavac is a lecturer in the School of Politics, University of Nottingham. She has worked as a consultant for the UN, the ODI, the OSCE and other international organisations and has published widely on human rights and international psychosocial approaches. She was awarded the Otto Klineberg Intercultural and International Relations Award 2003 for her article 'Pathologizing Populations and Colonizing Minds: International Psychosocial Programs in Kosovo', which appeared in the journal *Alternatives* in 2002.

Introduction

Global civil society and the future of world politics

Gideon Baker and David Chandler

For an increasing number of commentators, global civil society represents nothing less than the outline of a future world political order within which states will no longer constitute the seat of sovereignty, a status first bestowed on them by the Treaty of Westphalia in Europe (1648) and subsequently exported around the globe. For many, global civil society is revolutionising our approach to sovereignty as new non-state-based and border-free expressions of political community challenge territorial sovereignty as the exclusive basis for political community and identity (Falk, 1995: 100). This challenge 'from below' to the nation-state system is increasingly seen as promising nothing less than a reconstruction, or re-imagination of world politics itself (Lipschutz, 1992: 391). Whether in terms of the democratisation of the institutions of global governance, the spread of human rights across the world, or the emergence of a global citizenry in a world-wide public sphere, global civil society is understood to provide the agency necessary to these hoped-for transformations.

The 'stakes' in narrating global civil society – understanding its significance, analysing its potentialities – are therefore of the highest order. Yet, so far, much of this storytelling has been uncritical. For the most part, we find transnational movements and events 'beneath' the level of the state placed under the rubric of global civil society with barely a thought as to the significance of a move to label and categorise thus. In addition, much of what is written is prepared to uncritically celebrate the arrival of transnational citizen action. What is required is more sober reflection on whether this form of action is such a qualitatively new phenomenon after all – what we might term global civil society *past*; whether the transformation of the states' system is actually within its reach – the *contested futures* of global civil society; and what some of its down-sides might be – the *dialectic* of a global-civil-society-based form of enlightenment.

None of this is to say that there is not a critical literature on global civil society. The problem seems to be, rather, that the hopeful and critical voices never meet, instead talking past each other and becoming unhelpfully polarised in the process. This book seeks to counteract this trend, to bring together for the first time the whole range of voices on global civil society so that their various merits might be considered more carefully. In the process of this bringing together we also hope to clarify key positions within the burgeoning discourse of global civil society and the chief points of overlap and disagreement between them – to set a marker for the state of the debate today. However, this collection is not just about setting established voices in a framework for comparing and contrasting; alternatives to the recognised approaches are also put forward. Many of the authors provide *new* perspectives on what global civil society – either as discourse or practice – means today.

Having considered the aims of this book, we now seek to put it in its wider context, to provide a short introduction of what we see as the key points in the debate so far about global civil society. Following this, a brief overview of the structure of the book, and of the individual chapters, is provided.

Optimism in the world-transformatory potential of global civil society is grounded in the view that the nation-state, which long held a central position in the international order, has been increasingly sidelined by new international actors, some of these operating from 'above' in the form of the growth of new forms of global governance, but also from 'below' – witness the plethora of non-state actors and networks which operate on an international level. The boundaries of sovereignty, once seen to clearly structure world politics, now seem to be much more 'fuzzy' at the edges. As a result, though necessary to an understanding of the mechanisms shaping the international order in the twenty-first century, states are felt to be far from sufficient to such understanding. Rather than states bearing all the agency in the determination of world affairs, it appears to many that a new actor has appeared, an actor whose precise shape and contours may be indeterminate and disputed, but whose presence is not: global civil society.

Global civil society is seen by numerous analysts as the principle driver behind an extension of the rule of law and political community – *societas civilis* – beyond national boundaries; as something like a world citizenry in the process of constituting itself 'from below'. Mary Kaldor, for example, argues that the end of the global conflict of the Cold War 'allows for the domestication of international relations and the participation of citizens, and citizen groups at an international level' which was previously the preserve of governments (Kaldor, 2003: 13). For other commentators, while global civil society cannot yet be seen as a certain route to this global citizenship, at the very least it inspires us – requires us – to consider it as never before. Thus for John Keane, 'brand new democratic thinking – implicit in the theory of global civil society – is required' in the face of the growing lack of accountability of global governance (Keane, 2003: 126).

On the most optimistic readings, it appears that the international realm is in the process of a deep transformation as a result of this 'pressure from below'. No longer exclusively the sphere of violence and competition, of the 'war of all against all', the international realm is increasingly a space where transnational actors *and* the transnational values they sponsor – an emerging global ethic or 'law of humanity' orientated around human rights – work to overcome the narrow self-interest of national elites. For Jean Grugel, the global civil society approach therefore represents 'an overt attempt to blend normative theory with international relations' (Grugel, 2003: 275). This can be seen in the work of Kaldor, for example, who asserts that: 'The new meaning of civil society offers expanded possibilities for human emancipation' (Kaldor, 2003: 143). For John Clark, also, 'the time is ripe for "ethical globalisation" morally underpinned by new activist citizens' networks' (Clark, 2001: 18).

Global civil society theorists cover an increasingly wide range of perspectives and views. Yet despite their differences, most approaches focus on the break between old forms of 'citizenship' tied to the nation-state and new forms of moral and political community. Most also locate global civic actors as the source of ethical action in the world, and their break from conventional state-based politics as the strategic basis for radical political change. Below we sketch out the different levels on which this case is built, starting with the empirical.

The empirical case

The most important empirical trend since the end of the Cold War is alleged to be the development of a global civil society, bringing with it new ways of doing politics or of establishing moral-political communities. As Ann Florini states (2001: 30): 'The state system that has governed the world for centuries is neither divinely ordained nor easily swept away. It is, however, changing, and one of the most dramatic changes concerns the growing role of transnational civil society'.

The numbers of international NGOs had grown from 176 in 1909 to 28,900 by 1993 (CCG, 1995). The early 1990s witnessed a huge increase in the number of non-state actors involved in international policy. The number of development NGOs registered in the OECD countries of the industrialised 'North' grew from 1,600 in 1980 to 2,970 in 1993 and their total spending doubled, rising from US$2.8 billion to US$5.7 billion. In the 'South', the growth in the registered numbers of NGOs was even more impressive – for example, figures for Nepal show an increase from 220 in 1990 to 1,210 in 1993; in Bolivia, from 100 in 1980 to 530 in 1993; and in Tunisia, from 1,886 in 1988 to 5,186 in 1991 (Hulme and Edwards, 1997: 4).

Jessica Mathews argues that we are witnessing nothing less than a historic reversal of the post-Westphalian trend to increasingly concentrate power in the hands of states; so much so in fact that 'increasingly, NGOs are able to push around even the largest governments' (Mathews, 1997: 53). In another influential article, Lester Salamon, claimed that 'we are in the midst of a global "associational revolution" that may prove to be as significant to the latter twentieth century as the rise of the nation-state was to the latter nineteenth' (Salamon, 1994: 109).

It is in assessing the *significance* of these empirical trends, trends that few would dispute, that the normative approach to global civil society becomes enmeshed with this narrative of its growth. Thus according to many analysts the growth of the non-state sector, in threatening the political monopoly of nation-states in international decision-making, suggests nothing less than an emerging alternative view of political community from that suggested by states and the market – previously the only players in town. Global civil society represents a 'third force' capable of empowering citizens and possibly transforming the international system itself. Claims of this order come attached to an understanding that global civil society is indeed restructuring our sense of, and approach to, the political. For Kaldor, the *site* of politics itself 'has shifted from formal national institutions to new local and cross-border spaces and this is, to a large extent, the consequence of global civil society activities' (Kaldor, 2003: 148).

The normative case

Like the concept of human rights, few people today would argue against the normative or ethical concept of global civil society. Even those who may dispute the existence of global civil society in practice would not argue against the use of the concept to highlight a positive normative goal or ideal (see Van Rooy, 1998: 30; Kumar, 1993: 388).

What then are the goals or ideals suggested by the idea of a global civil society? Three seem particularly salient. First, the *extension of political community*, as international politics is no longer seen as a political sphere limited to the narrow national interests of states but as increasingly open to non-state actors working with a more universal human interest in mind. Second, positing the actions of global civil society as a major determinant of world politics re-emphasises *human agency* in the face of the determinism of a neo-liberal 'end of history'. Finally, global civil society appears to portend the *extension of democracy* beyond national boundaries, where it is perceived that decision-making has increasingly escaped 'above' and beyond the control of nation-state-based democratic institutions.

The extension of community

Global civic activism is seen as restoring collective values as a counterweight to the atomising individualism and political apathy reflected in the institutions of formal, state-based, politics. According to Richard Falk: 'globalisation from below extends the sense of community, loosening the ties between sovereignty and community but building a stronger feeling of identity with the sufferings and aspirations of peoples, a wider "we"'

(Falk, 1995: 89). For Mary Kaldor (2003: 2) too, such processes 'have opened up new possibilities for political emancipation':

> Whether we are talking about isolated dissidents in repressive regimes, landless labourers in Central America or Asia, global campaigns against landmines or third world debt . . . what has changed are the opportunities for linking up with other like-minded groups in different parts of the world, and for addressing demands not just to the state but to global institutions and other states . . . In other words, a new form of politics, which we call civil society, is both an outcome and an agent of global interconnectedness.

In such accounts, the promise of global civil society is not only that it offers up a new, more engaged and participatory way of doing politics, but also a new, more ethical, way of constructing political community. For normative theorists such as Andrew Linklater, the problem that global civil society is beginning to address is that the nation-state restricts the bounds of moral reasoning to the 'boundaries of political association' (Linklater, 1981: 27). Linklater argues that the obligations of citizens to states have acted as a historical constraint on humanity's moral and political development. In an internationalised social environment the self-determination of the individual, man's capacity to 'participate in the control of his total political environment', is restricted by the territorial limitations of sovereignty. Linklater suggests that these political and moral limits are historically conditioned (1981: 34). The solution is that of radical political struggle to resolve the tensions between the moral duties of men and the political duties of citizens through the 'actualization of a higher form of international political life [which] requires [a] radical critique of the state' and the formation of a broader, more inclusive community (Linklater, 1981: 35). For many, global civil society promises just such a community.

Human agency

The second attraction of the notion of a global civil society is that it posits the need for radical human agency in contrast to the perceived economic determinism of globalisation theory. As Naomi Klein reported from the first annual World Social Forum in Porto Alegre, Brazil: 'Many people said they felt history being made in that room. What I felt was something more intangible: the end of the End of History' (Klein, 2002: 193). By challenging the 'end of history' thesis, which suggests the end of radical alternatives to capitalist liberal democracy, global civic advocates reaffirm the potential for change (Heins, 2000: 37).

Globalisation is often considered to be the central problematic of international relations today. The neo-liberal perspective of the end of politics and domination of the free market, with states powerless to shape economic and social policy, is often presented as the backdrop which makes necessary the agency of global civil society and a restoration of the political on a new basis:

> Civil society is a process of management of society that is "bottom-up" rather than "top-down" and that involves the struggle for emancipatory goals. It is about governance based on consent where consent is generated through politics. In a global context, civil society offers a way of understanding the process of globalisation in terms of subjective human agency instead of a disembodied deterministic process of "interconnectedness".
>
> (Kaldor, 2003: 142)

The extension of democracy

Perhaps most popularly and enthusiastically, the project of global civil society is held to challenge the non-democratic structures of global governance emerging in the wake of globalisation. For Mary Kaldor, global civil society expands the sphere of 'active citizenship', referring to 'growing self-organization outside formal political circles and expanded space in which individual citizens can influence the conditions in which they live both directly through self-organization and through political pressure' (Kaldor, 2003: 8). Richard Falk also argues that global civic resistance 'from below' counters the problem of 'power' going global while traditional democratic institutions remain local. Global civil society movements 'carry the possibility of an extension of the movement for democratisation beyond state/society relations to all arenas of power and authority' (Falk, 1995: 35).

Rather than states being the space of democratic politics, the international sphere is increasingly viewed as the location of 'democratization from below through the articulation of radical and new forms of transnational citizenship and social mobilisation' (Grugel, 2003: 263). Mary Kaldor expands on these new mechanisms for world-wide democratisation created through global civic action, highlighting a role for global civil society in the representation of marginalised global constituencies and in providing internationalised spaces for a world-wide public to deliberate in:

> Global civil society does provide a way to supplement traditional democracy. It is a medium through which individuals can, in principle, participate in global public debates; it offers the possibility for the voices of the victims of globalisation to be heard if not the votes. And it creates new fora for deliberation on the complex issues of the contemporary world, in which the various parties to the discussion do not only represent state interest.
>
> (Kaldor, 2003: 148)

This book

As we have seen, Mary Kaldor is correct in noting that, despite the ambiguities involved in the concept of global civil society, all versions 'are both normative and descriptive'. Writers and advocates are both describing an emancipatory 'political project, i.e. a goal, and at the same time an actually existing reality, which may not measure up to the goal' (Kaldor, 2003: 11).

While all commentary on global civil society is implicitly or explicitly normative, there is nonetheless a useful heuristic distinction to be made between those commentaries that are mostly concerned with the ability of the concept to capture important aspects of how world politics *is* changing today, and those that are interested primarily in interrogating the concept of global civil society as an attempt to re-imagine what the future of world politics *might be*. Both such approaches are properly analytical, though the former analyses more directly the empirical evidence on global civil society, while the latter is concerned to a greater degree with how global civil society is imagined. The chapters in this book are accordingly divided into two parts that reflect this difference of approach. Part 1, the more empirical, brings together chapters *contesting current trends*, while Part 2, the more conceptual, includes chapters *contesting future possibilities*.

In the rest of this Introduction, a short resume of the chapters is provided.

In Part 1, Alejandro Colás's opening chapter argues for an alternative reading of global civil society to the dominant view that it is a (liberal) normative programme to be promoted and actualised. Colás seeks instead to develop an understanding of global civil society as a historical reality, rather than as a political project; as a specifically modern site of socio-political struggle which contains very diverse, often incompatible, ideological projects. Reading global civil society in this way requires identifying the concrete structures and processes which are bearers of the ethical norms and values associated with global civil society, rather than the other way round.

Colás illustrates this core argument by looking at the particular experience of civil society under colonial and post-colonial rule in the Maghreb, suggesting that the notion of global civil society has at once an older and more contested history than is usually allowed for in contemporary discussions. One consequence of this, he concludes, is that many expressions of contemporary global civil society can be seen as negative socio-political reactions to the very attempts at promoting global civil society as a liberal 'project to be realised'.

John Keane, in the second chapter, is in agreement with Colás that global civil society is not a single, unified domain, though this does not suggest to him that it is a meaningless construct either. Quite the contrary, since it contains within it a pressing constitutional agenda which must be conceptualised in fresh ways: the need to go beyond the present clutter of global political institutions in order to find new governing arrangements that enable something like effective and democratically accountable government, the rule of law and more equitable and freer social relations to develop on a global scale.

Keane argues that rising to the challenge of this new constitutional agenda for global governance – as suggested by global civil society in the making – requires in the first instance that we understand extant global governance. This will not be easy, but it must be done as a necessary precondition for the bold leap of imagination needed to achieve political change on a global scale. So it is to furthering understanding of global governance today which Keane devotes his chapter. The principal thesis here is that a new form of governmental power is emerging in the world today that Keane calls *cosmocracy*. Cosmocracy describes a type of institutionalised power that defies all previous accounts of different governmental forms. Cosmocracy is the first-ever world polity, a world-wide web of interdependence. It stands on the spectrum between the 'Westphalian' model of competing sovereign states and a single, unitary system of world government. Yet it also functions as something more and other than an international community of otherwise sovereign governments, being a much messier, more complex type of polity. For Keane, the essence of cosmocracy is a conglomeration of interlocking and overlapping sub-state, state and supra-state institutions and processes that have political and social effects on a global scale. And it is this form of governance that sets the scene for action in global civil society today.

For Vanessa Pupavac in Chapter 3, the ethos of global civil society is very far from pressing us towards more progressive forms of global governance, as Keane imagines it might. Instead, the discourse of global civil society is seen as echoing some of the worst features of the ideals of nineteenth-century liberal imperialism. Pupavac views the rights-based global governance sought by global civil society enthusiasts as promoting a demoralised, agency-free, image of the human subject who requires the promotion of his or her rights 'from without'. Pupavac contrasts this approach with classical social contract thinking, which she argues presupposed the moral agency of rights-holding citizens. Suspicion of the moral capacity of political majorities has led human rights advocacy to exhibit a preference for the codification of supranational frameworks beyond national political processes. In other words, there is a retreat from the modern ideal of law as derived from the will of legal subjects and a moral division is created between a global ethical elite of moral agents and the mass of citizens globally.

Pupavac seeks to expose this moral claim coming from global civil society as a will to power *by* global civil society. In claiming all virtue, global civil society is also disclaiming its own will to sovereignty. For none other than global civil society would be acting as sovereign by determining human rights norms and the conditions of their application. Under such a therapeutic ethos, Pupavac suggests, rights now denote rights of external therapeutic intervention rather than real freedoms.

In Chapter 4, Richard Falk provides a much more optimistic reading of global civil society in the world today, arguing for a view of its ethos and practices as progressive and emancipatory. Falk first sets out to chart the development of global civil society to date as a means to considering just what has been achieved and what might yet be achieved. Falk sees progression through three stages up until now. The first phase he associates with the activities of NGOs and popular movements in relation to specific issue areas, especially war/peace, the environment, human rights and women. Falk's second phase focuses upon the mobilisation of society to achieve democratisation and self-determination, including arenas of decision-making beyond the territorial state. This phase achieved prominence in the latter stages of the Cold War, exhibited in the form of movements (such as the Green Party in Germany) of opposition to the established order of the state and of geopolitics generally. Finally, the third phase of development for global civil society occurred in the period following immediately after the Cold War, and can be divided into two aspects: an anti-globalisation movement and a global justice movement. Civil society actors in this period became animated by the growing evidence that multinational corporations and international banks were escaping from the regulatory authority of sovereign states and shaping global policy on the basis of profits rather than human wellbeing.

In the remainder of his chapter, Falk considers three possible scenarios for the future of global civil society after September 11 and the subsequent 'war on terror'. In the first scenario, the United States generates a global resistance movement that is fearful of an American Empire. The second scenario is of a return to the approach of the 1990s and involves relying upon an improved framework for inter-governmental law enforcement against non-state actors engaging in transnational political violence. But though beyond the horizon of immediate plausibility, there exists for Falk a hoped-for third possibility – the potential for a non-utopian geopolitics premised on non-violence, governability, the rule of law and global democracy. It is Falk's view that the implicit ideology of global civil society is increasingly an affirmation of this vision of the future; to the extent that moves in this direction can be taken, therefore, the degree of implausibility is diminished.

Returning to a more sceptical view of the politics of global civil society, in Chapter 5 James Heartfield explores the interaction between 'anti-capitalism' as a celebrated example of global civil society activism, and the business, government and international financial institutional elites they seek to challenge. He argues that, far from being genuinely radical and suggestive of a renewed world-politics, anti-capitalist protest is actually motivated by the same doubts that beset international elites, only this time represented in oppositional form. Specifically, these doubts arise from the disappearance of the class-based organisations of the old left, which leads radicals, now shorn of a popular base, into a similar crisis of confidence to the capitalist elites who are increasingly aware of their own disengagement from any political constituency.

For Heartfield, the ironic convergence of interest of anti-capitalism and capitalist elites is then found in the emergence of Non-Governmental Organisations. The importance of NGOs for capitalist elites is that they represent a 'moderate bridge' between the protestors and those behind the barbed-wire defences. The importance of NGOs for anti-capitalism is that they are its organisational form, ensuring its coherence as a movement.

In Part 2 of the book, Mary Kaldor opens with a chapter (Chapter 6) arguing for the tradition of Kantian cosmopolitanism and suggesting that this is much more realistic than it was 30 years ago due to globalisation. Kaldor argues that this is because the growing interconnectedness of states, the emergence of a system of global governance, and, most importantly, the explosion of global civil society, have called into question the primacy of states.

After considering the re-emergence of civil society discourse and practice in the 1980s and its subsequent development in the 1990s, Kaldor turns to the question of the future of global civil society. She suggests that despite the setback of September 11 and the 'war on terror', global civil society, especially the activist strand, has not gone away. In particular, Kaldor celebrates new synergies between the anti-globalisation movement and the peace movement, which she sees bursting forth in a global anti-war movement of historically unprecedented size and geographical spread. For Kaldor, the idea of global civil society is thus an emancipatory one, since it suggests that whatever happens in the future depends on politics, on the agency of people who make history.

Gideon Baker's chapter (Chapter 7) follows on from Kaldor's, though in a more critical vein, by focusing its attention on her suggestion (and those who make a similar case) that global civil society suggests a future form of politics 'beyond' the state. He argues that the now dominant vision of how global civil society might achieve such a post-Westphalian order – what he terms the 'globalisation from below' view – actually fails to re-imagine world politics in any substantive way, instead collapsing back into a familiar liberal discourse which valorises a rights-based approach to the political.

Such a turn towards 'saying global civil society with rights' is problematic, Baker suggests, for requiring fixed points of sovereignty from which to bestow such rights (institutions of global government), which constitutes a return to statist politics at precisely the moment when an alternative vision and practice of world politics is being attributed to global civil society. Thus, for Baker, we have a concept of global civil society that does the most to celebrate its capacity to move us 'beyond' Westphalia while doing the least to suggest a real alternative.

Kimberly Hutchings' chapter (Chapter 8) is similarly concerned with the ways in which new ways of thinking about the political might be required by the idea of a global civil society. Hutchings identifies a common thread in the counter-narratives to realist accounts of international politics within which the promise of global civil society plays such a significant part. This common thread is the reconceptualisation of international political time in terms which admit the possibility of transnational or global historical progress. Hutchings sketches out the two most influential counter-narratives here: the theories of cosmopolitanism and post-Marxist postmodernism. In both cases, Hutchings argues, there is an inadequate framework for the analysis and judgement of global civil society, and this is to do with the specific kinds of closure inherent in the modernist philosophies of history on which these frameworks rely – specifically an orientation to the present that posits the possibility of a lasting and reliable improvement of the human condition. The problem here does not lie in the invocation of progress *per se*, but in the tying of the idea of progress to a unifying temporality, which is seen as universal and is therefore able to ignore (de-historicise and de-politicise) its own particular historicity and politics.

The challenge for Hutchings, then, is to find a way to think the time of global civil society as world political time, without either denying the possibility of progress or occluding the colonising logic of unitary philosophies of world history. The most important step in this direction, she argues, involves paying more attention to the philosophical problem of how to conceptualise 'world' politics simultaneously in both holist and pluralist terms. Modernist philosophies of history and their realist counterparts both impede forms of thinking which are not binary and reductive. In their place, we need a form of thinking adequate to the complexity, interconnection, division, plurality and hierarchy by which global civil society is characterised.

In Chapter 9, David Chandler also turns his attention to how best to 'think' global civil society in relation to world politics. Chandler considers the implications for international relations theorising of the shift away from the more traditional concern with liberal institutionalism and towards transnational networks operating in global civil society. Chandler sees the case for the existence of global civil society as a still open one. But he considers that the constructivist framework puts the strongest case for the influence and power of non-state actors. Constructivist theory de-centres the subject of traditional international relations, the nation-state. Rather than the structure of anarchy creating states and state interests, in which case the needs of 'power' constitute ideas which further these interests, constructivists assert that understanding international relations in purely structural or 'rationalist' terms is inadequate. The power of ideas, or 'discourse', to shape interest and identity in the international sphere must also be considered.

Vis-à-vis the notion of global civil society, constructivism is able to bring non-state actors back into international relations theorising by focusing on the ways in which 'moral entrepreneurs' in this sector are capable of influencing and changing the policies, interests and even the 'identities' of nation-states. Chandler accepts along with constructivists that the international agenda has been transformed since the end of the Cold War and that non-state actors have become increasingly involved in policy-making at the state and inter-state level. However, he argues that, to date, constructivist approaches to global civil society seem to be driven more by a normative desire to support the 'principled-issues' advocated by non-state actors than by any clear analysis of the complex relationship between state and non-state actors.

In his chapter (Chapter 10), Ronnie Lipschutz continues with the project of how to understand the significance of global civil society in world politics. Lipschutz draws on the work of Michel Foucault and situates global civil society in 'global governmentality'. Governmentality is understood as a system of management, regulation and normalisation, and Lipschutz argues that much of global civil society is one element in the globalisation of governmentality, being thus political only in a rather impoverished sense.

Lipschutz begins with a discussion of Foucault's concept of 'governmentality' and the ways in which it has become globalised under a neo-liberal regime of discipline and control. From this view, global civil society is less a 'problem' for power than a product of power. Being deeply imbricated with the market, it is enmeshed with practices of governmentality and is a means whereby those matters that cannot or will not be addressed by the state or inter-state institutions will, nonetheless, be dealt with by someone. Thus Lipschutz asks us to recognise how particular forms of (global) society and governmentality are constituted and reconstituted sometimes through the very (global) agency that, at first glance, appears to be a means of opposition and resistance, if not liberation. For Lipschutz, global civil society must seek to incorporate much more *politics* into its activism in order to present genuine challenges to global governmentality and its political economy.

In the final chapter (Chapter 11), Volker Heins is also alive to what we might term the dialectic of a global-civil-society-based process of enlightenment. Yet Heins' version of this dialectic draws on Oakeshott rather than Foucault. Heins argues that global civil society theorists offer an account of civic transnationalism which follows a distinct style of reasoning, a reasoning which British philosopher Michael Oakeshott called the 'politics of faith'. Contrary to the 'politics of scepticism', which detaches politics and the activity of governing from the quest for human perfection, the politics of faith places an absolute trust in human reason and sees government (backed by nongovernmental forces) as the agent that will lead society on the road to perfection.

However, Heins is willing to concede that the vocabulary of global civil society is linked to powerful collective beliefs which have to be analysed in their own right. The idea of global civil society therefore cannot be reduced to an intellectual construct misrepresenting reality, since the idea itself has become part and parcel of an emerging reality of transnational civic activism. In other words: the idea or imagination of global civil society has begun to inspire real groups by entering their self-conceptions and their agendas of social and political change. To a lesser extent, but similar to nations or ethnic communities – entities that do not exist outside the mutual expectations of their members – global civil society is real because of belief and the relationships these beliefs inspire. Be this as it may, Heins seeks to challenge what he sees as the ultimately faith-based certainties entertained by global civil society theorists, calling for a stronger emphasis on a 'politics of scepticism', which, though it would share many of the normative concerns of global civil society advocates, would resist subscribing to their overall project.

References

CGG (1995) The Commission on Global Governance, *Our Global Neighbourhood*, Oxford: Oxford University Press.

Clark, J. (2001) 'Ethical Globalization: The Dilemmas and Challenges of Internationalizing Global Civil Society', in M. Edwards and J. Gaventa (eds) *Global Citizen Action*, London: Earthscan.

Falk, R. A. (1995) *On Humane Governance: Toward a New Global Politics*, Cambridge: Polity.

Florini, A. M. (2001) 'Transnational Civil Society', in M. Edwards and J. Gaventa (eds) *Global Citizen Action*, London: Earthscan.

Grugel, J. (2003) 'Democratisation Studies Globalisation: the Coming of Age of a Paradigm', *British Journal of Politics and International Relations* 5, 2: 258–83.

Heins, V. (2000) 'From New Political Organizations to Changing Moral Geographies: Unpacking Global Civil Society', *GeoJournal* 52: 37–44.

Hulme, D. and Edwards, M. (1997) 'NGOs, States and Donors: An Overview', in *NGOs, States and Donors: Too Close for Comfort?* London: Macmillan/Save the Children Fund.

Kaldor, M. (2003) *Global Civil Society: An Answer to War*, Cambridge: Polity.

Keane, J. (2003) *Global Civil Society?*, Cambridge: Cambridge University Press.

Klein, N. (2002) *Fences and Windows: Dispatches from the Front Lines of the Globalization Debate*, London: Flamingo.

Kumar, K. (1993) 'Civil Society: An Inquiry into the Usefulness of an Historical Term', *British Journal of Sociology* 44, 3: 375–95.

Linklater, A. (1981) 'Men and Citizens in International Relations', *Review of International Studies* 7, 1: 23–37.

Lipschutz, R. (1992) 'Reconstructing World Politics: The Emergence of Global Civil Society', *Millennium: Journal of International Studies* 21, 3: 389–420.

Mathews, J. T. (1997) 'Power Shift', *Foreign Affairs* 76, 1: 50–66.

Salamon, L. M. (1994) 'The Rise of the Nonprofit Sector: A Global "Associational Revolution" ', *Foreign Affairs* 73, 4: 109–122.

Van Rooy, A. (1998) 'Civil Society as Idea: An Analytical Hatstand?', in A. Van Rooy (ed.) *Civil Society and the Aid Industry*, London: Earthscan.

Part 1

Global civil society – contesting current trends

1 Global civil society

Analytical category or normative concept?

Alejandro Colás

This chapter starts from the proposition that the idea of global civil society has been developed over the past decade or so as 'a project to be realised' (I adopt this term from Young, 1998). Liberal theorists ranging from the overtly cosmopolitan (Held, 1995; Kaldor, 2003) to the more sceptically communitarian (Frost, 2002; Walzer, 1996) have appropriated this term as a principally normative, or ethical category which should be promoted and nurtured across the world. In these formulations, global civil society has been presented as a set of actors, institutions and practices which are likely to reproduce liberal renditions of democracy, freedom, participation and citizenship on a global scale. To that extent, they seem to suggest that global civil society should be seen as a normative programme to be promoted and actualised.

In this contribution, I develop an alternative understanding of global civil society as a historical reality, rather than as a political project; and as a critical category devoid of any inherently liberal-democratic attributes, but more accurately portrayed as a specifically modern site of socio-political struggle which contains very diverse, often incompatible ideological projects. This does not preclude attaching a normative or ethical meaning to global civil society, but it does imply emphasising the need to ground any such attributes historically and sociologically by identifying the concrete structures and processes which are bearers of the ethical norms and values associated with civil society.

The brief section of the chapter which follows will elaborate on this relationship between the analytical and normative dimension of global civil society. The two central sections of the chapter then make the following core claims: first, that the globalisation of civil society is a process which has been unfolding – however unevenly – over the past three centuries, mainly as a result of the world-historical impact of the 'Age of Atlantic Revolutions'. Second, however, it will also be argued that this very unevenness in the global reproduction of civil society has generated complex and variegated expressions of a global civil society. By looking at the particular experience of civil society under colonial and post-colonial rule in the Maghreb, I hope to illustrate how the notion of global civil society has at once an older and more contested history than is usually allowed for in contemporary discussions. One consequence of this, I shall conclude, is that many expressions of contemporary global civil society can be seen as negative socio-political reactions to the very liberal attempts at promoting global civil society as a 'project to be realised'.

Global civil society: normative and analytical dimensions

Like most keywords of modern social and political theory, 'civil society' has from the outset contained both analytical (i.e. explanatory) and norm-ative (i.e. prescriptive) meanings. The seventeenth and eighteenth-century reinterpretation of this classical Greek concept initially emerged in con-trast to the largely mythical notion of the 'state of nature'. Civil society in the writings of Hobbes, Locke and Rousseau was therefore presented as a form of political contract – generally embodied in the coercive authority of the state – which could better guarantee peace, security and order within any given society. Toward the end of the eighteenth century, this predomi-nantly prescriptive use of the term civil society took on a more analytical inflection as thinkers like Ferguson, Smith and Hegel started to conceive of civil society as a concept denoting the systematic interaction of human beings mediated chiefly, though not exclusively, through the capitalist market. This understanding of civil society inaugurated a more socio-logical conception of the category by granting it an explanatory power which had until then eluded it: civil society on this reading referred to an increasingly mediated and historically unprecedented interaction between individuals outside both the affective domain of the family and the polit-ical ambit of the state. By the time Marx and his followers (most notably Antonio Gramsci) embraced the concept, civil society had matured into a category which could simultaneously denote a peculiarly modern way of organising social reproduction (the capitalist market) and a historically specific domain of socio-political protest connected to political parties, social movements and more broadly, a 'public sphere' incorporating written and audiovisual media, recreational clubs and a wide range of vol-untary associations.

Given this rich history, it is quite striking that contemporary appropri-ations of 'civil society' on a transnational or global plane tend to focus on the latter, more normative dimension of this concept. The influential *Global Civil Society Yearbook* for instance, certainly offers a wealth of empirical data on so-called 'third sector' activity at the global level; it is also astute enough to recognise that the prevailing understanding of global civil society involves 'a conflation of an empirical category, which is often referred to as NGOs or the non-profit or voluntary sector with a political project' (Anheier *et al.*, 2001: 15). The *Yearbook* editors are at pains to stress that global civil society 'has both normative and descriptive content and it is not always possible to find an exact correspondence between the two' (ibid.: 11). Notwithstanding all these important qualifications, global civil society emerges from the *Yearbook* as an idea and a reality 'in the making'; as a socio-political domain which, despite the editors' protestations of open-ended impartiality, actually aims to reproduce certain core liberal values including pluralism, non-violent contestation, dialogue and debate through global civil society: 'Rather than providing a definitive definition of global civil society, it has been our intention as editors to offer this and future Yearbooks as a continuing platform for exchange of ideas. We have opted for this approach because we believe that debating what global civil society means contributes to the emergence of an animated, open, and self-reflexive global civil society' (ibid.: 17).

In another recent contribution to these debates, John Keane (one of the Anglophone authors who has done most to both recover and develop the notion of civil society for our times) endorses an ideal-type definition of global civil society as '[a]n *unfinished project that consists of... actors who organise themselves across borders, with the deliberate aim of drawing the world together in a new way*' (Keane, 2003: 8 – italics in original). Once again, notwithstanding the numerous nuances and qualifications Keane attaches to this definition, it is dominated by a normative impulse whereby, 'Global civil society is ... an implied logical and institutional precondition of the survival and flourishing of a genuine plurality of different ideals and forms of life' (Keane, 2003: 202). The liberal notions of plurality, difference, freedom and individual rights thus constantly resurface in connection with global civil society, and so on this rendition the concept carries with it – however reluctantly – the burden of a liberal 'project to be realised'. On this reading, global civil society is an actually-existing socio-economic and political domain which nonetheless needs to be fostered and promoted as an arena where 'goods' such as non-violence, civility, transparency and compromise are more likely to flourish. It is, in Keane's words, '[n]ot just any old collection of ways of life that have nothing in common but their non-identification with governing institutions. Factually speaking, this society encourages compromise and mutual respect' (ibid.: 14).

While the musings on global civil society of Anheier *et al.* and Keane explicitly distance themselves from an exclusively prescriptive understanding of the concept, other scholars have sought to develop its normative content further. Mervyn Frost for instance eschews a 'political sociology' of global civil society and instead advocates a conception of this idea linked to right-holding citizens of democratic and democratising states: 'The social whole within which I claim basic rights for myself and recognize them in others ... I shall call *civil society*. This is a society without geographical borders – it is global in reach' (Frost, 2002: 7 – italics in original). Thus, for Frost, global civil society is a *practice* involving the *recognition* of democratic rights for oneself and others on a global plane, chiefly through non-violent, dialogic means. It therefore explicitly requires the global reproduction of such practices: 'For holders of citizenship rights the general answer to the ethical question: "What ought we as citizens to do under the circumstances?" is "Act so as to nurture and advance the practice of democratic and democratising free states within which citizenship, with its associated set of rights, is established as a valued form of ethical standing" ' (ibid.: 132).

What unites these otherwise quite disparate approaches to the notion of global civil society, then, is an insistence on the ethical promises attached to the concept. More specifically, the assumption is that the global reproduction of civil society in its liberal incarnation is likely to foster a more peaceful, lawful and plural world: 'Global civil society ... is about "civilizing" or democratising globalization, about the process through which groups, movements and individuals can demand a global rule of law, global justice and global empowerment' (Kaldor, 2003: 12). In what follows, I suggest that such an understanding of global civil society is potentially misleading both analytically and politically, for two basic reasons. In the first place, by presenting the 'globalisation' of civil society as a relatively recent phenomenon, the prevailing discourse on global civil society overlooks the longer history of this sphere of international activity. This is not just to suggest that we require an alternative periodisation which merely recognises the antecedents of contemporary global civil society; it is a more substantive claim about global civil society being a socio-economic and political domain structurally linked to the historical unfolding of modernity. As the next section will illustrate, the international expansion of civil society has been taking place since at least the eighteenth century, *and arguably contained globalising tendencies from its very inception.* Recognising the specifically modern nature of global civil society in turn raises a second problem for the predominantly liberal rendition of this term: namely, the highly variegated expressions of civil society across the world. As the historical experience of three non-western societies examined below will suggest, the international expansion of civil society has engendered very different (often virulently anti-liberal or antiwestern) civil societies across the world. This in turn places great strain on the prevailing view of global civil society as a set of practices and processes conducive to a more peaceful, lawful and tolerant world. On the contrary, I shall argue, the more the concept of global civil society is detached from any necessary association to 'civility', 'plurality' or 'democracy', the closer we will be to identifying both its full explanatory potential and its political/ethical limitations.

Global civil society and modernity

One of the characteristics of the historical epoch we today know as 'modernity' is the distinctive way of engaging in collective socio-political protest. Unlike earlier expressions of collective socio-political mobilisation, modern political movements tend to consist of a relatively open membership which generally pursues universalisable goals through secular activity of its members mediated chiefly (though clearly not exclusively) by the printed word. Accepting that the processes of historical transformation are never clear-cut or final, it can be said that the eighteenth and nineteenth centuries witnessed the generalisation in Europe and elsewhere of radically new forms of socio-political protest. In the evocative formulation of Louise and Charles Tilly: '[t]he food riot, the tax rebellion, the invasion of fields, and the other standard ways of voicing eighteenth-century demands give way to the strike, the demonstration, the public meeting, the electoral rally' (Tilly and Tilly, 1981: 21).

These new forms of mass socio-political mobilisation emerged in the course of complex and protracted historical transformations which cannot be addressed in detail here. Instead, attention will be drawn to two eminently modern social structures which were central to this process: the capitalist mode of production and the international system of states. While the latter increasingly became the focus of collective struggles for freedom, democracy and equality, the former revolutionised social relations by making huge swathes of the population dependent on the market for their own social reproduction. This in turn allowed for the reconfiguration of socio-political antagonisms in ways that encouraged for instance, the creation of labour representation committees, women's social and political unions or employers' associations. In other words, the gradual subjection of modern societies to the dictates of the labour-capital relation fostered the self-identification of socio-political movements along 'horizontal' lines of solidarity engendered through common experiences within civil society. As E. P. Thompson once put it in relation to his study of 'plebeian' protest in eighteenth-century England:

> It is necessary ... to go beyond the view that labouring people, at this time, were confined within the fraternal loyalties of the "vertical" consciousness of particular trades; and that this inhibited wider solidarities [...] In the scores of occupational lists which I have examined of food rioters, turnpike rioters, riots over libertarian issues or enclosure of urban commons it is clear that solidarities were not segregated by trade ... all these groups, during food riots, shared common consciousness – ideology and objectives – as petty consumers of the necessities of life. But these people were consumers also of cultural values, of libertarian rhetoric, of patriotic prejudice; and on these issues they could exhibit solidarities as well.
>
> (Thompson, 1974)

Similar observations could no doubt be made about the origins (and later development) of a whole host of other expressions of modern civil society – feminist public meetings, workers' libraries, employers' clubs – all of which emerged in the context of modern societies in the throes of radical transformations effected by capitalism. The point here is simply to emphasise that peculiarly modern forms of engaging in political protest can be identified with these 'horizontal' conceptions of solidarity.

A paradoxical outcome of such new-found expressions of political and socio-economic solidarity within civil society was that they developed in tandem with that other very modern structure of 'vertical' solidarity, namely the national state. In fact, modern social movements can in many ways be said to have been instrumental in legitimating and reinforcing the sovereign, territorial state as the dominant form of political authority in the modern epoch. For the territorial state has, from the early modern period, been the principal site for resolving (however imperfectly and temporarily) the socio-economic and political antagonisms within civil society. In other words, the national state has throughout the modern period served as a major locus in struggles over the democratisation of society, which have arguably engulfed social movements and political organisations of all ideological tendencies. Thus, most modern social movements – be it radical ecologists or religious fundamentalists – have engaged with, and often sought to take over, the state as the chief repository of political authority.

The foregoing is in many respects uncontroversial to most political sociologists. But, as I have argued elsewhere, if we consider the two aspects of modernity outlined above in conjunction a more challenging proposition arises, namely that modern social movements working in civil society have from the outset been international. This is so in two related senses. On the one hand, modern social movements have historically extended their 'horizontal' solidarities across state borders, and in the case of self-consciously 'internationalist' or 'cosmopolitan' organisations, across ethnic, religious or national boundaries. That is, they have conceived of (and generally acted upon) their political goals as being potentially universal. On the other hand, as was just suggested, the political struggles among modern social movements within civil society has historically reinforced the role of the national state as the major source of political authority. This in turn has generated a 'pluriverse' of formally independent political communities we have come to know as the modern international system. The combination of these 'horizontal' and 'vertical' forms of socio-economic and political solidarity have thus produced a global civil society which has from the beginning *simultaneously* undermined and reconfigured the international system of states. In this respect, the history of global civil society is not one of gradual separation from and contestation of the inter-state system, as is often suggested, but rather a process of creative destruction involving both the transgression of existing borders and their re-legitimisation through political protest. It is, in sum, a process constrained by the dual structures of the modern world: the system of states and the capitalist mode of production.

Global civil society in the periphery: the case of the Maghreb

If the arguments outlined above carry any weight, the liberal conceptions of global civil society as a domain which 'minimiz[es] violence at the global level, through the extension of global rules based on consent' (Kaldor, 2003) become more precarious. In fact, it is precisely by linking civil society with modernity and considering the global reproduction of civil society during this period that the protracted, variegated and often 'uncivil' nature of global civil society becomes apparent. For, insofar as there exists a global civil society today this is largely as a result of the violent overseas expansion of European societies during the 'Age of Empire'. As Partha Chaterjee has pointed out with regard to Indian history, it is useful to retain the modern European understanding of civil society and explore its differentiated and uneven global reproduction:

> [p]recisely to identify these marks of difference, to identify their significance, to appreciate how by the continued invocation of a 'pure' model of origin – the institutions of modernity as they were meant to be – a normative discourse can still continue to energize and shape the evolving forms of social institutions in the non-Western world.
>
> (Chaterjee, 2003: 172)

One such experience was the reproduction of civil society in the Maghreb region of northwest Africa. By briefly considering the origins and development of Maghrebi civil society under French colonial rule, some further light might be shed on the contradictory and fraught processes which constructed what we today call 'global civil society'.

The opening decades of the twentieth century witnessed the birth of a modern civil society in the Maghreb. As the Tunisian historian Béchir Tlili once suggested, this was a period of 'crises and mutations' in the Islamic-Mediterranean world (Tlili, 1978: 289). For the first time in the history of the region, collective political agency was channelled through distinctively modern mechanisms such as political parties, trade unions and cultural associations. The political vocabulary employed shifted from the exclusively religious – be it through the exegisis of sacred texts by qualified scholars or the messianic leadership of marabouts – to the modern language of constitutionalism, rights, representation, and eventually, national self-determination. Moreover, printed media (manifestos, programmes, petitions, newspapers) became the chief instrument for the propagation of these movements' ideas. As in the case of their European counterparts, the origins and subsequent development of these expressions of civil society lie in a number of international factors. Unlike the European experience, however, Maghrebi civil society was the product of imperialist penetration of the region. The violent processes of imperial subjugation and colonisation thus provided the necessary socio-economic and political conditions for the rise of a modern civil society in the region; but the 'uncivil' mechanisms which effected this change had momentous impact on the nature of civil society in that region during the colonial period and beyond.

The colonial state imposed itself in the Maghreb in three basic stages (see Bennoune, 1986 and Ruedy, 1992 for Algeria; Sammut, 1993 for Tunisia; and Parnell, 2000 for Morocco). Initially, the European conquerors used military force to 'pacify' resistance among the various North African peoples. In all three countries, this process unfolded through a combination of resistance and accommodation. As the French (and in the case of Morocco, Spanish) troops sought to extend their control beyond their coastal outposts, they generally encountered a fiercely hostile and well-organised adversary. Thus, the colonial state only affirmed its territorial control over these countries after long and bloody campaigns against rebel leaders: the names of Amir Adel Kader in Algeria and Abdel Krim in Morocco are the most famous among a host of generally tribal and millenarian – or *maraboutic* – rebellions. In other instances, however, the European colonisers used local power-holders such as *quaids* and tribal *shaiks*, in an attempt to reproduce the methods of indirect rule deployed by their Ottoman predecessors. Whatever the mechanism employed, the colonial state was able to exercise uncontested command over most of the local population, in Algeria by 1870, in Tunisia by 1910 and in Morocco by 1930. With the brutal single-mindedness which characterises most forms of imperial conquest, the Europeans had by the inter-war years (if not before) created three new territorially-bounded entities where they exercised exclusive political control.

The successful 'pacification' of the conquered peoples and territories paved the way for a second stage of the colonial state's development in the Maghreb, namely the creation of a civil society through the processes of 'primitive accumulation'. Again, this was a complex and uneven process, but the reproduction of the Second and Third Republic bourgeois society in North Africa was from the outset a transparent objective of the French colonisers. In Algeria, the extension of civil society was initially pursued through a policy of rural settlement as the French attempted to establish a republic of agrarian smallholders in the new colony during the first three decades after their arrival. The physical occupation of land which followed 'pacification' was soon accompanied by the 'destruction of the natural economy' through legal means such as the successive *sénatus-consulte* and the so-called Warnier law of 1873. In essence, this entailed the dispossession of the rural populations by replacing Islamic and customary systems of land tenure which often prohibited the alienation of property with a modern legal regime of commodified private property.

The early reluctance of European settlers to take up the 'pacified lands' forced the colonial state to invest greater resources in upholding law and order in the conquered regions, and so by the end of the century European landholders had secured over half of Algeria's arable lands. Colonisation was accompanied by substantial capitalist development and the concomitant rise of capitalist social classes, both in urban and rural Maghreb. Such capitalist development was 'articulated' politically and economically with non-capitalist forms of exploitation and political domination: tribal douars and other customary patterns of land tenure and political authority survived in the Maghreb well into the twentieth century, while sharecropping (*khammesat*) thrived under the colonial regime.

A third aspect (though not necessarily 'stage') of the colonial state's imposition on North Africa was simply the bureaucratic and legal extension and deepening of the latter's reach across each of the three territories. For not only did 'pacification' require the military occupation of conquered territories and its attendant legal-military infrastructure, it also involved the administration of the newly acquired peoples and territories. As was already suggested, a combination of direct and indirect rule was deployed in this exercise – Algeria in this respect falling more neatly into the first category. Through institutions like the *bureaux arabes*, European colonialism reinforced (and often reinvented) many of the pre-modern forms of political authority. There can be no doubt, however, that these 'native' institutions were integrated hierarchically into the centralised and uncontested power of the colonial state, and were therefore used as mechanisms of more effective subjugation. More significantly, as the imperialist project of reproducing civil society in the Maghreb consolidated itself, the administrative and bureaucratic infrastructure of the colonial state grew accordingly. Educational institutions, religious and sporting associations, even elements of the state's adopted social responsibilities (sanitation, health, labour law, public transport and so forth) came under the aegis of the colonial state. Thus, at the purely 'domestic' institutional level, the bourgeois state did erect itself in its full extension across North Africa.

Anti-imperialist resistance in the Maghreb initially took a pre-modern character: it was generally articulated by maraboutic shaiks in a fashion reminiscent of tribal resistance against successive foreign invaders – be they Christian Crusaders or Ottoman tax-gatherers. Yet by the turn of the twentieth century, several urban centres of the Maghreb witnessed one of the most important social and political transformations of their contemporary history. For the first time, autonomous associations with modes of organisation and a political idiom typical of modern civil society emerged in the region. North African civil society began moving away from more traditional sources of political mobilisation and gradually adopted modern forms of political engagement. The political party became the prevailing form of organisation; strikes, petitions, manifestos and demonstrations the tools of protest; and the language of rights, self-determination and representation the dominant political idiom.

It was these modern social movements which, through their (often violent or 'uncivil') contestation of French colonial rule, were ultimately responsible for the reproduction and consolidation of the modern state form in the Maghreb. The emergence of these early protagonists of Maghrebi civil society – bourgeois constitutionalist associations, the different trade unions and parties, the Islamist reformism of the salafiyya trend – must be explained with reference to the expansion of *capitalist* imperialism in the region. The social movements which operated within civil society were in this respect part of a broader pattern involving the internationalisation of class conflict. I shall very briefly consider three broad types of social movement which during the first half of the twentieth century represented the extension of 'global civil society' to this region.

The initial political expressions of Maghrebi civil society were cultural-educational associations like the Tunisian *Khalduniyya* and the *Sadiqiyya* or the Moroccan and Algerian 'free schools'. These served as hotbeds for the later bourgeois constitutionalism and Islamist reformism which underpinned the creation in 1920 of the *Destour* (Constitution) party, or the North African Star in 1927 – the first Maghrebi nationalist parties. Dubbed 'Young Tunisians' and 'Young Algerians' by the colonial press, the group of men which animated these associations drew their inspiration from a variety of sources including elements of European liberalism and, later, the Young Turk experience itself. In the early stages of its development however, two major tendencies were discernible in the programme of these organisations, particularly that of the vanguard 'Young Tunisians'.

The first was a tradition of constitutional reformism initiated by the enterprising Tunisian Prime Minister Khayr al-Din from 1873 until his dismissal in 1877. In establishing the elite Sadiki College in 1875, Khayr al-Din set out 'to develop civilisation [sic], in the interest of the population ... which the Muslim nation requires to develop its own affairs according to Islamic law' (cited in Sraïeb, 1995: 36 – my translation). As the French took over the Tunisian administration and the elite represented at Sadiki lost the prospect of securing an administrative position in the Beylical regime, the College gradually became a breeding ground for modern nationalist politics. The Sadiki students had, after all, acquired the necessary skills for confronting the colonial regime on its own terms: knowledge of a number of foreign languages; acquaintance with European history and political thought; widespread familiarity with the methods of modern science. By the mid-1900s the *Khalduniyya* and the *Sadiqiyya* had become the major centres of an incipient constitutionalist movement. Predictably, the ostensibly apolitical activities of the two associations had furnished a considerable number of Tunisian men with the ideological tools for the shaping of a nationalist consciousness.

Such consciousness was first translated into explicitly political activism through the elite Liberal *Destour* (Constitution) party. This party developed a reformist socio-economic and political programme moulded on the western bourgeois experience of the time. In this respect, its aim was not national independence, but rather the extension of citizenship rights to the Muslim population, and the proper capitalist development of the protectorate, all *within* the political community of the French Empire. As these aspirations appeared as increasingly unrealistic during the 1920s and 30s, mass nationalist organisations emerged in Tunisia and Algeria with the explicit aim of achieving greater popular sovereignty and eventually national liberation. Bourguiba's Neo-Destour and Messali Hadj's North African Star (later Algerian Popular Party) radicalised both the discourse and practice of constitutional reformism by replacing this bourgeois project with a much more populist stance informed by European working-class politics. Similarly, nationalist trade unions in the shape of the General Union/Congress of Tunisian Workers (CGTT/UGTT) and the General Union of Algerian Workers (UGTA) were established to mobilise in favour of national liberation a growing indigenous working-class disaffected by socialist and communist insensitivity to the 'national question'. In all these senses, French colonialism paved the way, through the extension of capitalist imperialism to the Maghreb, of the very socio-political forces which were responsible for national self-determination in the region.

A second important influence came from the so-called 'salafiyya' movement which claimed that an adequate response to European imperialism could only be achieved through a re-evaluation of the central tenets of Islam, and through the substantial reform of the existing Islamic institutions. Many young North African activists felt the salafiyya doctrines offered the ideal political language with which to disseminate their modernising programme without jeopardising the cultural legacy of Islam. The outstanding civilisational achievements of Islam – its profound political, spiritual and cultural force – had for several centuries provided Maghrebi society with a firm reference-point for the maintenance of social cohesion and moral order. Faced with the deepening of imperialist penetration by the latter half of the nineteenth century, North Africans naturally turned to Islam as the most immediate source of resistance. The way Islam served as a vehicle of political mobilisation, however, varied a great deal according to the place and moment of its occurrence.

The most coherent and historically significant expression of this trend was embodied in the salafiyya movement. Derived from the concept of *al-salaf al salih* ('the virtuous forefathers'), the term 'salafiyya' refers to those Muslim thinkers of the nineteenth and early twentieth century – names like Jamal al-Din Al-Afghani, Mohammed Abduh and Rashid Rida are usually associated with the trend – who argued for the return to the values which had guided the Prophet Muhammad and his companions during their exile at Madina. The leitmotif of their argument was that the original

postulates of Islam had been abandoned through the centuries by hetero-
dox practices like Sufism and by corrupt governments. The results, according to the Salafis, were plainly visible in the Muslim world's feeble
response to European imperialism, and the remedy lay in the revival of
the pristine culture of the first Islamic community. The Salafis did not
reject European values and achievements *per se*, but on the contrary,
sought to reconcile Islam with modernity. Their objective was to combine
elements of European industrial society – positivistic science, technology,
rationalised organisation – with the heritage of Islam – moral order, spir-
ituality and just governance (Al-Azmeh, 1994).

As opposed to earlier reactions to imperialism, the salafiyya trend
became a 'movement' in that it actually established a permanent network
of institutions characteristic of civil society. Interestingly, this was particularly true of the Maghreb where the Salafis had a considerable social and
political impact essentially transmitted through two vehicles: educational
institutions and cultural or religious associations. The most powerful of
these were the so-called 'free schools' (*maktab al-hurriyya*) or '*Kuttab
réformés*', which took their name by virtue of being independent from
colonial regulation. By offering a curriculum comprised of both traditional
and modern subjects taught mostly in Arabic, the schools provided an
alternative to both the secular francophone institutes and the declining
Koranic schools. With considerable foresight, the Salafis had identified the
Kuttab réformés as the cornerstone of future Muslim resistance against
European imperialism. By 1925, Morocco boasted a dozen such institutions (distributed between Fez, Rabat, Casablanca, Tetouan and Mar-
rakesh) while in Algeria, the movement pioneered by Ibn Ben Badis in
1917 accounted for the country's 100 free schools by the mid-1930s. An
important off-shoot of all this activity was the circulation of a number of
journals and newspapers – both in Arabic and French – such as Ben Badis'
al-Shihab (The Meteor) or the Tunisian *As-Sa'da al'Uzma* (The Greatest
Good).

The Salafi component in Maghrebi civil society waned with the growing
power of mass secular movements during the interwar period, but it still
made a significant practical and ideological contribution to the postwar
nationalist movements such as the Moroccan *Istiqlal* (Independence) party
or the Algerian National Liberation Front, and today informs much of the
Islamist activity in the Maghreb. Either way, there is little doubt that, once
again, it was the violent and unsolicited imposition of European political
rule in the region which encouraged this resurgence of Islam as a source of
nationalist activism.

Parallel to this gradual emergence of Tunisian and Algerian nationalism was the slow implantation of working-class movements in these two
countries. Various European working-class parties opened sections in the
Maghreb from 1907 and while trade unions were not formally legalised
until the 1930s in the region, most of the European workers had been

affiliated to the local branch of the *Confédération Générale du Travail* (CGT). The indigenous membership of these organisations was curtailed by both the limited development of the indigenous proletariat and by the administrative obstacles placed on Muslim workers wishing to join trade unions and political parties. The root cause for the overwhelmingly European character of the Maghrebi working-class movements during this period, however, lay in the racist attitude which pervaded much of their early activity. Most branches of the CGT and the *Section Française de la Internationale Ouvrier* (SFIO) were unwilling to attack head-on the various forms of discrimination faced by indigenous working people, nor to embrace the political issues which motivated this population. Despite this glaring insensitivity for the social and political aspirations of the majority of North Africans, the European working-class organisations managed to attract a growing number of Muslims to their ranks. During the interwar years, Arab and Berber workers participated in strikes and demonstrations side by side with their European comrades, while their presence became more noticeable in the governing bodies of working-class organisations. The founding of the Communist International in 1919 as an explicitly international anti-imperialist organisation further accelerated this process and with the rise of the Popular Front government in France in the Spring of 1936, communist organisations across the Maghreb challenged the nationalist parties as the chief mass political actors in North African politics. This disproportionate influence of communist parties on the Maghrebi political landscape continued into the postwar years, inflated in part by the USSR's prestige in anti-imperialist circles at that time. The communist ambivalence toward national liberation in the region and its association with elitist or 'westernised' *évolués* combined with an uncompromising stance on the part of the socialist administrations in Paris to turn the mass of the politicised population toward the nationalist movements.

The preceding overview throws up three general conclusions on the reproduction of civil society in the Maghreb which are relevant to the broader discussion on the contemporary nature of global civil society. First, civil society initially emerged in this region as a result of the transnational reach of capitalist social relations, and their accompanying legal, bureaucratic and ideological infrastructure. To that extent, civil society in its various guises certainly took root in the Maghreb, but it did so under the auspices of the coercive power of the imperial state. This in turn was to give civil society in that part of the world a very particular inflection: one marked – as in other colonial civil societies – by the resort to armed struggle and discourses of political unity in the pursuit of national self-determination, and by the peculiarities of a colonial capitalism which, rather than reproducing itself in the 'pristine' form of Marx's famous double-freedom, actually grafted its own logic of surplus extraction onto pre-existing modes of exploitation and oppression. Second, the social movement which made up Maghrebi civil society drew on a very broad range of transnational influences and material support, many of them arriving from the Arab East and Turkey. Thus, the 'pure' model of civil society alluded to by Chaterjee not only combined with local socio-cultural structures such as, for instance, the networks of Sufi brotherhoods, but also developed through contact with and inspiration from the wider Arab and Muslim world. Kinship, ethnicity and regional provenance certainly acted as resilient constraints on the nature of Maghrebi civil society, but these local features were challenged and often remoulded by external forces arriving not only from the capitalist West, but also via pan-Arab and pan-Islamic ideologies. Finally, as in most other regions of the world, civil society in the Maghreb was forged through the interaction with the international system of states. As was suggested above, the colonial state and inter-state institutions of the period played an instrumental role in the reproduction of civil society in this region: 'political' and 'civil' society were not in absolute opposition here, but rather deeply implicated in their mutual development. The postwar period in particular witnessed extensive campaigns at international fora like the UN Assembly or the newly-formed League of Arab States to further the nationalist cause in all three Maghrebi countries.

In each of these senses, we can reasonably speak of the integration of the Maghreb into a global or international civil society during the colonial period. Crucially, however, this must be swiftly followed by the recognition that such an integration was highly uneven and contradictory, thereby opening up the crippling paradox in liberal renditions of global civil society: the historical reproduction of civil society across the world can itself generate virulent reactions against the project of global civil society. As the concluding section to this contribution will argue, this liberal paradox should act as the starting point of contemporary discussions on the nature of global civil society.

Global civil society as domain of conflict

The core proposition of this chapter has been that global civil society is most usefully understood as a historical and sociological domain characterised by peculiarly modern forms of political mobilisation and protest. Normative values or ethical principles certainly emerge and develop within this sphere, but they are not structurally tied to the notions of pluralism, non-violence, consensus-building and rule of law which liberals tend to associate with global civil society. Rather, global civil society is best conceived as a domain of political struggle and social antagonism where various ideological and normative projects fight out (sometimes all too literally) their competing visions of society. The international and transnational dimensions to these struggles make global civil society a complex and multi-layered sphere, mediated by a number of hierarchical social structures, two of which have been especially highlighted in this contribution: the global capitalist market and the international system of states. By way of conclusion, this last section will suggest that close attention must be paid to these two structures and their interaction when considering the political and ethical content of global civil society.

The globalisation of the capitalist market, it was suggested above, has been the mainspring of global civil society. The imposition of capitalist social and property relations across the globe – principally through imperialist domination – has, for good or ill, set the terrain for the development of social movements and political organisations we associate with modern civil society. However, as the illustrations from the colonial Maghreb indicate, this has been a highly differentiated process, often allowing for the persistence or, better still, re-articulation of existing modes of exploitation and oppression within the context of global capitalism. In many respects, the post-colonial history of the Maghreb conforms to Mahmood Mamdani's celebrated theorisation of the 'bifurcated' state in sub-Saharan Africa which combines 'Direct rule as the form of urban civil power' with 'Indirect ... rural tribal authority' so as to generalise a form of 'decentralised despotism' (Mamdani, 1996). For many observers of the contemporary Maghreb, the emergence of modern civil society in the region has (like in other parts of the Third World) also been refracted through this 'bifurcated' imperial experience in ways that render contemporary Maghrebi politics especially over-determined. Indeed, one recent study on political authority in Morocco argues that:

> The ideological sources of popular protest in Morocco are complex and not readily disaggregated; to a certain extent, they rest on a deep historical sense of social justice made up of memories of past glories, a collective image of the exemplary leader, and a popular notion of moral purity and material generosity arising from the Islamic traditions. In the political arena, this historical sensibility arising from below meets the ambiguities of power disseminated from above, creating a polyphonic, frequently discordant setting for political life.
>
> (Bourqia *et al.*, 1999: 12)

As I have argued elsewhere (Colás, 2001), much of the popular protest emanating from Maghrebi civil society is characterised by a thoroughly undemocratic, anti-Western and 'uncivil' character, which nonetheless (and contrary to its own claims) owes a great deal to the historical interaction with other civil societies. Thus, the resurgence of political Islam in the region over the last two decades is both comparable to, and in some senses inspired by, other forms of 'populist' opposition to capitalist globalisation and, more importantly, can, in its ideological content and social base, be traced to the very specific conjuncture of global neo-liberal reform of the 1980s and 1990s. Such social movements are demonstrably part of that historical-sociological domain we have come to call 'global civil society', but they simultaneously stand and fight against everything liberals – and indeed other progressives – associate with this sphere of world politics.

The historical and contemporary experience of the Maghreb – like that, I would insist, of other post-colonial societies – clearly challenges the idea of global civil society as a realm of non-violent, consensual and lawful social intercourse. It also underlines the paradoxical centrality of the inter-state system in the reproduction of global civil society. For, not only were the historical origins and evolution of Maghrebi civil society closely tied to anti-imperialism and national liberation, but crucially, the contemporary expressions of civil society are very much focused on the reforms and reconstitution of the post-colonial state. Notwithstanding the important variations in forms of rule and post-colonial trajectories of Maghrebi states, in all of the three cases considered above, the state remains the primary locus of authority among competing political projects. Somewhat ironically, it is precisely those social movements most inclined toward a liberal understanding of civil society as a sphere of freedom, equality and non-violent debate, which are most vociferous in demanding that the state live up to its claims as ultimate guarantor of social welfare and the rule of law. One of the more dynamic expressions of civil society in the region, the Moroccan associations of 'unemployed graduates' (*chômeurs diplomés*) have shown up – in a series of uncompromising but peaceful sit-ins, occupations and demonstrations during the 1990s – a state incapable of catering for the needs of even those Moroccans with the privilege of higher education: 'In the eyes of Morocco's unemployed college graduates, the state has yet to fulfil its part in the social and political contract' (Burton-Rose, 1998: 9). More recently, feminist movements and their Islamist opponents have been responsible for impressive mobilisations for and against, respectively, the state reforms extending women's rights in those countries. These cases perfectly illustrate the enduring dilemma of liberal renditions of global civil society: a democratic civil society requires a strong (i.e. legitimate and extensive) state; but an all-encroaching state runs the danger of snuffing out a democratic civil society. This is clearly a dilemma which all democrats – not just liberals – must live with. Yet in associating the notion of civil society in its various dimensions – local, regional or global – with civility, plurality, legality and consent, liberals run the risk of glossing over what John Keane (1998: 135) has called the 'endogenous sources of incivility' inherent to the category. It might, then, be more accurate, and ultimately more enabling for democratic politics, to think of global civil society not as a project to be realised, but rather as a socio-political space where democrats have over the past three centuries competed and conflicted with their adversaries.

References

Al-Azmeh, A. (1994) *Islam and Modernities*, London and New York: Verso.

Anheier, H. K., Glasius, M., Kaldor, M. (eds) (2001) *Global Civil Society Yearbook 2001*, Oxford: Oxford University Press.

Bennoune, M. (1986) *The Making of Contemporary Algeria*, Cambridge: Cambridge University Press.

Bourqia, R. and Gilson Miller, S. (1999) 'An Introduction to the Discussion' in R. Bourqia and S. Gilson Miller (eds) *In the Shadow of the Sultan: Culture, Power and Politics in Morocco*, Cambridge, MA: Harvard University Press.

Burton-Rose, D. (1998) 'Room to Breathe: Creating Space for Independent Political Action in Morocco' *Middle East Report* 28, 3, Winter 8–10.

Chaterjee, P. (2003) 'On Civil and Political Society in Postcolonial Democracies' in S. Kaviraj and S. Khilnani (eds) *Civil Society: History and Possibilities*, Cambridge: Cambridge University Press.

Colás, A. (2001) 'The Reinvention of Populism: Islamist Responses to Capitalist Development in the Contemporary Maghreb' (Unpublished paper delivered at the BISA Annual Conference, Bradford, December).

Frost, M. (2002) *Constituting Human Rights: Global Civil Society and the Society of Democratic States*, London: Routledge.

Held, D. (1995) *Democracy and the Global Order: From the Modern State to Cosmopolitan Governance*, Cambridge: Polity.

Kaldor, M. (2003) *Global Civil Society: An Answer to War*, Cambridge: Polity.

Keane, J. (1998) 'Uncivil Society' in Keane, J. (ed.) *Civil Society: Old Images, New Visions*, Cambridge: Polity Press.

Keane, J. (2003) *Global Civil Society?*, Cambridge: Cambridge University Press.

Maghraoui, A. (2001) 'Political Authority in Crisis: Mohammed VI's Morocco' *Middle East Report*, 218, Spring.

Mamdani, M. (1996) *Citizen and Subject: Contemporary Africa and the Legacy of Late Colonialism*, Princeton, NJ: Princeton University Press.

Ruedy, J. (1992) *Modern Algeria: Origins and Development of a Nation*, Indiana: Indiana University Press.

Sammut, C. (1983) *L'impérialisme capitaliste français et le nationalisme tunisien (1881–1914)*, Paris: Publisud.

Sraïeb, N. (1995) *Le Collège Sadiki de Tunis, 1875–1956: Enseignement et nationalisme*, Tunis: Alif, Editions de la Méditterannée.

Thompson, E. P. (1974) 'Patrician Society, Plebeian Culture', *Journal of Social History* 2, 7: 382–405.

Tilly, L. A. and Tilly, C. (eds) (1981) *Class Conflict and Collective Action*, London and Beverly Hills, CA: Sage Publications.

Tlili, B. (1978) *Crises et mutations dans le monde islamo-méditerranéen contemporain (1907–1912)*, Tunis: Université de Tunis.

Walzer, M. (1996) *Thick and Thin: Moral Argument at Home and Abroad*, Notre Dame, IN: University of Notre Dame Press.

Young, T. (1998) ' "A Project to be Realized": Global Liberalism and Contemporary Africa', *Millennium: Journal of International Studies*, 24, 3: 527–46.

smocracy and global civil
:iety

hn Keane

Global civil society is a 'syndrome' of processes and activities which have
multiple origins and multiple dynamics, some of them more conjunctural
than deep-seated. Together, these forces ensure that global civil society
is not a single, unified domain, and that it will not be turned into something that resembles a combined factory, warehouse and shopping mall
retailing consumer products on a global scale – let's say, a version of
Disney's *It's a Small World After All* or Naomi Klein's (2000) 'international rule of the brands'. Global civil society is not simply reducible
to the logic of commodity production and exchange, which helps to
explain both its semantic promiscuity and its normative appeal to an
astonishing variety of conflicting social interests, ranging from groups
clustered around the World Bank to broad-minded Muslims defending
their faith and radical ecological groups pressing for sustainable development.

If the institutions of global civil society are not merely the products of
civic initiatives and market forces then is there a third force at work in
nurturing and shaping it? It can be argued that global civil society is also
the by-product of governmental or intergovernmental action, or inaction.
Contrary to those for whom global civil society is driven by a single social
logic, like voluntary action or turbocapitalism, it is important to see the
ways in which many global non-governmental organisations and actors
are both framed and enabled by – and sometimes heavily dependent
upon, in matters of funding and influence – governmental organisations of
various kinds (Risse, 2002). In fields like telecommunications and air,
land and sea traffic, political bodies such as the International Postal
Union and the World Intellectual Property Organisation, most of them
resting formally on agreements to which states are signatories, exercise
formidable regulatory powers that enable many parts of global civil
society to keep moving, at a quickening pace. Governmental agencies,
much more than corporate philanthropy, also currently play a major,
positive-sum role in protecting, funding and nurturing non-profit organisations in every part of the earth where there is a lively civil society
(Salamon, 1999). Included in this category are civil organisations that

operate on the margins of the governmental institutions that license them in the first place. Examples include a body like the International Committee of the Red Cross which, although nongovernmental, is mandated under the Geneva Convention and is linked to states through the organisation of the International Federation of Red Cross and Red Crescent Societies; similarly, the International Association of Religious Freedom, a forum for interreligious dialogue, has accredited NGO status at the UN and UNESCO levels.

To cite such examples at random is not to say that global civil society is describable as a para-governmental body. It is not a 'court society', of the kind that prevailed before the eighteenth-century emergence of civil societies, when concentric rings of social life were typically attached like barnacles to the hulls of monarchic states, which distributed favours and privileges to members of 'society' roughly in direct proportion to their proximity to the centres of administrative power (Pérez-Diaz, 1999: 10–21). The feisty institutions of global civil society are on the whole more dynamic and independent than the court societies of old. There is another key difference, which is that, unlike the early modern civil societies, which typically hatched within the well-established containers of empires and territorial states, global civil society has emerged and today operates in the absence of a global state, a world empire, or comprehensive regulatory structures that are describable in the state-centred terms of political 'realism'.

Some observers quickly conclude from this generalisation that the term 'global civil society' is meaningless; for them, the term is logically the Siamese twin of the term global state. The point that they want to drive home is: no global state, no global civil society (Brown, 2000: 7–26). Such reasoning is unconvincing, if only because it overlooks the utter novelty of our situation. It is true that there is currently no global state. It is also most improbable that in future one could be developed, even on the doubtful assumption that it would be desirable to do so. Our situation is different, and without historical precedent. The current growth spurt of global civil society under 'anarchic' conditions certainly outpaces governments of all descriptions, but that is why it contains within it a pressing constitutional agenda which must be conceptualised in fresh ways: the need to go beyond the present clutter of global political institutions, in order to find new governing arrangements that enable something like effective and democratically accountable government, the rule of law and more equitable and freer social relations to develop on a global scale.

Cosmocracy

Any possibility of going beyond this present clutter of interacting and overlapping structures of governance, however, requires first that we understand them. Summarising extant global governance is not easy, but for various strong reasons that will become clear it can and must be done. Its necessary precondition is a bold leap of political imagination. Some groups within global civil society have spotted this. Transparency International's image of good global government as like a Greek temple – with foundations built from publicly-shared values, pillars comprising separate branches of government and a roof structure that supports the world-wide rule of law and a sustainable, high-quality way of life – points in this direction (Interview with Miklos Marschall, 2002). A new theory of the emerging world polity is indeed urgently needed. And so a principal thesis of this chapter: our world is today coming under the influence of a new form of governmental power that can be called a *cosmocracy*. The neologism (from *kosmos*, world, order, universal place or space; and *kratō*, to rule or to grasp) is used here as an *idealtyp*. It describes in simplified form a type of institutionalised power that defies all previous accounts of different governmental forms – beginning with Aristotle's attempt to develop a typology of states and continuing today in various efforts to distinguish among 'Westphalian', 'post-modern' and 'post-colonial' states or 'modern', 'post-modern' and 'pre-modern' states. Although cosmocracy was not conceived as part of a grand design – it is much more a combined product of will, luck, accident and unintended effects – and although it has old roots, over time it has come to display a certain coherence and distinctiveness. Understood as an emerging system of political power, cosmocracy is without precedent. It defies all previous typologies because it is a form of government *sui generis*, with the following features:

Cosmocracy is the first-ever world polity. Despite the fact that it does not appear as such on maps of the world, cosmocracy is a system of world-wide webs of interdependence – of actions and reactions at a distance, a complex melange of networks of legal, governmental, police and military interdependence at world-wide distances. These chains of interdependence are oiled by high-speed, space-shrinking flows of communication that have a striking effect: they force those who wield power within the structures of cosmocracy to become more or less aware of its here-there dialectics. The power structures of cosmocracy are constantly shaped by so-called butterfly effects, whereby single events, transactions or decisions somewhere within the system can and do touch off a string of (perceived) consequences elsewhere in the system. Those who wield power know not only that 'joined-up government' is becoming commonplace – that governmental institutions of various function, size and geographic location, despite their many differences, are caught up in thickening, fast-evolving webs of bilateral, multilateral and supranational relations. They also know that 'splendid isolation' is impossible, that their decisions are potentially or actually unrestricted in scope and effect – that what they say and do (or do not say or do) impinges upon the lives of others elsewhere on the face of the earth. Both wilful and unintended political intervention in the affairs of others is a chronic feature of cosmocracy, as is meddling's opposite: regrets of abstentions and missed opportunities, even expressions of shame and public apologies (like that of President Clinton's to the survivors of the 1994 Rwandan genocide) for not having intervened politically into others' affairs.

Cosmocracy stands on the spectrum between the so-called Westphalian model of competing sovereign states and a single, unitary system of world government. It functions as something more and other than an international community of otherwise sovereign governments. It is not understandable in terms of the nineteenth-century idea of balance-of-power politics. It is also wrong to understand it as a two-tiered, proto-federal polity that has been formed by the gradual 'pooling' of the powers of territorial states under pressure from arbitrage issues and cross-border spillovers. Cosmocracy is much messier, a far more complex type of polity. It is better understood as a salmagundi of multiplying, highly mobile and intersecting lines of governmental powers. It is *a conglomeration of interlocking and overlapping sub-state, state and supra-state institutions and multi-dimensional processes that interact, and have political and social effects, on a global scale.*

Legality

Cosmocracy is a conglomeration of political power cemented together with laws and legal procedures. Especially during the past half-century, there has been a definite trend towards not only the *legalisation of governmental structures*, but also the development of new forms of *multilateral legal networks* that highlight the passing away of the fiction of the legal sovereignty of territorial states. Talk of sovereignty and claims that it remains at the core of the world's political system certainly survive in the era of cosmocracy. Its protagonists point out that since the founding of the United Nations in 1948, the number of officially-recognised states has nearly quadrupled, a state-centric trend that is reinforced by international law. Appearances are however deceptive, or at least paradoxical. For in policy areas like the management of the commons (outer space, Antarctica and the oceans, for instance), or global crime, weapons systems and environmental protection, three highly complex, often overlapping forms of multilateral legal regulation are now becoming standard (Shelton, 2001). Some multilateral agreements, such as the Antarctic Treaty and the Montreal Protocol on the protection of the earth's ozone layer, contain provisions that are aimed not only at the contracting parties, but at third parties as well. Other arrangements, exemplified by the International Tribunal for the Former Yugoslavia, the judgment of the European Court of Human Rights in *Al-Adsani v the United Kingdom*, and the well-known *Pinochet* case, are guided by the doctrine of *jus cogens*, according to which there are definable global norms – a 'common interest of humanity' – from which no dissent or derogation by governmental or non-governmental parties is justified. Still other agreements, such as the UN General Assembly resolutions to ban driftnet fishing and the 1979 Bonn Convention on the Conservation of Migratory Species of Wild Animals, take the form of agreed measures, declarations, programmes, final acts and other types of non-legally binding 'soft law', whose purpose is to induce others to change or reinforce their behaviour (Chinkin, 2000).

These polycentric forms of legal regulation have sprung up in a higgledy-piggledy or sector-by-sector fashion, in consequence of which the legal norms and jurisdictional boundaries of the cosmocracy are in a constant state of definition and re-definition, conflict and compromise. Their principal trajectories are nevertheless clear. Most obvious is that the various units of cosmocracy, including territorial states, are caught up in thickening webs of sub-national, intergovernmental and global law. There is also growing world-wide awareness that the whole process of ordering, enabling, restraining and legitimating the cosmocracy by means of law is (so to say) taking on a life of its own and that, for that reason, it stands in need of tighter synchronisation of currently conflicting laws and jurisdictions, perhaps even their 'harmonisation' (in the form of initiatives like the Organization of the Supreme Courts of the Americas, ratified in 1996) through the principle of a hierarchy of global norms. This dynamism, and the first efforts to integrate it, help to explain why the nets of legal regulation are now beginning to be cast over various parts of global civil society, so that matters once considered 'private' or subject to territorial state prerogatives – from the migration patterns of birds to genocidal crimes and violence against women to corporate mergers – are now subject to legal regulation. Finally, the complex pattern of multiple jurisdictions is reinforced by moves by e-commerce firms to claw back regulatory powers through so-called mechanisms of *alternative dispute resolution*: in effect, they are pushing for a new market-based system of private laws, which would enable companies to operate outside of the courts, within a minimum framework of 'safe harbour' rules guaranteeing privacy and consumer protection (*The Economist* 2001: 25–7).

This trend towards the 'legalisation' of global civil society is by no means a zero-sum relationship in favour of governmental power. More legal attention is certainly being paid to non-state actors, coupled with expectations that their behaviour will be subject to norms and procedures previously applied to governments and their agents. But developments like the World Court Project (a coalition effort to obtain an opinion from the International Court of Justice on the legality of nuclear weapons) and the UN-sponsored Indigenous Forum (comprising representatives of member states and of indigenous groups) point to a different conclusion: by being drawn into governmental affairs, parts of global civil society are now regularly exercising influence on the institutions of cosmocracy itself.

This rule of effect and counter-effect certainly applies to the slow erosion of both the immunity of sovereign states from suit and the presumption that statutes do not extend to the territory of other states. There are many tendencies in this direction. INGOs are licensed by bodies like the Council of Europe and the United Nations. Non-governmental groups participate in election monitoring and as *amici curiae* in the proceedings of such bodies as the European Court of Justice and the Inter-American Court of Human Rights. War crimes cases are given global publicity, thanks to new bodies like the Hague Tribunal; an International Criminal Court has been agreed; and local courts, under pressure from citizens' groups, show ever greater willingness to prosecute symbolically 'foreign' acts of wrongdoing.

The empowerment of global civil society is also evident in the fields of power of the turbocapitalist economy. While criticisms of the 'anarchy' of 'unregulated' global markets remain justified, the domination of turbocapitalist firms is now routinely subject to contestation and resistance. Not only are they subject to the 'top-down' rulings of governmental institutions like the WTO, a free-standing body with legal personality (the same politico-legal status as that, say, of the United Nations) and self-executing dispute mechanisms that are binding on all its members. The turbocapitalist economy is subject as well to various legal pressures initiated 'from below', including plaintiffs' efforts in the United States to use the Alien Tort Claims Act to hold turbocapitalist firms liable for environmental damage and human rights violations in far-away countries like Nigeria, India, Burma and South Africa.

Clumsy government

As a compound form of government wrapped in law, cosmocracy has a definite durability. Especially within its heartlands, there is a strong tendency towards a stable and non-violent, if dynamic equilibrium. This stability is paradoxical, especially because, throughout the system, from the macro- to the micro-domains, there is a heavy preponderance, and sometimes deliberate reliance upon, decision-making procedures that involve 'muddling through' and 'clumsiness'. Cosmocracy might be described as a dynamic system of clumsy institutions (Schapiro, 1988: 1555–69). Indeed, from either a strategic or a normative standpoint – the *idealtyp* of cosmocracy is used in this context primarily for the purpose of descriptive interpretation – much can be said in its favour. Clumsy government has all sorts of desirable features – like the power-sharing that comes with a plurality of institutions – certainly when compared with the unworkable normative ideal of designing institutions that are rigidly geometric in style and strategy. There are certainly many policy areas in which clumsy governing structures enable civil society organisations and actors to practise the arts of *divide et impera* from below, so ensuring positive-sum effects. Working in the interstices of government, nongovernmental bodies take advantage of its resources by finding ways of bending and manipulating that system for the purposes of strengthening the hand of global civil society itself (Wapner, 2000).

The processes through which this happens are highly complex. Many different governmental forms function as catalysts of global civil society. This consequently results in a wide continuum of different relations enjoyed by nongovernmental bodies with their governmental counterparts. Hence, an important rule: that global civil society should not be thought of as the natural enemy of political institutions. The vast mosaic of groups, organisations and initiatives that comprise global civil society are variously related to governmental structures at the local, national, regional and supranational levels. Some sectors of social activity, the so-called anti-government organisations (AGOs), are openly hostile to the funding and regulatory powers of state institutions. In certain contexts, this resistance or cantankerousness of social organisations is important in loosening up and humbling governmental structures. Charter 77 in Czechoslovakia and KOR in Poland and similar bodies certainly had this effect during the last years of the Soviet empire, especially on its western fringes. Elsewhere, the gradual strengthening of non-governmental organisations, some of them directly linked to global civil society, has had the effect of questioning arbitrary and/or pompous exercises of governmental power – as in Japan, a country in which the old word for public (*ōyake*, literally the house of the emperor) and terms like *okami* (the government or the authorities, literally 'those above') and familiar proverbs like 'the nail that sticks out gets hammered' (*Deru kugi wa utareru*) once sat comfortably alongside popular maxims such as 'respect for authorities, contempt for the people' (*kanson minpi*) (Deguchi, 1999: 11–20).

In other sectors of global civil society, for instance those in which the acronym NGO rather means (according to the South African joke) 'next government official', relations between social organisations and political power are openly collaborative. Civil society organisations either serve as willing contractors for governments or aim at dissolving themselves into governmental structures (Tendler, 1982). Still other nongovernmental organisations (GRINGOs or GONGOs, like the International Air Transport Association and the World Conservation Union) are the dependent creations of state authorities. In between these two extremes stand those social actors (e.g., Médecins sans Frontières, Oxfam, Greenpeace) who slalom between self-reliance and legal and political dependency. They form *ad hoc* partnerships with governments; lobby donor intergovernmental bodies like the World Bank to change their policies; and work with other nongovernmental organisations in rich and poor countries, zones of peace and war alike.

Public-private partnerships between sectors of global civil society and governing institutions are strongly evident in one of the major supranational political developments of the twentieth century: the formation of the United Nations. Its history is often told from above, from the standpoint of the behaviour of governments and their diplomats. This is unfortunate because, during its gestation period, civic organisations took advantage of its arrival by playing a small but vital role in shaping its future identity. In the spring of 1945, for instance, the Roosevelt administration included some 40 NGOs as 'consultants' within the American delegation to the United Nations Conference on International Organization. Although the aim was to use these civil society groups to win public support for the United Nations Charter to be agreed in San Francisco, they were joined by others – an estimated 1,200 of them, from all around the world – who together went on to contribute to the drafting process itself. Meanwhile, inside the newly established Human Rights Commission, a small group of legal experts and diplomats, led by Eleanor Roosevelt, hammered out the world's first international bill of rights. As the major powers squabbled and concentrated on political methods of war prevention through new territorial guarantees and collective security arrangements, the declaration – written in a language that could not be dismissed as simply 'Western' – won the necessary backing of religious and peace groups, legal activists, and political figures from smaller countries, all of whom were convinced that the disregard of civil and political freedoms and social justice had produced the barbarities of the Second World War.

Considering that key powers, including the United States, were opposed to UN entanglements in the domestic affairs of states implied by NGO activity, the power of the supposedly powerless civil society actors was considerable. They were not merely an inspiration for a generation to come. Their immediate influence was evident in the inclusion of human rights provisions in the Charter: Article 55(c) confirms, for example, that the UN will promote 'universal respect for, and observance of, human rights and fundamental freedoms for all'. Article 71 of the Charter affirms that the UN Economic and Social Council (ECOSOC) 'may make suitable arrangements for consultation with non-governmental organizations which are concerned with matters within its competence'. While such arrangements were subject to the approval of the member states and intergovernmental organisations, the formal legitimation of civil society involvement – note the striking contrast with the League of Nations, which lacked such a provision – was to set the rules for the subsequent growth of governmentally-framed, cross-border civil initiatives. So Article 71 served as the basis for the formation of the World Health Organisation (WHO), whose constitution and conduct fostered the involvement of civic organisations, and of UNESCO, under whose activist Director-General – Julian Huxley – provision was made for the 'consultation and co-operation' of INGOs and, in cases where they did not exist, time and money were invested to nurture new NGOs. Soon after its formation, UNESCO also convened a path-breaking conference on the protection of nature, at which global NGOs like the International Committee for Bird Preservation recommended that the problem of pesticides be tackled by calling upon the UN to establish a joint commission of its relevant agencies.

The catalytic effects of the United Nations during its earliest years should not be exaggerated. It certainly recognised the existence and information and nuisance values of NGOs, but little positive recognition was initially given to their potential role in structuring the postwar global environment along the lines of a global civil society. The birth of the UN was nevertheless a symbol of hope for a more civilised world – a world that lay beyond the textbook descriptions of territorial state politics. In its early years, the UN was also a vital training ground for civil society organisations, many of which came to learn that political/legal regulation is often a vital precondition of their survival and effectiveness. The latter-day complexity within the patterns of regulation is staggering. Many thousands of civil society organisations are now officially recognised by the United Nations, and by supranational governing bodies, like the Antarctica Treaty System (Clark *et al.*, 1998). Political institutions and agreements meanwhile play a vital role in fostering the growth of turbocapitalism, for instance the 'Final Act' of the Uruguay Round of trade negotiations, a 1994 agreement that had the backing of 145 states and that led to the establishment of both the World Trade Organisation and the extension of the principle of freer trade into such areas as copyrights, patents and services. Governmental institutions also sometimes operate as important catalysts of non-profit activity within global civil society. This logic of catalysis was famously evident in the proliferation of human rights groups like Charter 77 after the 1975 signing of the Helsinki Accords, one of whose 'baskets' required signatories to guarantee the civil and political rights of their citizens. Similar catalytic effects resulted from the much-publicised 1992 Global Forum and Earth Summit, held in Rio de Janeiro, and the follow-up women's and population conferences in Beijing and Cairo; and the 1993 Vienna Conference on Human Rights, where 171 states reaffirmed their commitment to the principle of the 'universal nature of the rights and freedoms' specified in the International Bill of Human Rights.

Instabilities

There are rare times, in response to major global crises, like that of September 11, when the whole system of cosmocracy – resembling what is called in physics the Bose-Einstein condensate – is so chilled down with concern that its different components momentarily sing together in unison.[1] Under more normal conditions, however, the complex, multi-layered, dynamic and open-ended totality called cosmocracy displays several fault-lines. These zones of tension and slippage periodically produce shock-effects on the whole system, especially when they are highlighted as such by collective actors and journalists operating through communications media. Such instabilities strongly suggest that cosmocracy's description as a multi-level governance system or system of 'transgovernmentalism' is inappropriate. Theorists of multi-level governance and transgovernmentalism concede that complexity – multiple actors, variable patterns, unpredictability – are among its leading qualities, yet they tend to downplay or neglect the idea that a system of multi-level governance or transgovernmentalism can suffer destabilising contradictions. This idea is profoundly relevant for any examination of cosmocracy, which is currently marked by patterns of danger and deep incoherence that highlight the ways in which it is an inadequate form of government. The governing institutions of cosmocracy (as we have seen in the case of the United Nations) certainly have positive enabling effects upon global civil society. But cosmocracy also chronically lets global civil society down. It does not bring peace and harmony and good government to the world, let alone usher in calm order. Its hotchpotch of rules and institutions produce negative – disabling and destabilising – effects.

What are these contradictions or structural problems of cosmocracy? What are their symptoms? To what extent do they have paralysing effects on the whole system? To answer these questions, we need to look carefully at the principal overlapping, but identifiably different, structural problems lodged within the structures of cosmocracy. A sample of four – they are among the most pertinent – are outlined below.

Political entropy

In affairs of government, as in physics, confusion and ineffectiveness are the offspring of entropy, the condition of inertness and self-degradation that results from formlessness. Whatever advantages bless its clumsy structures, the system of cosmocracy displays definite signs of entropy. In this sense it poses challenges that are the opposite of those confronted during recent centuries by the influential separation of powers doctrine. That doctrine, famously associated with Bolingbroke and Montesquieu, proposed solutions to the over-concentration of power that typically plagued the absolutist states of early modern Europe. Bolingbroke remarked: 'The love of power is natural; it is insatiable; almost constantly whetted; and never cloyed by possession'. Montesquieu, marked by his training as a magistrate of a provincial *parlement*, added: 'Pour qu'on ne puisse abuser du pouvoir, il faut que, par la disposition des choses, le pouvoir arrête le pouvoir' (Montesquieu, 1979: book XI, Chapter 4).

This kind of language may in future come to be strikingly relevant for the system of cosmocracy, but for the moment, and for the foreseeable future, this system is hampered by the under-concentration of powers. The serious lack of driving seats and steering mechanisms, and the ineffectiveness of many that currently do exist – note that no unfavourable comparison with an imaginary perfect form of state is here being secretly made – is one of cosmocracy's striking weaknesses. Cosmocracy has no proper functioning parliament or network of parliaments through which demands from global civil society could be peacefully channelled. There exists no executive power, for instance an elected, fixed-term and impeachable president of the world. There are no political parties that campaign globally, on a regular basis, trying to gather support for certain policies among business and non-business NGOs and receptive governments (Kreml and Kegley, 1996). There is no global army or police force that could act decisively to bring about order and maintain peace within and across the territorial boundaries of states and regions. There is not yet a global criminal justice system – with sharp teeth.

Where global steering mechanisms do exist within the cosmocracy, they are often hampered by four related impediments – which highlight their serious need of overhaul and pleaching. First, they are often marked by impotence caused by funding shortages, under-staffing, jurisdictional disputes, and consequent lack of reputation. A case in point is the main global agency for monitoring and preventing world-wide money laundering, the Paris-based Financial Action Task Force (FATF). Set up by the Group of Seven governments in 1989, mainly to counter money laundering by global drug cartels, it operated (in 2001) with a staff of only five and a budget of only FFr5.8m (US$810,000) – despite its obvious strategic importance for turbocapitalism and cosmocracy, and despite its formal backing by the European Commission, the Gulf Co-operation Council, and 29 states (but not including important countries like Russia, Indonesia and Egypt). Political entropy also results from bureaucratic sclerosis and inertia caused by demarcation disputes and the opacity and paralysis that results from the tangled, rhizomatous (or rootstalk-like) structures of decision-making.

Unaccountability problems

Quite a few of the institutions that comprise the system of cosmocracy are publicly unaccountable. Cosmocracy is not quite a species of absolutism, since its core contains rich networks of democratic procedures designed to expose and oppose hubris. Yet when considered overall, as an integrated polity, cosmocracy definitely has an affinity with authoritarian, rather than representative-democratic procedures. It is full of what the English call rotten boroughs, whose political processes are invisible to many millions of eyes. The ingredients of representative democracy are in short supply, and often entirely absent. Time-limited power granted on the basis of open and equal electoral competititions, effective complaints and evaluation procedures, the obligation of power-wielders to solicit different, openly expressed opinions and to explain and justify their actions publicly to stakeholders (wherever they are on the face of the earth), and to resign in cases of gross mismanagement or misconduct – these vital rules, well-outlined in initiatives like the Global Accountability Project and the Campaign for a More Democratic United Nations (CAMDUN), are often flouted by the structures of cosmocracy, many of which are obscure and secretive. Whether in Beijing or Berlin, those who wield power within these structures – like all exercisers of power – tend to feed upon the two standard justifications for concealing its motives and moves. They say that it is foolhardy to reveal one's hand to one's opponents and enemies (let us call this the Rumsfeld Rule: 'In difficult situations, governments do not discuss pressing matters' (Rumsfeld 2001)). They repeat as well some version of Plato's Rule that affairs of government are too complex and difficult to explain to publics, who would not in any case understand what is at stake. Sometimes these two alibis converge, as when the institutions of cosmocracy deliberately shield themselves from public scrutiny because their aim is openly to favour a certain power group within the global civil society, using such techniques as secrecy, spin, and legal coercion.

There are unfortunately plenty of examples where for instance cosmocratic institutions resemble management boards for turbocapitalism. The tribunals set up under NAFTA – sarcastically condemned by the Canadian trade lawyer Steven Shrybman as a 'revolutionary development in international law' – enable corporations to veto governmental restrictions upon corporate power by bringing a case before a tribunal that operates *in camera*. If a company considers that its commercial rights have been violated, and if the tribunal finds in favour of the company and its complaint, then a government is legally obliged to make a pay-out to the corporation. Such authoritarian arrangements give a bad name to global governance. They fuel the suspicion that turbocapitalist firms, and the global economy in general, have been unfairly granted unlimited grazing rights that threaten the authority of democratically elected governments. The power of property feels unchecked; it seems that the global economy has become master to none, that hard-won citizens' rights at home are being gobbled up by unchecked world-wide 'market forces'. This conclusion easily fuels fatalism: as John Ralston Saul (1995) has pointed out, the *ad hoc* alliance between turbocapitalism and the enabling and compliant power of cosmocratic institutions potentially destroys the one institution that citizens can identify with as their own: representative government. A sense spreads that governments are powerless in the face of mysterious forces operating 'out there', in the buccaneering, nineteenth-century-style global economy.

Within the system of cosmocracy, these familiar alibis of unaccountable power are regularly supplemented by two less familiar dynamics. One of them is related to the problem of complexity: the fragmentation of political authority, combined with a technocratic mind-set among officials and a lack of public-friendly, well-trained administrative staff, ensures that many parts of the cosmocracy are closed off from either mutual or public scrutiny of any kind. They come to feel like an impenetrable jungle of acronyms. Matters are worsened by the tyranny of distance: despite the noblest of public-spirited motives, decision-makers tend to lose track of their decisions, which are whizzed around in a cyclotron of global structures and events, with many different and unpredictable effects. Governing at a distance tends to 'disjoin remorse from power' (Shakespeare). Responsibility is overpowered. It becomes just a word.

A dominant power

The body politic of cosmocracy contains a destabilising anti-body: a dominant power, the United States. Like all previous modern dominant powers – from Habsburg Spain to the *Pax Britannica* of the nineteenth century – this one seeks mastery over the whole system. Yet the United States differs from these previous dominant powers in two fundamental ways. It is the first such power in human history that finds itself, partly thanks to a measure of historical luck, of being in the position to lay claim to world hegemony. It is also unusual because it is a dominant power equipped with a revolutionary world-view: a vision of itself, and the whole world, as a unique constitutional order based upon the republican, federal, democratic principles first crafted in the 1776 revolution. In its embrace of the Philadelphia model, America differs, say, from the House of Habsburg, which was a dynastic confederation of states (stretching from Portugal and the Netherlands to Naples and Milan through to Bohemia and Hungary) that gathered at the altar of international Catholicism. The new dominant power also differs from nineteenth-century Britain, the driving force behind the previous phase of globalisation. Even at the height of its power, those who governed Britain sensed the folly of risking everything, including its fleet, to conquer the world. Where they perceived that they could not intervene successfully, in continental Europe or South America, they refrained from doing so (Hobsbawm, 2001). The United States shows few signs of acting in this way. Like revolutionary France and Soviet Russia before it, the United States is a territorial power dedicated to transforming the whole world in its favour. True, its political leaders and diplomats are often embarrassed by talk of 'empire'; they speak and act as if the United States were only one state among others. Such efforts of an empire to masquerade as a state are nevertheless wearing thin: the days when it could be said (by Gore Vidal and others) that the success of the American empire depends in part upon keeping it a secret are coming to an end. Its leaders now see themselves more and more as the world's first unchallenged global imperial power, as a sequel and effective replacement of the old system of nineteenth- and twentieth-century imperial powers that once ruled the world, and have now collapsed.

The United States tends to behave in this way, despite historical evidence that all previous dominant powers produce geopolitical instability, and despite growing evidence, reinforced by the theory of global civil society, that the world has become too large and complicated to be governed by a single power. The dominant power often operates bullishly, and it does so because its governing class perceive strength as the principal way in which it can secure its flanks and protect its dominant power privileges, if need be by exercising the right of direct intervention into others' affairs. This perception is not inaccurate. Considered as a political subsystem of cosmocracy, the dominant power is the heartland of the turbo-capitalist economy (despite the fact that its share of world production has fallen from one-third to one-fifth during the past half-century), the driving force of the global telecommunications and entertainment industries, and the homeland of the mightiest army in the world. During the Clinton presidencies, it completed the transformation of its strategy of global containment into the capacity 'nearly simultaneously' to fight two major regional wars (Department of Defence, 1994). The Gulf War of 1991, the Bosnian pacification of 1995, and the overthrow and arrest of Milosevic after the war in Kosovo all showed that decisive military action at the global level depended on the United States. So too did the 2001 war against the government of Afghanistan, which collapsed quickly under the impact of the most advanced military technology known to humanity: state-of-the-art bombing, missiles fired through doorways by unmanned Predator aircraft, interception of the enemy's every telephone call and radio transmission, bombs that burst open the deepest bunkers. The dominant power's war-fighting budget for 1999 was only two-thirds of what it was in 1989, but still it accounts for 35 per cent of the world's total military spending (Russia's share was ten times less); expenditure on the armed forces is equal to the sum total of the next largest eight states in the world. The United States has meanwhile consolidated its role as the biggest arms dealer, with sales in the year 2000 worth US$18.6 billion, more than half the $36.9 billion global arms trade figure (*New York Times*, 21 August 2001).

The dominant power can and does throw its weight around – most recently, in Serbia, Afghanistan and Iraq. Its leaders know that money, information, kilobytes, blood and iron count in world affairs. Its politicians are tempted, like every previous dominant power of the modern era, to act as a vigilante power, to see their power as the ability, especially when push comes to shove, to measure their strength against all of their rivals combined (Wight, 1978). They do so partly through arrogant presumptions – summarised in the closing words of presidential speeches, 'May God bless the United States of America' – and straightforward designs of aggrandisement and neglecting or cherry-picking international agencies and agreements at their own convenience; and partly through the quite different insistence that everybody has an 'urgent and binding obligation' to gather beneath the Stars and Stripes, and to march forwards with America in its world-wide struggle for democratic freedoms (George Bush Jr, 2001).

Cosmopolitan democracy?

When comparing monarchies and republics, the great Dutch political commentator, Jan de Witt, claimed that the former (in line with Machiavelli's *Il principe*) encouraged princes to act using the force of lions and the cunning of foxes. By contrast, de Witt said (cited in Venturi, 1970: 35–6), those who are elected and in charge of republics are encouraged to act with stealth, like cats, which are both 'agile and prudent'. De Witt's rule-of-thumb today retains its heuristic value. For whether the United States will succumb to the temptation of lion-and-fox world aggrandisement, or whether, like the British before them, it will instead take measures to behave carefully, like a cat, and to avoid hubris, for instance by playing the role of catalyst of a more effective and democratic form of cosmocracy, is among the great, if dangerous political issues of our time. Its resolution will help to determine the life span of global civil society. If the hegemonic power turns out (unusually) to be a self-limiting global force for 'constitutional order' guided by principles like power-sharing, multilateralism and the rule of law, then global civil society could well thrive during the coming years. If, on the other hand, the American empire consistently behaves as if it is morally entitled to run the whole world, and to act on its behalf, then almost certainly that roguery would have the effect of stirring up geopolitical troubles. That roguery would in turn work against global civil society, perhaps even wrecking the chances of its survival.

The problem of whether (or how) the dominant power can be tamed is compounded by the pressing need to develop a more effective and legitimate form of cosmocracy. What can be done to tame and control the zones of unaccountable power within the actually existing cosmocracy? Following the world's largest death squad atrocity directed at two key symbols of the emerging global civil society and cosmocracy, it is to be hoped – forlornly, in all probability – that the classical tactic of tyrant-killing by monarchomachs, as the Scot Barclay famously called it, has lost all legitimacy. Whatever transpires, the search for solutions to the problem of unaccountable power on a global scale will continue; the members of global civil society cannot expect the perpetrators of incompetence and hubris to be destroyed automatically by the angry gods. Other, human, all-too-human remedies will be needed.

It is obvious to many that a pressing constitutional agenda confronts both the actually existing cosmocracy and global civil society: the need to find the appropriate methods for enabling something like effective, publicly accountable government to develop on a global scale. Alas, there is currently no consensus about what form this agenda might take. This is partly because of the inordinate strength of the neo-liberal forces that champion free market turbocapitalism *über alles*. It is also partly because some of their opponents slam 'globalisation' in the name of stronger and more nationalist territorial states, or by means of vague notions of 'de-globalisation' and the 'deconcentration and decentralization of institutional power' through 'the re-empowerment of the local and the national' (Bello, 2000). Matters are not helped by the far-fetched thinking that foolishly turns its back on the actually existing system of cosmocracy, in order to predict (and in the process recommend) the arrival of 'world government'. Meanwhile, political thinkers are divided about what should or could be done. Some defend the neo-Kantian principle of a transnational democratic legal order, a community of all democratic communities, something resembling a global *Rechtstaat*, of the kind implied in Article 28 of the Universal Declaration of Human Rights: 'Everyone is entitled to a social and international order in which the rights and freedoms set forth in the Declaration can be fully realised'. Others anticipate a second-best scenario that owes everything to Emmerich de Vattel: a complex international system of nominally sovereign, democratic states that are the voting members in a variety of international fora. Still others foresee a new compromise between these two options: a cosmopolitan process of democratisation, through which citizens gain a voice within their own states and in sites of power among their states (Archibugi and Held, 1994).

This latter approach – the appeal to 'cosmopolitan democracy' – currently enjoys some popularity in academic circles. Its early exponents proposed a 'system of geo-governance unlike any other proposed to date'. This approach (perhaps without intending to) tried to bring a rather unconventional meaning to the word cosmopolitan, to indicate 'a model of political organization in which citizens, wherever they are located in the world, have a voice, input and political representation in international affairs, in parallel with and independently of their own governments'. Cosmopolitanism measures itself against historical examples. It aims to steer a course between and beyond, on the one hand, NATO-style arrangements, whose transnational power structures are a law unto themselves, and at odds with the mainly democratic structures of their member states; and, on the other hand, Congress of Vienna-style arrangements, which displayed the inverse mismatch: generous inter-state consultative mechanisms among states that were mostly autocratic. Cosmopolitan democracy looks forward instead to 'the parallel development of democracy both within states and among states'. It is noted that this double democratisation requires the building of 'authoritative global institutions', like the reform of the Security Council, the creation of a second chamber in the United Nations, the strengthening of international law, even the creation of 'a small but effective, accountable, international military force' (ibid., 1994).

The early version of the cosmopolitan democracy approach summarised here is stimulating, but unconvincing. Its definition of democracy is vague and tautologous ('the distinctive feature of democracy is ... not only a particular set of procedures [important though this is], but also the pursuit of democratic values involving the extension of popular participation in the political process') and rests ultimately on the questionable, arguably outdated principle that democracy equals 'popular participation'. And note, above all, the not-so-secret attachment to an originally Kantian, two-level or 'double democratisation' schema. 'What is necessary', it is argued, 'is to deprive states of some of their more coercive and restrictive powers: in the former case, those powers which are deployed against the welfare and safety of citizens; in the latter case, those powers which are deployed to forestall or inhibit collaborative relations among states on pressing transnational questions'. Then comes a revealing conclusion: 'Cosmopolitan institutions must come to coexist with the established powers of states, overriding them only in certain, well-defined spheres of activity' (ibid., 1994).

The proposed peaceful co-existence between two levels of government is problematic, if only because, empirically speaking, the complex and contradictory structures of cosmocracy are against it. The model of cosmopolitan democracy supposes that we are still living in the age of Kant – or the age that spawned Tennyson's vision of 'the Parliament of Man, the Federation of the World'. It rests, unfortunately, upon what can be called the Law of the Excluded Middle: an object of theoretical reflection, it is supposed, can or may be here or there, but not in both places at once. It can be A or not-A, but not both, or not somewhere in-between. Things, events, people have their place: they belong to separate and pure realms. Such dualistic thinking is unhelpful in the task of theoretically understanding how substantially to increase the level of public accountability of governmental institutions on a global scale. Such a theory not only needs to be clearer and more persuasive about the normative meanings of democracy; on descriptive grounds, it also needs to be much more sensitive to the 'messy', self-contradictory, criss-crossing, dynamic networks of mediated power that are a basic feature of cosmocracy.

Note

1   Bose-Einstein condensates, so named and predicted to exist by Satyendra Nath Bose and Albert Einstein some 70 years before their actual laboratory creation, are bundles of atoms that sing in unison, in that they lose their individual identities and join together in a single energy state after being cooled down to just a few billionths of a degree above absolute zero.

References

Archibugi, D. and Held, D. (eds) (1994) *Cosmopolitan Democracy*, Oxford: Blackwell.

Bello, W. (2000) 'The Struggle for a Deglobalized World', www.igc.org/trac/feature/wto/8-bello.html.

Brown, C. (2000) 'Cosmopolitanism, World Citizenship and Global Civil Society', *Critical Review of International Social and Political Philosophy* 3: 7–26.

Bush, G. Jr (2001) From the speech of President George Bush Jr at the United Nations, as reported in the *Financial Times*, London, 23 November 2001: 13.

Chinkin, C. (2000) 'Normative Development in the International Legal System', in D. Shelton (ed.) *Commitment and Compliance: The Role of Non-Binding Norms in the International Legal System*, Oxford: Oxford University Press.

Clark, A. M. *et al.* (1998) 'The Sovereign Limits of Global Civil Society: A Comparison of NGO Participation in UN World Conferences on the Environment, Human Rights, and Women', *World Politics* 51, 1.

Deguchi, M. (1999) 'A Comparative View of Civil Society', *Washington-Japan Journal* VII, I: 11–20.

Department of Defense (1994) *Annual Report to the President and Congress, 1994*, Washington, D.C.

Hobsbawm, E. (2001) *On The Edge of the New Century*, New York: New Press.

Klein, N. (2000) *No Logo*, London: Flamingo.

Kreml, W. and Kegley, C. W. Jr (1996) 'A Global Political Party: The Next Step', *Alternatives* 21: 123–34.

Interview with Miklos Marschall, Executive Director of the Hungarian Chapter of Transparency International (Berlin, 3 June 2002).

Montesquieu (1979) *De l'esprit des lois* (1748), edited by Victor Goldschmidt, Paris.

Pérez-Diaz, V. (1999) 'La formación de Europa: nacionalismos civiles e inciviles', *Claves* (Madrid), 97, Noviembre 1999: 10–21.

Risse, T. (2002) 'Transnational Actors and World Politics', in W. Carlsnaes *et al.* (eds) *Handbook of International Relations*, London: Sage.

Rumsfeld, D. from a press conference featuring Donald Rumsfeld, United States Defense Secretary, *CNN* (7 October 2001).

Salamon, L. (1999) 'Government and Nonprofit Relations in Perspective', in the publication of the Urban Institute, *Nonprofits and Government: Collaboration and Conflict*, Washington, D.C.

Saul, J. R. (1995) *The Unconscious Civilization*, Concord: House of Anansi Press.

Schapiro, M. (1988) 'Judicial Selection and the Design of Clumsy Institutions', *Southern California Law Review* 61: 1555–69.

Shelton, D. (2001) 'The Nature and Role of International Law in a Globalised World', paper presented to the conference *Globalisation and Its Possibilities*, University of Sydney, December 12–14.

Tendler, J. (1982) *Turning Private Voluntary Organizations into Developmental Agencies: Questions for Evaluation*, USAID Program Evaluation Discussion Paper 12, Washington D.C.

Venturi, F. (1970) *Utopia e riforma nell'illuminismo*, Turin: Einaudi.

Wapner, R. (2000) 'The Normative Promise of Nonstate Actors: A Theoretical Account of Global Civil Society', in R. Wapner and L. E. J. Ruiz (eds) *Principled World Politics. The Challenge of Normative International Relations*, Lanham, Md.: Rowman & Littlefield Publishers.

Wight, M. (1978) *Power Politics*, H. Bull and C. Holbraad (eds), Leicester: Leicester University Press.

3 The demoralised subject of global civil society[1]

Vanessa Pupavac

The idea of global civil society gained significant ground in the 1990s following the end of the Cold War. Advocates were encouraged by the strides in international human rights regimes and the foundation of an international criminal justice system in which human rights were invoked as transcending national sovereignty. Kenneth Roth, director of Human Rights Watch, proclaimed in 1999 that human rights had now trumped national sovereignty (Roth, 1999). However, since September 11 and the inauguration of the war on terrorism, global civil society advocates identify reversals in developments towards global civil society. In contrast to the global civil society literature, this chapter identifies problems with the concept of global civil society and its concept of the rights-holding subject. The chapter's core argument is that global civil society advocacy projects a demoralised vision for humanity, which constrains human aspirations and inverts rights and freedoms. A profound scepticism of citizens as moral beings underlies the global governance sought by advocates of this model. First, the chapter analyses the demise of belief in humanity as progressive history-making subjects. Second, it analyses global civil society's concept of rights. Third, it assesses the contemporary model of aid and development. It concludes that global civil society advocacy represents a retreat from universal rights and reinforces official donor government policies disciplining populations. However, the disciplining of populations is mystified under the contemporary therapeutic mechanisms of self-articulation.

The demoralised political subject

The ideals of global civil society reflect the broader political crisis in Western societies revealed in the wake of liberalism's triumphant proclamation of the end of history following the Cold War's conclusion (Fukuyama, 1992). The crisis of liberalism, understood loosely as the West's underlying political philosophy affirming the individual and individual freedoms, has affected contemporary Western societies' understanding of the human condition with profound implications for the nature of politics and political subjectivity. Liberalism's crisis arises from the inherent tensions in a civic virtue founded on the affirmation of the individual and the privatisation of beliefs and conscience (Hunter, 2000). Liberalism has always confronted the dilemma of how to prevent citizens turning inward and withdrawing from involvement in the public sphere. This phenomenon has been analysed variously as 'demoralisation', 'the fall of public man' (Sennett, 1976), the rise of a 'culture of narcissism' (Lasch, 1979) or as constituting a 'therapeutic ethos' (Nolan, 1998; Furedi, 2003). How does society maintain a civic consciousness through an ethos which makes a virtue of the individual? For a civic virtue which takes the self as its moral reference point and which promotes individual fulfilment risks imploding as citizens seek personal realisation and disengage from politics.

Historically the risks of liberalism's solipsism have been countered by its struggle against tradition and competing political ideologies, or in its defensive recreation of tradition. But liberalism risks the erosion of its civic ethos following the death of tradition, secularisation and its triumph over alternative ideologies. What is to prevent the slide from the public into the personal? For it is not only civic life but ironically individuals also that risk becoming impoverished (Furedi, 2003; Hunter, 2000; Nolan, 1998, Sennett, 1976). The logic of liberalism threatens its own foundation: the individual. Thus sociological studies have referred to the 'death of character' (Hunter, 2000) or the 'minimal self' (Lasch, 1984). Consequently, liberalism's ideological triumph and its declaration of the end of history involves the end of the history-making subject, as Michael Dillon and Paul Fletcher have explored (2003). The demise of political or ideological contestation involves the demise of citizens as political beings. Having withdrawn from civic activities, citizens are reduced to passive consumers or victims of their environment seeking perpetual affirmation and protection. Citizens, Dillon and Fletcher argue, retreat to a more biological condition governed by biological instinctual desires. The citizen becomes infantilised by the diminishing of political subjectivity and adult maturity is no longer expected or achieved. The social distinction between adulthood and childhood is blurred as adulthood loses its social aspect and adult pursuits are trivialised as arbitrary, socially irrelevant activities. The moral capacity of citizens, whose maturity is in doubt, can no longer be taken for granted.

Liberalism's secular governance has been based on a social division between groups considered to have the capacity to determine their own lives and those deemed unable. Liberal states have been willing to use force to secure its vision of peace against groups or populations deemed immature and unfit (Dillon and Fletcher, 2003; Dillon and Reid, 2000; Duffield, 2001; Furedi, 1994). The liberal state, reluctant to interfere in the private lives of individuals deemed fit, developed new secular technologies to govern the personality and behaviour of those deemed unfit. Political movements challenged liberalism's exclusions, and rights were incrementally extended to new groups who could demonstrate their maturity and fitness. But if citizens are no longer assumed to have a developed moral capacity and cannot be trusted to make appropriate judgements, then liberalism's privatisation of beliefs and conscience no longer makes sense. Consequently, technologies of governance previously reserved for sections of society categorised as unfit become viewed as universally relevant and are generalised for the whole of society. With the erosion of adult maturity, citizens in general, not just a residuum, are regarded as at risk of psychosocial dysfunction and as requiring therapeutic governance (Pupavac, 2001; 2004). Therapeutic governance tends to invert rights, rather than explicitly withdrawing them, at least domestically. Rights are thus being reconfigured as rights of external interventions on behalf of infantilised citizens to avert psychosocial dysfunction and support them in becoming good citizens.

The rest of the chapter suggests that global civil society advocacy globalises a demoralised subject and a demoralised vision. The next section examines the implications of global civil society advocacy for sovereign equality.

The demoralised human rights subject

I will begin by examining the ideal of global civil society and what makes the concept so attractive. The key attraction of the concept of global civil society is its avowed affirmation of the individual over states. For global civil society advocates, as David Held has stated, 'the ultimate units of moral concern are individual people, not states or other particular forms of human association' (Held, 2003: 470). Proponents seek to challenge a Realist paradigm based on states as the only legitimate actors and denying individual subjectivity in the international sphere. Global civil society's elevation of the individual is contrasted to a conceptualisation of international society based on national sovereignty. Thus proponents have argued against a Realist paradigm making national politics paramount over global morality (Held, 2003: 469; Midgely, 1999). For cosmopolitans, as for other global civil society advocates, 'Humankind belongs to a single moral realm in which each person is equally worthy of respect and consideration' (Held, 2003: 470), in contrast to the particularist morality of Realists. Again, in the Realist world of states as the only legitimate actors, there is no space for the rights of the individual in the international sphere. Against this model, global civil society is denoted as 'the ethical and political space which sets out the terms of reference for the recognition of people's equal moral worth, their active agency and what is essential for their autonomy and development' (Held, 2003: 473).

States are condemned in global civil society discourse today both for lacking the capacity to guarantee the security of their citizens under glob-alisation and for all too frequently actually imperilling their security. These accounts typically portray states as inadequate and/or immoral actors. Global civil society is envisaged as transcending the failures of states. The immorality or at best moral minimalism of a state-centric Realpolitik is contrasted with the ethics of global responsibility informing the concept of global civil society. In particular, global civil society aspires to give a voice to the marginalised through entrenching supranational human rights. But underlying the imperative to codify human rights today is a retreat from confidence in the moral and political capacity of ordinary citizens. Strikingly, contemporary human rights advocacy is founded on a demoralised subject who has to be constituted and empowered by external advocates. External human rights advocacy has come to the limelight, whereas earlier external human rights advocacy played a subordinate, largely offstage or witness role to national political activists facing political oppression from authoritarian regimes.

At the same time contemporary human rights advocacy is creating new hierarchies and divisions. The moral and political divisions accompanying human rights advocacy do not simply arise in its practice but at the con-ceptual level. Proponents are re-conceptualising the rights-holder and the meaning of rights in their aspiration to entrench supranational rights trumping national sovereignty. This re-conception seeks to extend rights to excluded groups but its significance is to empower unaccountable exter-nal advocates. How does this phenomenon arise? The international system based on national sovereignty is associated with a social contract model of political and civil rights founded on the notion of the rights-holder as having the power or capacity to guarantee his or her own rights. Here the subject of rights and the agent of rights are one. However, this conception of rights has been criticised as immoral for excluding persons who lack capacity, that is, those who are most vulnerable and worthy of moral claim. Within the traditional understanding of rights, where the possession of rights follows capacity, the problem of those lacking capacity has been addressed, first, through developing prohibitions on the use of force and, second, by developing national economic and social welfare protection.

The novelty of human rights discourse is that rights are conceptualised as not merely offering welfare protection but as empowering those who lack capacity. But conferring the language of rights onto subjects who depend on external advocacy only *appears* to move beyond protection and resolve the problem of their lack of political and social agency. For who is the agent of human rights-holders? The social contract model does not pose this conceptual problem, for it presupposes that the rights-holder and the guarantor of rights are the same person. However, the human rights-holder depends on an external advocate. But who is entitled to speak on behalf of the human rights-holder? Who decides what is codified as human rights? How do human rights-holders determine what rights are codified in their name? How do human rights-holders hold the agent of human rights accountable for how human rights are interpreted, and whether and how human rights are enforced? The issue of the designation and accountability of the agent of human rights is not properly addressed by global civil society proponents.

In making claims for the superiority of global civil society, the impression is often conveyed that the sphere has a monopoly on virtue and is free from the temptations that afflict nation-state politics. A dualism is set up between a virtuous global civil society and a dirty world of national politics. Thus, for example, Derek Heater talks about the temptations of national allegiance encouraging the use of violence (Heater, 1999: 188). Proponents often voice their distrust of their own publics to ratify their conception of the good, and propose the necessity of bypassing national politics to secure this vision of the good. On the one hand, we are to believe that in the sphere of global civil society the efficacy of policy-making is guaranteed by ethical advocates. On the other hand, the claim to virtue is informed by a loss of faith in the moral agency of national electorates who are commonly depicted as inimical to the good. Human rights advocates' assumption of moral agency against electorates involves de-recognition of the moral agency of citizens nationally, whereas classical social contract thinking presupposed the moral agency of rights-holding citizens. Allowed to exercise their own free will, it is feared the majority of citizens will fail to endorse the ethical global life. Suspicion of the moral capacity of majorities has led human rights advocacy to exhibit a preference for judicial decision-making and the codification of supranational frameworks beyond national political processes. In other words, there is a retreat from the modern ideal of law as derived from the will of legal subjects. A moral division is thereby created between a global ethical elite of moral agents and the mass of citizens globally.

In claiming all virtue, global civil society is also disclaiming its own will to sovereignty, albeit a demoralised sovereignty. Yet global civil society would be acting as sovereign by determining human rights norms and their application. In aspiring to transcend national sovereignty, proponents are effectively evading national accountability, rather than the exercise of sovereignty *per se*. Furthermore, global civil society advocacy legitimises the demise of sovereign equality between states and the expansion of the sovereignty of the most powerful states that are designated as enforcer states against the rest. Effectively, global civil society is conceptualised on the basis of a new moral division between responsible and irresponsible states, and between a global ethical elite of moral agents and the mass of humanity. So even at the ideal level there are fundamental problems with the universalist claims made of global civil society and its transcending of sovereignty.

The problem of unequal states can hardly be blamed on global civil society advocacy. However, earlier architects of an international system considered that, in an unequal world where some states were manifestly weaker than others, then outlawing the use of force and interference in the internal affairs of states was the best available mechanism for curbing sovereign abuse by powerful states. The prohibitions on the use of force and non-interference were honoured more in the breach than respected. Nevertheless, these prohibitions did represent a high point in aspirations towards a more equal world in their attempts to bolster sovereign equality. Global civil society advocates, however, are overturning this injunction and in the process eroding the principle of non-interference in the internal affairs of states, thereby extending the writ of the most powerful states.

Moreover, Southern states are destined to be weak demoralised subjects under global civil society's conception of good development, which has abandoned the vision of economic advancement of the South to the level of the Northern industrialised states. Realisation of sovereign equality for Southern states was regarded as dependent on their economic advancement through industrialisation. Without substantial economic advancement, Southern states lack the capacity to become moral agents domestically securing their population's welfare, nor can they be equal subjects internationally. Consequently, the possibility of Southern states becoming moral and political equals has been abandoned in the conception of global civil society order. The abandonment of industrialisation has not however meant the abandonment of international development policy, but its re-invention as psychosocial governance of the South.

Demoralised humanitarianism

As we have seen, global civil society proponents give an idealised account of global civil society as the realm of virtue in contrast to the immorality of states. Yet the irony of this idealised account is the profound soul-searching and misgivings over its role that the NGO sector has experienced over the last decade. NGOs have been distinctly uncertain about their own virtue and the ethical principles they espouse, even as global civil society proponents have invoked them as key actors in their vision. NGOs have received strong backing from western governments since the end of the Cold War as these governments have shifted from bilateral aid to channelling aid through NGOs. This official endorsement has significantly increased the NGOs' profile and the scope of their activities in Southern states, but it has also tended to heighten the NGOs' internal crises of legitimacy.

The demoralisation of humanitarian ideals is captured in critical accounts written by former aid workers. The aid worker is characterised as *The Selfish Altruist* in a personal account by former Oxfam field officer, Tony Vaux (2001), an account which contrasts sharply with the projection of global civil society as the realm of virtue. Numerous reports express fears over NGOs having lost their earlier degree of independence, being increasingly co-opted by donor governments. Accounts such as Michael Maren's *Road to Hell: The Ravaging Effects of Foreign Aid and International Charity*, or David Sogge's *Compassion and Calculation: The Business of Private Foreign Aid*, characterise the NGO sector as having become a bloated industry. NGOs are portrayed as being more concerned with building their own business empires, protecting their share of the aid market and cultivating relations with donor governments, than aiding beneficiaries.

Indeed, the very ideals of humanitarianism have been at issue, since these ideals reflect evolving liberal norms. Historically, the purpose of charitable-giving under liberal secularisation shifted from being primarily about the salvation of the giver to being concerned with the needs of the recipient. In this shift there has always been a tension between the affirmation of a common humanity versus a judgement as to fitness; in other words, a tension between the provision of relief to the needy and their moral improvement. To be dependent on the receipt of welfare was commonly associated with a failing of character. Liberalism, with its elevation of the individual has essentially understood social change in terms of individual change. We can see how the individual is taken as the starting point for social explanations in Anglo-American social psychology, which has had a growing influence on social policy (and international development). Anglo-American social psychology traces back the root of social problems to the socialisation of individuals. Passionate campaigns were conducted in the nineteenth century against irresponsible alms-giving, which was condemned for undermining industriousness and encouraging irresponsibility and dependency. Instead, charity was to distinguish between the deserving and undeserving poor and foster recipients' moral improvement. So the charitable work was to take into account the character of the potential recipient and, where good character was lacking, charity was to be directed towards their moral rehabilitation. A core theme of charity work was the importance of instilling work habits to develop the moral character of the poor.

Debates over international humanitarianism echo these preoccupations. The origins of key western humanitarian organisations, founded in response to European wars, demonstrate an aspiration to recognise a common humanity transcending politics and nation. Humanitarianism has traditionally aspired to treat people as ends in themselves and provide aid to needy people irrespective of the politics of their situation. For example, Save the Children was founded in Britain in 1919 to provide relief to German children, transcending the national politics which opposed the provision of aid to a former enemy nation. Similarly, Oxfam was founded to provide aid to famine-stricken Greece under allied blockade during the Second World War, seeking to establish a humanitarian space transcending the politics of war. The traditional principles of humanitarian aid, of neutrality, impartiality and consent embodied in the International

Committee of the Red Cross, did not make the character of the recipients an issue. Moral approbation was not attached in the same way to those communities whose distress was seen as exceptional and temporary, whether in war or natural disaster.

The crisis of legitimacy in the NGO sector has arguably hit hardest on its traditional humanitarian relief role, despite the public support it has enjoyed here. The humanitarian space outside of politics and its treatment of people as ends has been squeezed under the imperative of global governance's security and developmental concerns. The erosion of the humanitarian space and its principles may be traced to the re-orientation of aid organisations towards development. Western humanitarian organisations had re-invented themselves as development agencies following resolution of the European refugee crisis and decolonisation, and subsequently re-directed their work to the developing world.

Turning then to a fuller discussion of development aid, it is important to note that the developmental orientation has been critical of humanitarian aid for being inadequate and short-termist. Once vulnerability to war and disaster was seen not as exceptional but as endemic to particular societies – which then had to be addressed through long-term development – then developmental criteria began to be applied to humanitarian aid. As Hugo Slim has shown (1998; 2000), there has been a shift in humanitarianism from deontological ethics, which treats people as ends in themselves, to consequential ethics, which considers the long-term social impact of aid and not just the immediate relief of individuals. Moral judgements about the worthiness of recipients, and aid conditionality to improve recipient societies, have crept into humanitarian work where previously moral and political judgements were suspended. These judgements were held in check by the Cold War solidarist framework operating within the aid sector, which emphasised support for the decolonised states. However, the traditional humanitarian relief role has come under systematic attack since the end of the Cold War. Critiques such as Mary Anderson's *Do No Harm*, or Alex de Waal's *Famine Crimes*, have accused humanitarian relief of being short-termist, for 'feeding the killers', and for prolonging conflict and undermining development.

The new humanitarianism, which emerged in the 1990s from the critique of traditional humanitarianism, corresponds in key respects with contemporary global civil society advocacy and its championing of human rights and impatience with national sovereignty. Attacks against traditional humanitarianism came to a head over the Rwandan genocide of 1994. Aid agencies following traditional principles were accused of being complicit in the Hutu massacres of Tutsis and of providing aid to genocidaires. These accusations arose because of their initial silence over the killings and treatment of the Hutu flight from Rwanda in the wake of the killings as an ordinary humanitarian crisis. In the debacle over humanitarian responses in Rwanda, aid organisations sought to reject the traditional humanitarian principles, in particular the principles of neutrality and consent vis-à-vis the warring parties. The new humanitarianism that superseded traditional humanitarianism evolved from the 'without borders' organisations, which deliberately sought to challenge national sovereignty and bear witness against states over their human rights abuses (Chandler, 2002; Duffield, 2001; Macrae, 2001). The new rights-based humanitarianism seeks to take up the cause of the human rights victim and is premised on the idea that aid should further human rights, security and development. These imperatives have led aid agencies to seek to be more discriminating in their provision: to make a distinction between sides, to be mindful of not feeding the killers, to promote the voices of victims, and all the while to not create dependency. At the same time, humanitarianism has been more willing to engage with politics and pursue enforcement of human rights.

However, the new rights-based humanitarianism has not proved to be the magic bullet for humanitarian organisations and has immediately created new ethical dilemmas for aid agencies. The starting point of the new rights-based humanitarianism is the human rights victim, but yet the developmental imperatives of rights-based humanitarianism can collide with the interests of the individual human rights victim. Making humanitarian aid conditional on the fulfilment of human rights risks sacrificing the immediate needs of vulnerable individuals in the uncertain hope of promoting social justice. Yet the human rights victim cannot hold the self-declared human rights agent accountable for how his or her interests are interpreted and potentially denied. That rights-based humanitarianism may deny recognition to some groups was illustrated in the continuing Rwandan crisis. Humanitarian aid was withdrawn from Hutu refugees in camps outside Rwanda following concerns over providing aid to Hutu genocidaires. Yet withdrawing aid from these camps involved causing up to 200,000 preventable deaths, including an estimated 75,000 infants under five who could in no way be culpable for the massacres in Rwanda (Stockton, 1998). This is by no means an isolated example of how an approach seeking to affirm the human rights victim can risk the lives of vulnerable groups. Oxfam found itself doing just that when its gender rights policy clashed with the Taliban government's stance towards women. Oxfam's principled withdrawal from a water project in the name of gender justice withheld access to clean water to an area of Kabul, an action estimated to have resulted in many deaths due to waterborne disease (Vaux, 2001). In sum, rights-based ethics can be criticised for not treating people as ends in themselves and for creating divisions between deserving and undeserving victims, subordinating them in the process to uncertain political and developmental ends (Chandler, 2002; Duffield, 2001; Macrae, 2001).

If a rights-based withdrawal of aid raises serious moral dilemmas, humanitarian enforcement jeopardises the very identity of humanitarian organisations as moral actors. The imperatives of rights-based humanitarianism, such as liberal peace, have led to NGO demands for the use of military force in the name of human rights victims – notably in Kosovo, characterised as the first humanitarian war. The advent of humanitarian war has raised fundamental questions about the meaning and future of humanitarianism. The demand for military enforcement in the absence of an international military force presumes an international division between responsible liberal human rights enforcer states and non-liberal human rights violating states. NGOs have been prepared to endorse humanitarian enforcement by Western states, bypassing the United Nations and existing international law which prohibits the use of force without prior Security Council authorisation (except in the case of self-defence). NGOs are thereby legitimising the use of force by the most powerful states outside of international law and, by extension, the expansion of their sovereignty.

Humanitarian war is like any war in that it suspends peacetime concepts of the rule of law and inevitably risks innocent deaths, namely the deaths of those in whose name humanitarian war is conducted. Moreover, humanitarian organisations, having supported humanitarian war as legitimate though illegal, have quickly found that they are unable to determine how humanitarian war is conducted militarily, and that their own humanitarian role is called into doubt. The concept of humanitarian war blurs the division between humanitarian organisations and the military, more specifically the division between humanitarian organisations and Western military forces. What is the meaning of being humanitarian if humanitarians go to war and the military are being humanitarian by going to war? NGOs have defined themselves as being non-violent, but does not rights-based humanitarianism violate its fundamental principle of the right to life? What is left of the humanitarian space in a conflict if humanitarian organisations are a party to that conflict? While NGOs may feel that they can cope with the ethical niceties of their new situation, their roles have already become compromised in the minds of potential recipients on the ground. The warnings of the ICRC's Jean Pictet of the dangers of humanitarianism becoming 'indistinguishable from political partisanship' are apposite. While Western NGOs risk being cast as merely representing the interests of the West, Islamic relief organisations are asking whether Islamic relief has a future after September 11, as they find themselves under suspicion in the new security situation. It is significant that in Iraq, the US as occupying power felt little need to give NGOs any great role, but even when the occupying administration conceded some role for them, NGOs found themselves targeted along with the occupying forces. In summary, critiques coming from within and without the NGO sector argue that NGOs reflect and reproduce the inequalities of the world of states.

We turn next to an examination of how the international development championed under the banner of global civil society holds out no prospects for advancing the South and overcoming international inequalities.

Demoralised development

I have contended that global civil society advocacy is informed by a degraded view of humanity which associates the unfettered exercise of human will with abuse. The idea of an apocalyptic future awaiting humanity because of humanity's very power over nature has been a preoccupation of global policy-makers and global citizenship education since the 1970s. The Brandt report proclaimed its remit as *A Programme for Survival* (ICID, 1980), and it remains striking how proponents of global ethics on both sides of the Atlantic have characterised their work in terms of survival rather than progress since the 1970s. In this vein, the US peace educator Betty Reardon called for policy-makers to face up to a survival crisis and make survival education strategies central to the school curriculum (Reardon, 1973: 127). 'The age of confidence is dead. We live in an age of pessimism' proclaim the opening words of Derek Heater's *World Studies: Education for International Understanding in Britain* (1989: 3), giving a flavour of the negativity which has pervaded Western global citizenship education.

This pessimism is apparently contradicted by a radical human rights social agenda. Nevertheless, the human rights agenda too embodies a demoralised subject as victim/abuser whose emotions and desires are to be disciplined and authenticated by professional enablers. The contradictions lie rather in the conception of rights and development and how rights-based development is to be realised in circumstances of pre-industrial scarcity. To begin with a general observation: paradoxically global civil society advocacy favours a form of development that prefers rural development over industrialisation and urbanisation when the very concept of civil society itself is associated with the development of cities. Mark Duffield has observed that from the beginning of their involvement in development, NGOs have favoured rural development and been wary or hostile of industrialisation. Indeed, NGOs' entry into international development policy coincided with its retreat from industrialisation with all the implications that this contains for the Southern state. In this, NGOs have followed British colonial preferences for the rural over the urban arising from their attempt to contain the urban basis of Third World nationalism. As Duffield (2001) points out, previous generations of NGO staff were drawn from the ranks of former colonial officials. It is against the background of the retreat from the aspiration of developing the South to equal the North that I will now discuss international development as psychosocial governance.

The ascendancy of global civil society advocacy has been theorised as a response to the global risks generated by reflexive modernity, and as creating a new active global citizenry (Beck, 1999). Global advocates' alarm over human progress has encouraged a sustainable development philosophy concerned with containing human ambition and restraining human action over nature. Since the 1970s, global advocates have dropped the idea of the industrialisation of the South and embraced development thinking, essentially seeking to moderate material expectations and prevent frustration over the failure to realise material aspirations (see, for example, Eric Schumacher's *Small is Beautiful*). In this embrace of restraint, global advocacy parallels Western official preoccupations with the dangers of a 'revolution of rising expectations' becoming a 'prescription for violence' (National Commission on the Causes and Prevention of Violence, 1969: 41). Indeed, one can trace the thinking underlying contemporary needs-based strategies to interwar social psychological theories of frustration and aggression. Re-reading Schumacher, Duffield observes how development activities appear less to create things, than to keep people occupied for their moral improvement. In this reading, participatory or rights-based development is more about psychosocial management than significant material improvement. As such, development policy echoes Western domestic welfare policy concerns 'to strengthen the characters of the poor by forcing them to work, no matter what work they d[o]' (Sennett, 2003: 109). The stress on psychosocial needs has long been apparent in peace and development education (Aspelagh, 1979; Burns and Aspelagh, 1996). Indicatively, psychosocial needs have increasingly come to the fore as the basic needs approach has been codified into rights-based development, the approach favoured by global civil society advocates. Development policy increasingly conceives needs in psychological rather than material terms, which is to say that therapeutic wellbeing is displacing universal prosperity as the goal of international development policy (Pender, 2002; Pupavac, 2004).

At the same time, abandoning industrialisation of the South implies abandoning the aspiration for the South to become sovereign equals, as highlighted above. Yet there is a surprising silence on the implications of this for international relations in the development and global civil society literature. Rights-based development focuses on addressing national inequalities rather than international inequalities. But a further dichotomy exists between rights-based development's aspiration for wholesale transformation of social relations within the South, without the South having experienced substantial economic transformation. Consequently, whether rights-based development can overcome national inequalities is in doubt. The fundamental contradictions of global advocacy's radical social agenda and its conservative economic agenda are possible because of its flight from the material and because it implicitly or explicitly conceives of social transformation in terms of cultural and personal change. The character of rights-based development as psychosocial governance arises logically from its abandonment of industrialisation. At best, rights-based development in the absence of economic advancement means the redistribution of poverty and the lowering of societal expectations. Yet how are redistributive policies realisable in circumstances of an undeveloped economy, a precarious state with a weak relationship to the population, and a society characterised by a personalised public sphere? There are inherent limitations to the realisation of social and economic rights in circumstances of underdevelopment, as accounts of the development of modern law demonstrate. For the evolution of modern law and the redistributive welfare state were preceded by the industrial revolution, which fostered an impersonal public sphere and the necessary infrastructure to make redistribution a possibility (Weber, 1954). However, rights-based development thinking evades how distributive rights are to be realised in the absence of economic advancement. Consequently, the rights-based development model signals the moral worth of the needy to the needy and the rest of society, but fails to constitute a serious redistributive strategy. Social justice is essentially to be achieved through creating awareness of the worth of the needy which fosters their self-esteem and social inclusion, empowering them with the confidence to act to secure their own needs. At the same time, recognition is seen as promoting a sense of inclusion and undermining alienation which could foster conflict (Burton, 1997: 31).

Under rights-based development, treating self-esteem as a distributable good is linked to microeconomic strategies, such as microcredit, in which people are expected to create their own employment and material welfare, even as they are distrusted to act as moral agents without external intervention. Grievances are either criminalised as greed or pathologised as manifestations of stress, skills deficits or feelings of exclusion. Low self-esteem is treated as a cause of poverty or even its very meaning. In sum, contemporary development thinking as psychosocial governance proposes emotional adjustment for societies, rather than material advancement of their circumstances. Fostering self-esteem has become a core theme of international peace and development strategies, but self-esteem does not signify having high ambitions and being emotionally self-reliant: ambition and emotional independence are mistrusted under international therapeutic governance. Rather, policy to tackle low self-esteem seeks to moderate emotion, to temper frustration, not fire ambition. In accordance with frustration and aggression theories, international development projects today typically strive to avoid raising unrealistic and high expectations among participants (Pender, 2002; Wahlberg, 2003). This lowering of societal expectations through rights training is apparent in Bosnia, with participants instructed by Western human rights lawyers that, for example, they have a human right to basic health provision, but not to cancer hospitals. However, the disciplinary nature of international global governance is mystified by the seemingly radical reference to self-actualisation and empowerment. Meanwhile, globally, people increasingly rely on their informal networks and informal economic activities to address their needs and ambitions (Duffield, 2001).

Conclusion: the demoralised subject of global civil society

Global problems are regarded essentially by global civil society proponents in normative terms and as deriving from personal or cultural deficits. The promotion of global human rights has been argued for as providing a moral vocabulary (Rorty, 1993). However, there is a lack of confidence in 'sentimental education' arising from misgivings over the sentiments of people (expressed, for example, in the preoccupation with compassion fatigue). Thus, evolving global human rights regimes do not only concern 'education in the sentiments', but seek ever-more detailed regulation and monitoring of human interactions. This negative view of people's moral capacity is underscored by the ways in which the remit of human rights work is increasingly directed towards intervening in interpersonal relations. So whereas human rights work in earlier decades was concerned with documenting abuses by states, human rights work has turned towards the actions of private actors and individuals. Much human rights activism in the 1990s seems directed towards depoliticised and demoralised subjects whose existing political leaders are pathologised and whose very moral agency is in doubt. Global good governance is premised on humanity's propensity for barbarity and depravity in which we are all potentially victims or perpetrators. By contrast, earlier classical rights thinking, for all its faults, at least assumed the moral agency of individuals and held out the potential for freedom.

In some respects, the ethos of global civil society echoes the ideals of nineteenth-century liberal imperialism. Yet there are important distinctions. Whereas the past ideal invoked the strong character and the robust ego – as embodied in Charlotte Brontë's portrayal of St John Rivers in *Jane Eyre* – today's sense of the self is one of the vulnerable id ever at risk of psychosocial breakdown. Global governance promotes a demoralised subject as victim/abuser who has to be empowered through lifelong therapeutic interventions by professional enablers. Extensive therapeutic interventions informed by Anglo-American social psychology are becoming globalised across societies to address the ever-perceived risk of psychosocial dysfunction (Pupavac, 2001; Pupavac, 2004). Under this therapeutic ethos, psychosocial wellbeing is becoming one of the duties of the global citizen and rights are being therapeutised, denoting rights of external therapeutic intervention rather than freedoms. Instead of empowering individuals, global governance as therapeutic governance can only demoralise individuals and erode their rights. Treatments of global civil society globalise the demoralisation of Western societies and propound a deeply misanthropic vision of humanity.

Note

1 Earlier versions of this chapter were presented at the Department of Politics, Open University and BISA Annual Conference, University of Birmingham,

December 2003. I am grateful for the discussion at these events for stimulating my ideas. However, responsibility for the views expressed here lies with me.

References

Anderson, M. (1999) *Do No Harm: How Aid Can Support Peace – Or War*, Boulder: Lynne Rienner.

Aspelagh, R. (1979) 'Basic Needs and Peace Education'; *Bulletin of Peace Proposals*, 10, 4: 403–6.

Beck, U. (1999) *What is Globalization?*, Cambridge: Polity Press.

Bracken, P. (2002) *Trauma: Cultural Meaning and Philosophy*, London: Whurr Publishers.

Burns, R. and Aspelagh, R. (1996) 'Peace Education and the Comparative Study of Education', in R. Burns and R. Aspelagh (eds) *Three Decades of Peace Education Around the World*, New York and London: Garland Publishing.

Burton, J. (1997) *Violence Explained: The Sources of Conflict, Violence and Crime and Their Prevention*, Manchester: Manchester University Press.

Centre for the Study of Global Governance (2003) Seminar on 'Legal Imperialism: The New Heart of Darkness?' Centre for the Study of Global Governance, London School of Economics, 29 January. Synopsis available at: http://www.lse. ac.uk/Depts/global/Yearbook/legalimpersynop.htm.

Chandler, D. (2002) *From Kosovo to Kabul: Human Rights and International Intervention*, London: Pluto.

De Waal, A. (1997) *Famine Crimes: Politics and the Disaster Relief Industry in Africa*, Oxford: James Curry/Indiana University Press.

Dillon, M. and Fletcher, P. (2003) 'Perfect Dark: Liberalism, Life and War', British International Studies Association Annual Conference, University of Birmingham, December 2003.

Dillon, M. and Reid, J. (2000) 'Global Governance, Liberal Peace and Complex Emergency', *Alternatives* 25, 1.

Duffield, M. (2001) *Global Governance and the New Wars: The Merging of Development and Security*, London: Zed Books.

Fukuyama, F. (1992) *The End of History and the Last Man*, London: Hamish Hamilton.

Furedi, F. (1994) *Colonial Wars and the Politics of Third World Nationalism*, London and New York: I. B. Tauris.

Furedi, F. (2003) *Therapy Culture: Cultivating Vulnerability in an Age of Uncertainty*, London and New York: Routledge.

Heater, D. (1984) *Peace Through Education: The Contribution of the Council for Education in World Citizenship*, London and Philadelphia: The Falmer Press.

Heater, D. (1989) *World Studies: Education for International Understanding in Britain*, Basingstoke: Harrap.

Heater, D. (1999) *What is Citizenship?*, Cambridge: Polity.

Heater, D. (2002) *World Citizenship: Cosmopolitan Thinking and its Opponents*, London: Continuum.

Held, D. (2002) 'Globalization, Corporate Practice and Cosmopolitan Social Standards', *Contemporary Political Theory* 1, 1, March: 59–78.

Held, D. (2003) 'Cosmopolitanism: Globalisation Tamed', *Review of International Studies* 29, 4, October: 465–80.

Hunter, J. (2000) *The Death of Character: Moral Education in an Age Without Good or Evil*, New York: Basic Books.

Independent Commission on International Development Issues (ICID) (1980) *North-South: A Programme for Survival* (The Brandt Report), London: Pan Books.

Klein, N. (2002) *Fences and Windows: Dispatches from the Front Lines of the Globalization Debate*, London: Flamingo.

Lasch, C. (1979) *Culture of Narcissism: American Life in an Age of Diminishing Expectations*, New York: W. W. Norton.

Lasch, C. (1984) *The Minimal Self: Psychic Survival in Troubled Times*, New York: W. W. Norton.

Macrae, J. (2001) *Aiding Recovery? The Crisis of Aid in Chronic Political Emergencies*, London: Zed Books.

Marcuse, H. (1968) 'Liberation from the Affluent Society', in D. Cooper (ed.) *The Dialectic of Liberation*, Harmondsworth: Penguin.

Maren, M. (1997) *Road to Hell: The Ravaging Effects of Foreign Aid and International Charity*, New York: Free Press.

Maslow, A. (1970) *Motivation and Personality*, New York: Harper & Row.

Midgely, M. (1999) 'Towards an Ethic of Global Responsibility', in T. Dunne and N. Wheeler (eds) *Human Rights in Global Politics*, Cambridge: Cambridge University Press.

National Advisory Commission on Civil Disorders (1968) *Report of the National Advisory Commission on Civil Disorders (Kerner Commission)*, New York: Bantam Books.

National Commission on the Causes and Prevention of Violence (1969) *Report of the National Commission on the Causes and Prevention of Violence to Establish Justice, to Insure Domestic Tranquillity*, Washington D.C.: U.S.G.P.O.

Nelson, J. M. (1969) *Migrants, Urban Poverty, and Instability in Developing Countries*, Occasional Papers in International Affairs, No. 22, Center for International Affairs, Harvard University.

Nolan, J. (1998) *The Therapeutic State: Justifying Government at Century's End*, New York: New York University.

Pender, J. (2002) 'Empowering the Poorest?: The World Bank and "The Voices of the Poor" ', in D. Chandler (ed.) *Rethinking Human Rights: Critical Approaches to International Politics*, Basingstoke: Palgrave.

Pupavac, V. (2001) 'Therapeutic Governance: Psycho-social Intervention and Trauma Risk Management', *Disasters* 25, 4, December: 358–72.

Pupavac, V. (2004) 'The Emotionology of the New International Security Paradigm', *European Journal of Social Theory* 7, 4, February: 149–70.

Reardon, B. (1973) 'Transformations into Peace and Survival: Programs for the 1970s', in G. Henderson (ed.) *Education for Peace: Focus on Mankind*, Washington: Association for Supervision and Curriculum Development.

Rieff, D. (2002) *A Bed for the Night: Humanitarianism in Crisis*, Simon & Schuster, New York.

Rorty, R. (1993) 'Human Rights, Rationality and Sentimentality', in S. Shute and S. Hurley (eds) *On Human Rights: The Oxford Amnesty Lectures*, New York: Basic Books.

Roth, K. (1999) 'Human Rights Trump Sovereignty in 1999', Human Rights Watch, 9 December. Available at: http://www.hrw.org/press/1999/dec/wr2keng.htm.

Schumacher, E. F. (1973) *Small is Beautiful: A Study of Economics as if People Mattered*, London: Blond & Briggs.

Sennett, R. (1976) *The Fall of Public Man*, New York: W. W. Norton.

Sennett, R. (2003) *Respect in a World of Inequality*, New York and London: W. W. Norton.

Slim, H (1998) 'Sharing a Universal Ethic: The Principle of Humanity in War', *International Journal of Human Rights*, 2: 28–48.

Slim, H. (2000) 'Fidelity and Variation: Discerning the Development and Evolution of the Humanitarian Idea', *Fletcher Forum of World Affairs*, 24: 5–22.

Sogge, D. (ed.) (1996) *Compassion and Calculation: The Business of Private Foreign Aid*, London: Pluto.

Stockton, N. (1998) 'In Defence of Humanitarianism', *Disasters* 22, 4: 352–60.

Vaux, T. (2001) *The Selfish Altruist*, London: Earthscan.

Wahlberg, A. (2003) 'The Teleology of Participation', *Anthropology in Action*, 10.

Weber, M. (1954) *Max Weber on Law in Economy and Society*, M. Rheinstein (ed.), Cambridge, Massachusetts: Harvard University Press.

4 The changing role of global civil society

Richard Falk

Rethinking the role of global civil society

The invention of *global* civil society as a framing construct can be dated in various ways, but its time of existence is certainly no greater than a decade or so (Lipschutz, 1996). Of course, the lineage of 'civil society' is older and far more convoluted, and its role in achieving social change is becoming more frequently acknowledged and affirmed (Edwards, 2004; Kaldor, 2003). Alejandro Colás argues that the agency of civil society has actually been prominent in the social and political spheres for centuries ('from the American Revolution to the current experiments in global governance'), and has always possessed overseas links and been strengthened by 'practices of transnational solidarity' (Colás, 2002: 1). In this rather basic behavioral sense, 'global civil society' is not altogether an innovation, leaving aside the recent coinage of the phrase. Yet I think it is helpful to demarcate this current period as introducing a radically new dimension into our understanding of global governance, consisting of a variety of transnational undertakings by voluntary associations of citizens seeking to influence the *global setting* of politics, rather than to work for changes in particular states. In this respect, global civil society is best understood as part of the overall globality of the post-Westphalian world, although it is equally important to give due weight to the resilience of Westphalian sovereignty, including patterns of state governance and statist diplomacy. The existing framework of world order, then, can be best grasped from a perspective of organizational and normative hybridity, the overlapping of differing logics and ordering formats (Falk *et al.*, 2002).

This positing of global civil society as a new political reality can be understood, in the first instance, as a matter of highlighting – describing intensifying long-term trends that are giving greater prominence to transnational actors and activity. It also involves prescribing a global future to be constructed through social action that would be far more shaped by civic forces than, as at present, through a collaborative relationship between states and market forces (Keohane and Nye, 1989). The descriptive dimension has been associated especially with transnational social movements, initially in this era with respect to environmental issues and the status of women, and with transnational civic organizations that appeared to be influential on matters of human rights, environmental policy and concerns about war, nuclear weapons and intervention. Prescriptively, these movements and actors were viewed as vehicles for the realization of liberal values, norm creation and policy formation, as well as providing positive sources of information and pressure that helped offset the widely perceived failure of governments and international institutions to address effectively a range of global challenges. Such assessments also reflected a growing realization that electoral democracy was not achieving either meaningful participation for citizens or accountability of leaders in relation to fundamental policy concerns (despite the encouraging repudiation of authoritarian rule at the state level). From a more academic perspective, this attention given to global civil society was also a more formal way of adapting the conceptual framework of world politics to the growing inadequacy of a Westphalian statist worldview (Falk, 2002b). Specifically, these developments involved an acknowledgement that the interplay of social and political forces needed to be understood on the basis of a range of participants and arenas relevant for norm-creation and policy formation additional to sovereign states.

As with other organizing concepts, global civil society is a mental construct that is held to give insight into the workings of the political order. By bringing this idea to bear there is an implicit challenge directed at the statist world picture, but there is also an interpretative debate that is often not made explicit. Those that emphasize global civil society are usually motivated by a cosmopolitan vision of global democracy, while those who refrain from employing such terminology are usually adherents of a realist geopolitics that is dismissive of democratization situated *beyond* the borders of the state, so much so as to not even mention the rise of non-state, transnational social forces in their depiction of the global political framework (for the former see Archibugi *et al.*, 1998; for the latter see Mearsheimer, 2001; for Hedley Bull's intermediate formulation of a 'new medievalism' see Falk, 2000). At best, the element of subjectivity is particularly central to this debate because the existence and influence of global civil society is only indirectly capable of validation by such statistical indicators as numbers of NGOs, meetings, budgets, media references, size of membership and so forth. Other kinds of evidence include anecdotal reports of how global policy was formed on a case study basis – for instance, those who advocate a wider lens than that of statism tend to attribute a large role to global civil society in mobilizing support for particular international treaties (Rosenau, 1990). Because promoters of global civil society also believe generally in global democracy they sometimes exhibit a tendency to proclaim prematurely the death of the state; to treat as already established what are really *wishes* for shifts in powers, influence and status away from the sovereign state to transnational arenas controlled by social forces. Critics note the exaggerations of influence attributed to these transnational social forces and complain about utopianism – then putting aside altogether any conceptual or political role for global civil society. The position taken here is more moderate, arguing that there is sufficient evidence of impact to insist on an identity and role for global civil society, but not yet such a shift in power relations as to describe world order as transformed. The transformative project of global democracy and humane governance remains to be achieved through social and political action of great magnitude (Falk, 1975; Falk, 1995). If anything, developments in world society since 1990 have made these goals seem more remote than ever.

The growth of the global civil society idea in this period has progressed through three stages up until now, recognizing that there was considerable overlap and interplay, as well as variation of perception depending on circumstances and angle of perspective. One phase does not end when the next begins, the dynamic being more complex and confusing. It is still useful to offer these distinctions for the sake of identifying evolving patterns and their interaction with changes in the overall global setting. The first phase can be associated with the activities of NGOs and popular movements in relation to specific issue areas, especially war/peace, environment, human rights and women; and to consider the relevance of the growth of global advocacy networks to promote change for these concerns (Keck and Sikkink, 1998). Two important areas of concern were associated with opposition to reliance for security on nuclear weaponry, including nuclear testing and the transnational popular demonstration against the American role in the Vietnam War. The social science discussion was presented primarily in the language of 'new social movements' that achieved prominence in the 1980s, although it had been in gestation over the course of a decade or more previously. In this phase, whose origins can be traced most persuasively to the Stockholm UN Conference on the Environment (1972), where a formal conference of governments under UN auspices found itself shadowed by a set of parallel events organized by an array of civil society activists associated with NGOs, giving rise then and there to a *global* environmental social movement. Before Stockholm there had been a variety of *national* environmental initiatives, some with transnational connections, but no systematic identification of global goals and processes. What became clear at Stockholm, and even clearer subsequently, was the challenge being posed to governments and international institutions as adequate *representatives* of the human interest in these new areas of growing concern. It became apparent that a serious tension existed between governmental immobilism based on the inhibiting influence of industrial capitalism, and civil society expectations of far reaching adjustments that seemed to correspond with empirical necessity and evolving and widely endorsed world order values. The expression of this tension was generally dialogic and performative, with civil society actors mounting transnational pressures demanding *reforms*, not *revolutionary change*. The main impact of global civil society was to alter somewhat the global policy debate; to encourage governments to do more on their own to solve problems generally acknowledged as posing urgent societal challenges; and to push governments to pursue more diligently goals they had already affirmed by their own policy initiatives in areas such as environmental protection, human rights and peace. In the background of these initiatives was a commitment to non-violent approaches to international problem-solving, as well as a belief in the need for and potentialities of enhanced patterns of cooperation.

The second phase, especially in its European expressions, was concerned with the mobilization of society to achieve democratization and self-determination, including arenas of decision-making beyond the territorial state. This phase achieved prominence in the latter stages of the Cold War, exhibited in the form of movements of opposition to the established order of the state and of geopolitics generally. The formation of the Green Party in Germany was inspirational in many ways. The Green slogans 'neither East nor West', 'neither Left nor Right but in front', captured some of the mood of this time that appealed particularly to youth. By the mobilization of civil society, its initiatives tied to confronting the regimes of East Europe as well as the nuclearism of the two superpowers, and transnationally reinforced by relations with the West European peace movement, a political climate was generated favorable to change and challenge. Other factors supported this mounting challenge to state control over political destiny. Opponents of oppressive forms of governance no longer seemed engaged in a hopeless enterprise even in major states. The overthrow of the Shah of Iran in 1979 was one indication that popular mobilization could successfully challenge strongly entrenched state power without resorting to massive violence. Above all, the softening of Soviet rule in the Gorbachev era contributed to a series of sea changes that brought about the peaceful transition from authoritarian rule to conditions of political independence in those countries that had constituted the Soviet empire, certainly one of the great modern transformations. Of course, a heated debate goes on about causal factors. And statists point with pride to the Helsinki intergovernmental process that emboldened societal opposition, and to the assertive security approach of the Reagan presidency that they claim lured the Soviet Union into a bankrupting arms race that was beyond their means to sustain, inducing societal collapse. It is difficult in this mélange of considerations to disentangle the impact of civil society from the wider setting, and it is especially difficult to measure the impact of *global* civil society.

This experience in Europe inspired and was parallel to pro-democracy movements in several Asian countries, illustrating both the transnationality of influence and the growing leverage exerted by civil society actors. In this regard, the changes wrought to South Africa assume a particular importance, changes associated with the governmental decision to release Mandela after 27 years in jail and with the subsequent dramatic pattern of reconciliation that produced the dismantling of the apartheid structures without the prelude of armed struggle. This dynamic was encouraged by a global anti-apartheid campaign that called effective attention to the degree that the racism of the South African government amounted to a Crime Against Humanity. The surprising transition in South Africa without bloodshed seemed best explained by a combination of internal and transnational factors moving in the same direction, but again we should note the critical point that global civil society was a socially constructed reality that helped make unexpected things happen under the right conditions.

The third phase of development for global civil society occurred in the period following immediately after the Cold War, and can be divided into two aspects: an anti-globalization movement and a global justice movement. Even before the 1990s, civil society actors were disturbed by the growing evidence that multinational corporations and international banks were escaping from the regulatory authority of sovereign states and shaping global policy on the basis of profits rather than human wellbeing. But it was in the aftermath of the Cold War that it became ever clearer that the world economy was capital-driven in accordance with a neo-liberal ideology based on according priority to market forces and reflecting American ideological triumphalism in the aftermath of the Soviet collapse. This perception was reinforced by the prominence achieved by the World Economic Forum in Davos that brought business leaders together, as well as by the media attention given to the annual economic summits of heads of state from the Group of Seven, an association of advanced industrial countries. State actors seemed to accept a growing measure of subordination of territorial priorities while deferring to the imperatives of capital formation, world trade and investment. International institutions such as the World Bank and IMF facilitated this outlook, with disturbing results for the 50 percent or more of the world's people who remained impoverished despite a steady expansion of the global economy (Falk, 1999). The Asian financial crisis, which produced disastrous currency gyrations for several countries that had seemed perfect embodiments of the neo-liberal growth model championed by the IMF and World Bank, challenged the ideologues of world capitalism who had been arguing that world markets were self-regulating in a manner that best promoted the human interest. These developments and perceptions stimulated the deepening and widening of an anti-globalization movement vividly launched on the world stage in Seattle during the ministerial meetings of the World Trade Organization in late 1999. This movement further exhibited its militancy at major intergovernmental meetings associated with world economic policy (Broad, 2002). The expanding size and growing intensity of the demonstrations, together with their global resonance, suggested that global civil society was a political force to be reckoned with. This process of reckoning was also a result of civil society initiatives that were actively seeking to establish policy-shaping and network-building networks of their own. The impetus here was partly an adjustment to an economistic backlash led by leading actors bent on making unavailable to this civil society movement the venues of the United Nations in the course of global conferences. The early 1990s had borne witness to the degree to which UN global conferences on environment, human rights, population and women could be strongly mobilizing occasions for civil society (which incidentally could prefigure some of the contours of a participatory *global* democracy). Leading states had been shown willing, and even eager, to compromise their autonomy with respect to corporate and financial markets during the 1990s, but not in relation to civil society – using their influence within the UN to block future events of this kind. In turn civil society, mindful of both the need for global arenas and their disappearance, took initiatives to establish arenas under their own auspices. In this spirit, the Hague Appeal for Peace brought together a wide assortment of activists to establish their own network, and, even more formidably, NGOs in the South creatively brought into being the World Social Forum that has been meeting annually in Porto Allegre, Brazil, and which moved in early 2004 to Mumbai, India. Another initiative worthy of mention is held every second year in the Italian city of Perugia, under the banner of 'The UN Assembly of the Peoples', making the central point that direct representation of society produces a different set of attitudes and priorities than does representation by governments in the formal organs of the United Nations. At Perugia, representatives of civil society from one hundred or more countries, who first interact with both local Italian civic communities throughout the country and then gather for days of discussion and networking, definitely establish an agenda of their own.

In this same period, a global justice agenda emerged in the years following the fall of the Berlin Wall. Partly this reflected sweeping political changes that ended the rule of many dictatorial leaders in different regions, and even more so it expressed receptivity to grievances that had long been suppressed during the Cold War. Claims of Holocaust survivors were suddenly enjoying success. The calls for redress of historic grievances by indigenous peoples began to be listened to. For the first time, reparations claims put forward by descendants of African slaves were taken seriously, along with the cries of abuse associated with 'comfort women' who served the Japanese military in the course of their imperial venturing throughout Asia. Human rights became a central goal of American foreign policy, and lost its bad image as a tool of East/West propaganda. The wrongs done to peoples by their own governments increasingly seemed to engage the responsibility of the world community to protect such vulnerable populations. From the failed states of sub-Saharan Africa to genocidal actions in the Balkans and Rwanda, there was a growing sense that territorial sovereignty had to be trumped by humanitarian intervention so as to protect vulnerable populations from catastrophe. This process reached its climax with the intervention by NATO in Kosovo, which was controversial because a non-defensive use of force was undertaken without the mandate of the UN, and under conditions in which the motives for the use of military force were somewhat suspect. Another manifestation of the global justice movement was the revival of the Nuremberg idea of holding leading individuals accountable for crimes during their official tenure. This impulse received an unexpected boost with the detention of the deposed Chilean tyrant, Augusto Pinochet, when he came to Britain in 1998 to receive medical treatment. Although Pinochet was never prosecuted, his pursuit galvanized human rights activists throughout the world, producing an extraordinary collaboration between a coalition of civil society actors and like-minded governments. The establishment of the International Criminal Court in mid-2002 due to this 'new globalism' was little short of remarkable, requiring governments to accept a wide array of potential claims relating to the accountability of territorial leaders. Highly revealing was that this reformist move in the direction of institutionalizing global governance and the global rule of law provoked a hostile reaction on the part of the United States Government. The US as the global hegemon and ardent advocate of its own sovereign prerogatives – while at once pursuing an increasingly interventionary diplomacy – wanted to set the rules and procedures of accountability for others but without being bound by them (Bobbitt, 2002). I have argued elsewhere that this combination of developments and their flourishing during the 1990s was on the verge of giving rise to a 'normative revolution' of unprecedented character, lending genuine weight to ethical concerns in the formation of global policy and achieving some degree of global democracy through the effective participatory role of these transnational civic actors (Falk, 2002a; also Barkan, 2000).

There is no doubt that the September 11 attacks cast a long shadow over both aspects of this third, and most consequential, phase of the emergence of global civil society. The attacks themselves revealed the dark potency of what might be called transnational *uncivil* actors, actors capable of, and willing to, inflict severe symbolic and substantive harm on Westphalian states, no matter how formidable their military capacity in a state-to-state setting. Significantly also, September 11 shifted attention from social and economic policy back in the direction of security concerns, in the process re-endowing states and borders with a central role in protecting their populations. In addition, the United States somewhat opportunistically seized the occasion to declare a global war on terror, claiming an assortment of novel rights to treat the world as a single battlefield and to disregard the constraints of international law. When these claims began to materialize as moves towards a war of choice against Iraq without support from the United Nations, alarm bells went off in civil society around the world. On February 15, 2003, millions marched against an Iraq War in hundreds of cities and towns around the world, a unique event in world history. The scale of this public outpouring to prevent the war together with its failure to alter the course of events suggests both the robust reality of global civil society, and its current weakness as a challenge to geopolitical prerogatives at least in the area of war and peace. At minimum these developments, complicated and still taking shape, call our attention to the changing role of global civil society under differing world conditions. Specifically, it seems useful to discuss the future of global civil society in relation to the American global domination project as undertaken before and after September 11. To what extent will the phase three emphases on globalization (and more broadly, the world economy) and the pursuit of global justice be superseded by a phase four that is oriented around 'security' concerns?

Three scenarios for phase four

It seems certain that the magnitude of the al-Qaeda attacks, combined with the declaration of an unbounded jihad against America, Americans, and their allies creates the sort of threat that cannot be ignored by a government whose society has been targeted and struck in this manner. But the direction and scope of the response is not pre-determined, and could still assume different forms. It was the immediate decision of the Bush presidency to treat the attacks as analogous to the 1941 Pearl Harbor attacks, and opt to wage war on a worldwide scale against 'global terrorism', which has never been delimited in a careful or consistent manner. There are many reasons, as well, to suppose that the Bush entourage of neocon advisors saw September 11 as 'a blessing in disguise', to quote the Secretary of Defense, Donald Rumsfeld during a TV interview on the second anniversary of the attacks. The celebrated document of the Project for a New America entitled 'Repairing America's Defenses' also suggests that America needs a Pearl Harbor to wake itself up to the dangers and opportunities of the world after the collapse of the Soviet Union and the end of the Cold War.

These scenarios treat the response of the US Government as important for situating the probable role of global civil society. It is undoubtedly the case that there will be deep cleavages in global civil society reflecting differing perceptions and priorities across the globe, and these should be taken into account. It is also highly likely that phase four will reflect the experiences of political violence on both sides of the struggle. To what extent has the massive American military response inclined the political extremists who planned the September 11 attacks to change their tactics? To what degree has the hostile resistance to the American occupation of Iraq since the fall of Saddam Hussein's regime caused a rethinking of reliance on war and regime change in Washington?

Scenario I: the neocon project for global security and the role of global civil society

The Bush administration has so far blended its pursuit of global security with claims of defensive necessity with respect to al-Qaeda. The results are confusing, but the claim is rather simple, although far reaching in its implications. These results are evident both in the Afghanistan and Iraq Wars, and in the doctrinal formulations that explain the new American approach to national security. The most revealing document is undoubtedly the National Security Strategy of the United States of America (NSS) issued by the White House in September 2002. I think it is apt to compare the comprehensiveness of NSS with the formulation of the American security doctrine during the Cold War as famously set forth in National Security Council 68 (White House, 2002; Etzold and Gaddis, 1978). This new document spells out the implications of earlier statements, especially President Bush's commencement address at West Point delivered in June 2002.

The most relevant features of the document can be enumerated rather briefly, although their impact on the global setting would require a longer discussion than is possible here:

1   the prior century ended with 'a decisive victory' for the 'forces of freedom' aligned with American values;
2   this victory produced 'a single sustainable model for national success: freedom, democracy, and free enterprise';
3   these circumstances create a situation of unprecedented American preeminence in economic, political, diplomatic and ideological spheres of influence, but especially as exhibited by military dominance;
4   this favorable global setting is endangered by non-state 'terrorism' and by 'axis of evil' states that pose severe dangers to American wellbeing;
5   those states that 'harbor' terrorists will be held fully responsible for 'terrorism' that emanates from their territory, and those states that do not join in the 'war against terrorism' will be viewed as hostile, and treated accordingly;
6   to meet these dangers justifies preemptive warfare, intervention to achieve regime change, counter-proliferation diplomacy, coalitions of the willing, and military and para-military capabilities adapted to these post-Westphalian threats;
7   global security will be enhanced by promoting American political values and extending the benefits of market-driven economic policies; and
8   with the absence of strategic conflict among major states, reinforced by a margin of American military dominance that is beyond credible challenge by a rival *state*, 'the international community has the best chance since the rise of the nation-state in the seventeenth century to

build a world where the great powers compete in peace instead of continually prepare for war'.

This framework of thought was converted to action initially by the United States' recourse to a war against Afghanistan. The rationale for the war was that Afghanistan was both the headquarters and base area of al-Qaeda and that the Taliban regime was oppressive and implicated in political violence unleashed from within its territory, including the September 11 attacks. Taliban offers of negotiation were ignored, as were proposals to deliver Osama Bin Laden for indictment and trial, provided evidence was presented showing responsibility for the attacks. Diplomacy was rejected. The Taliban regime was replaced by a leadership chosen in Washington, and an American occupation, with some support from the UN and other states, has followed. No sooner had the Afghanistan War ended than the drumbeats for a second war against Iraq were launched by Pentagon advisors and the neocon cabal. The story of this mobilization over a period of months in 2002 and early 2003 is long and complicated, but it involved misrepresentation of dangers associated with the Iraqi government, disregard for constraints on the use of force embodied in international law, and failure to heed procedures designed to prohibit non-defensive wars contained in the UN Charter.

In the context set by these developments, the energies of global civil society turned in an anti-war direction, with a secondary stress on governments avoiding superfluous interference with civil liberties on a domestic level. The main effort of this new peace movement was to oppose the Iraq War as an undertaking that could not be convincingly justified by reference to the al-Qaeda threats nor reconciled with international law governing the use of force and protecting the sovereign rights of Iraq. The pre-war effort was to exhibit an overwhelming anti-war public opinion around the world, including in such countries as Italy, Britain, Spain and Portugal whose governments supported the Bush approach to Iraq. The Internet facilitated a coordination of efforts involving 100 countries and mounting mass demonstrations on the common date of February 15. The media took note of these demonstrations and of anti-war public opinion, but the American and British leaderships went ahead with their war plans, proceeding in defiance of UN procedures. Since the occupation of Iraq by American forces as of May 2003, the focus of anti-war sentiment has been on the criminality of the war, and the individual responsibility of American leaders. Several war crimes tribunals have been held or planned in such diverse places as Tokyo, London, Berlin and Istanbul over the course of 2003–04. Such legal proceedings are attempts by global civil society to fill the gaps created by the lack of political will of governments or the UN to take seriously the recourse to war by a major geopolitical actor such as the United States. Such initiatives are undertaken as projects of global civil society, without any governmental backing and in the face of a hostile mainstream media, but with broad transnational solidarity.

It is notable that such an attempt to activate global civil society as a source of law enforcement runs directly counter to the climate of opinion associated with the response to September 11. The enactment of the Patriot Act, the treatment of detained al-Qaeda suspects in Guantanamo Bay, and the hostility to the emergence of an International Criminal Court, exhibit a willingness to override private rights – especially of non-Americans – under the banners of anti-terrorism and security. At the same time, with the capture of Saddam Hussein, the US Government was immediately comfortable with a criminal trial under the auspices of the Iraq Governing Council, a body notable for viewing the former ruler as responsible for an endless chain of atrocities. To achieve a fair trial would require international auspices, which would further expose the hypocrisy of the American refusal to accept external accountability for its own conduct.

In this first scenario, then, the United States generates a global resistance movement that is fearful of an American Empire. The other dimensions of concern that were present in global civil society before September 11 remain, especially the promotion of human rights, but are muted by the salience of the war/peace agenda. It is possible that two sets of circumstances would lend credibility to the second scenario, which would entail a return to the essential approach of the 1990s, but with some modifications associated with subsequent developments. These would include a renewed effort to deal with the security challenge without embarking on a program of regime change for governments deemed hostile or whose activities cause regional and global instabilities.

Scenario II: globalization, governance and global security

Several possibilities exist for a return, with crucial modifications, to the world of the 1990s – dominated as this was by global economic policy and a deepening controversy over the balance between market freedoms and social goals – including especially the reduction of poverty and environmental protection. This controversy was taking many forms before September 11, and continues to do so in the face of the global militarization scenario outlined above, but at the margins of global security concern rather than, as earlier, at the center. If, however, three main developments ensue, these issues may again rise to the surface of the global policy process. These developments are a pronounced failure of the American occupation of Iraq, the defeat of George Bush in the 2004 presidential elections, and the containment of al-Qaeda political violence through cooperative law enforcement. Failure in Iraq, which will be determined by a prolonged hostile occupation with continuing American casualties and a failure to achieve political stability, will inhibit further non-defensive

military operations, especially associated with regime change. The electoral defeat of Bush, especially if associated with criticisms of the approach
taken to al-Qaeda after the World Trade Center attacks, will also encourage a different approach to American and global security. Such a different
approach would be further encouraged if it appears that al-Qaeda has
either abandoned or moderated its violent jihad, and also if a law enforcement approach is understood to be more effective than a war approach.
This latter point would be strengthened to the extent that anti-terrorist
law enforcement and policies are disentangled from a reliance on military
intervention in pursuit of the American global domination project.

   This second scenario of a return to the approach of the 1990s involves
adjustments of policy but not fundamental changes. The main amend-
ments would be to rely more on an improved framework for intergovernmental law enforcement against non-state actors engaging in
political violence, especially those with transnational agendas and networks. A related adjustment would involve a return to diplomacy in hand-
ling relations with governments that appear to resist the American vision
of world order, and a disentanglement of the al-Qaeda challenge from a
series of intergovernmental conflicts. Such a demilitarization of American
foreign policy would not imply an abandonment of the global domination
project. This goal of using American preeminence to establish an accept-
able form of world order for the twenty-first century would produce a
much greater reliance on 'soft power' than during the Bush presidency. It
would stress global economic policy, multilateralism and the advocacy of
human rights – in a manner that resembles the American global role
during the Clinton presidency. But such an emphasis should not be exaggerated. As in the 1990s, the American effort included a commitment to
the militarization of space and the maintenance of a position of military
dominance with respect to any possible challenge from a rival state in any
part of the world. The dispute with neocon geopolitics was somewhat
exaggerated in its fundamental aspect and centered on the level of investment in military capabilities required to achieve these agreed goals (plus
the extent to which military intervention and regime change was possible
and necessary).

   The role of global civil society would become stronger and more varied
in this global setting of reduced militarization. The stress would again be
placed on creating a more equitable distribution of the benefits and
burdens of world economic growth, as well as on influencing such institutions as the International Monetary Fund and the World Bank to view
their roles as mediating between capital efficiency and the promotion of
social justice. The problems associated with the prospect of American
global dominance would challenge civil society actors around the world in
a more profound manner than previously. A renewed stress by grassroots
actors on global governance with humane features is likely to avoid some
of the humanitarian catastrophes that occurred in the 1990s. It is also

likely that initiatives associated with the International Criminal Court and the establishment of a regime to regulate the release of greenhouse gases would be given greater attention, as might new institutional innovations such as the creation of a Global People's Assembly (or Parliament) and a UN Enforcement Brigade (to address humanitarian emergencies).

In this second scenario, certain lessons are likely to have been learned by US political leaders, particularly the importance of cooperative approaches to global security, which would include an increased reliance on the United Nations. Yet the main priorities of global civil society would still be at odds with the patterns and structures of American global leadership. This is especially true of the commitment to 'global democracy' by the World Social Forum and analogous civil society actors, seeking participation, accountability and equity in the way that global policy is formed and implemented. The US Government, and most other major governments, would continue to oppose democratization for global policy arenas, ensuring a sharpening encounter between states and civil society with respect to world order. The extent to which the UN system is willing to provide civil society actors with meaningful participation and representation should reveal whether the old Westphalian actors pursue an accommodationist or conflictual approach. In essence the second scenario, as with the first, challenges global civil society with the specter of American global dominance, but does so in a manner that recognizes a more limited role for military power in the twenty-first century than earlier.

Scenario III: achieving humane global governance

Beyond the horizon of immediate plausibility there exists the potential for a non-utopian geopolitics premised on non-violence, governability, the rule of law and global democracy. It is beyond the horizon because there is no demarcated path that has any assurance of making the journey from here to there. It is non-utopian as it is a continuation of the Enlightenment project to subject human experience to rationality and there are no insurmountable obstacles to such a reconfiguration of world political life. It is my view that the implicit ideology of global civil society is increasingly an affirmation of this vision of the future; to the extent that moves in this direction can be taken the degree of implausibility is therefore diminished. Further, there exists an opportunity for participants in global civil society to initiate a cross-civilizational dialogue depicting this vision, and to struggle to embody it in concrete undertakings. Whether these undertakings, borrowing from the past, can enlist collaborators from existing governments remains to be seen, but it would be one way to gain momentum. At present, as even more so immediately after the Cold War, there is a sense that no alternatives exist to an American-led neo-liberal world order. In the last few years the World Social Forum has thus adopted as its defining motto the phrase 'there are alternatives!'.

A non-violent geopolitics does not imply pacifism, but it does entail adherence to the UN Charter framework prohibiting wars of choice, and it limits war-making to circumstances of defensive necessity or under the auspices and control of the United Nations (as in response to humanitarian emergencies). It also depends on the willingness of leading political actors to seek a fair resolution of disputes arising from *legitimate* grievances, such as the unresolved Palestinian quest for self-determination. It further requires building up the institutional capabilities that enable patterns of regional and global governance in a manner that strengthens the rule of law and gives reality to the demand for global democracy. In this regard, establishing autonomous capabilities for protection of human rights and enforcement of international law would be an essential part of freeing regional and global procedures from manipulation by leading state actors, as occurs at present. Also important would be moves in the direction of allowing civil society actors to participate directly and indirectly in global policy making arenas, as well as the widest possible acceptance by states of accountability in relation to international criminal law.

In comparison with the other two scenarios, this third scenario does require the abandonment by the United States of its quest for global dominance – whether, as presently, by reliance on hard power tactics or, as in the 1990s, by a much greater use of soft power in the course of implementing an economistic worldview. To realize this third scenario will depend on the forces of global civil society managing to alter the climate of opinion sufficiently to shake current levels of confidence in Westphalian and neoliberal approaches to world order, and to do this by depicting a coherent alternative that does not appear to be as risky as continuing on the present path. What makes such a prospect more attainable is the likelihood that the old geopolitics will experience a series of self-destructive dead-ends and that the clarification of a new geopolitics will begin to engage the political and moral imagination of individuals around the world who are frightened and frustrated by current trends (Schell, 2003; Mahathir, 2003).

Conclusion

It is difficult to escape from the hegemony of the present moment, with its special mixture of challenges and responses. One benefit of considering the role of global civil society actors by reference to stages of emergence and through the projection of future scenarios is to emphasize the relevance of a changing world context and thereby heighten the awareness of new possibilities. Given the turbulence of this historical period, including the rise of civil and uncivil non-state actors as major players on the global stage, there is deep structural uncertainty. In such an atmosphere, the pursuit of unlikely yet desirable patterns of reform and transformation seems almost like a moral imperative of citizenship in the twenty-first century, rooted in the dilemmas of the historical political community yet necessarily engaged with wider non-territorial communities of aspiration and fear.

There are some contingencies, especially bearing on the American response to the al-Qaeda challenge, that accentuate this sense of uncertainty about the future. Of particular importance for the rest of the world is how the American citizenry view their own wellbeing and security, especially the extent to which a dysfunctional militarism continues to control the political imagination of the mainstream approaches. If such dysfunctionality persists it will highlight the artificiality of territorial democracy, subjecting the peoples of the world to the tribalism and imperial ambitions of the United States without allowing participation in its political processes. A new perspective for global civil society may then be to redraw the lines of citizenship to seek representation on the basis of impact rather than as a mechanical reflection of geography.

References

Archibugi, D., Held, D. and Köhler, M. (eds) (1998) *Re-Imagining Political Community: Studies in Cosmopolitan Democracy*, Cambridge: Polity.

Barkan, E. (2000) *The Guilt of Nations: Restitution and Negotiating Historical Injustices*, New York: Norton.

Bobbitt, P. (2002) *The Shield of Achilles: War, Peace, and the Course of History*, New York: Knopf.

Broad, R. (ed.) (2002) *Global Backlash: Citizen Initiatives for a Just World Economy*, Lanham, MD: Rowman & Littlefield.

Colás, A. (2002) *International Civil Society: Social Movements in World Politics*, Cambridge: Polity.

Edwards, M. (2004) *Civil Society*, Cambridge: Polity.

Falk, R. (1975) *A Study of Future Worlds*, New York: Free Press.

—— (1995) *On Humane Governance: Toward a New Global Politics*, College Park, PA: Penn State University and Cambridge: Polity.

—— (1999) *Predatory Globalization: A Critique*, Cambridge: Polity.

—— (2000) 'A New Medievalism?', in G. Fry and J. O'Hagen (eds) *Contending Images in World Politics*, Basingstoke: Macmillan and New York: St. Martin's.

—— (2002a) 'The First Normative Global Revolution: The Uncertain Future of Globalization', in M. Mozaffari (ed.) *Globalization and Civilizations*, London: Routledge.

—— (2002b) 'Revisiting Westphalia, Discovering Post-Westphalia', *Journal of Ethics* 6: 311–52.

Falk, R., Ruiz, L. and Walker, R. B. J. (eds) (2002) *Reframing the International: Law, Culture, Politics*, New York: Routledge.

Kaldor, M. (2003) *Global Civil Society*, Cambridge: Polity.

Keck, M. and Sikkink, K. (1998) *Activists Beyond Borders: Advocacy Networks in International Politics*, Ithaca, NY: Cornell University Press.

Keohane, R. O. and Nye, J. S. (1989) *Power and Interdependence*, Glencoe, IL: Scott, Foresman/Little Brown.

Lipschutz, R. D. (1996) *Global Civil Society and Global Environmental Governance*, Albany, NY: State University of NY Press.

Mahathir, M. (2003) 'Welcoming Address', Meeting of the Non-Aligned Movement, Kuala Lumpur, February 2003.

Mearsheimer, J. J. (2001) *The Tragedy of Great Power Politics*, New York: Norton.

'NSC 68: United States Objectives and Programs for National Security' [1950] (1978), in Etzold, T. H. and Gaddis, J. L. (eds) *Containment: Documents on American Policy and Strategy, 1945–1950*, New York: Columbia University Press.

'National Security Strategy of the United States of America' (2002) Washington, D.C.: White House.

Rosenau, J. N. (1990) *Turbulence in World Politics*, Princeton, NJ: Princeton University Press.

Schell, J. (2003) *The Unconquerable World: Power, Nonviolence, and the Will of the People*, New York: Metropolitan.

5   Contextualising the 'anti-capitalism' movement in global civil society

James Heartfield

Anti-capitalist protest: a time-line

19 June 1999:
The 'Carnival Against Capitalism', City of London.

21 June 1999:
G8 summit in Cologne: demonstrators held hands to form a ring around the city.

28 November 1999:
Protests against the World Trade Organisation meeting in Seattle.

15 June 2000:
Italian riot police fired tear gas and used batons against an estimated 1,500 protesters outside an Organisation for Economic Co-operation and Development summit in Bologna.

22 July 2000:
Pressure groups 'direct their anger at the sumptuous scale of the G8 summit' on the Japanese island of Okinawa.

12 September 2000:
2,000 anti-globalisation protesters blockaded the opening of the World Economic Forum, Melbourne, chanting 'Power to the people' and 'WEF kills'.

18–26 September 2000:
Prague becomes armed camp for IMF talks. There are fears of widespread violence as 50,000 radical protesters try to disrupt the meeting.

10 December 2000:
Young people rioted in Nice outside the European Union summit.

6 May 2001:
Across the world groups of demonstrators took to the streets on May Day to protest against globalisation, Third World debt and pollution.

17 June 2001:

Swedish authorities had planned a peaceful protest against the visiting US President George Bush but ended up firing live rounds on demonstrators when they lost control.

22 July 2001:

Carlo Giuliani, a 23-year-old Italian anarchist was shot by Carabinieri who then proceeded to run over his dead body during protests outside the summit of the Group of Eight world leaders in Genoa, Italy. His parents hoped that his 'absurd death would not be in vain'.

September 2003:

Korean farmers' leader Lee Kyoung-hae takes his life in protests at the World Trade Summit in Cancún, Mexico.

The 'anti-capitalist/anti-globalisation' movement that came to prominence in the late 1990s seems at first to be an unlikely contribution to the development of global civil society. All the same, the anti-capitalist protests at world summits, the alternative summits and international cooperation the movement exhibits, as well as the involvement of civil action groups in the movement, all qualify it as an important component of international civil society. This chapter looks at the interaction between the 'anti-capitalists' on the one hand, and the business, government and international financial institutional representatives they set out to challenge (Keegan, 2000: 37). It argues that, despite appearances, the motivations of the anti-capitalist revolt are not so far from those of the attendees at the international summits they protest at. The doubts that beset international elites are the soil that nurtures the anti-capitalist movement, which represents those inner worries in an external and oppositional form.

In 1998 the Organisation for Economic Co-operation and Development prepared its Multilateral Agreement on Investment, only to see it ambushed by the protests of the anti-capitalist movement. As activists leaked details of the MAI on the Internet, Western leaders retreated from proposals which would have enhanced the power of business over government (Monbiot, 2000: 302–7). The *Financial Times* complained that the MAI had been 'ambushed by a horde of vigilantes whose motives and methods are only dimly understood in most national capitals' (30 April 1998). *New York Times* columnist Thomas Friedman called the anti-capitalist movement 'a Noah's Ark of flat-earth advocates, protectionist trade unions and yuppies looking for their 1960s fix' (1 December 1999). The former Overseas Development Minister Clare Short called them 'misguided, white middle-class activists' in the same month. Yet their impact appeared clear: *Time* worried that the movement was 'winning the battle of ideas' (Kingsnorth, 2003: 63).

But while the – relatively sudden – impact of the anti-capitalist protests is clear and tangible, its goals are more ambiguous. The manifesto of

People's Global Action, the group which played a key part in organising the summit protests, is tentative: 'We need to develop a diversity of forms of organisation at different levels, acknowledging that there is no single way of solving the problems we are facing' (People's Global Action manifesto, pt. 2, para. 2). *Ecologist* Deputy Editor Paul Kingsnorth describes the protest at Genoa thus: 'the makeup of participants is hugely diverse: unions, environmentalists, church representatives, middle-aged anti-debt campaigners, teenage anarchists, party politicians, and many thousands upon thousands of non-aligned but passionate people.' Kingsnorth adds: 'No one person or organisation is in charge of this sea of humanity; it will move as it sees fit' (ibid.: 53).

In this account, the anti-capitalist movement fulfils the characterisation of the new social movements made by Claus Offe. They are diverse, and:

> the process by which multitudes of individuals become collective actors is highly informal, ad hoc, discontinuous ... they have at best rudimentary membership roles, programs, platforms, representatives, officials, staffs, and membership dues. The new social movements consist of participants, campaigns, spokespersons, networks, voluntary helpers and donations. Typically, in contrast to traditional forms of political organisations, they do not employ the organisational principle of differentiation in either horizontal (insider versus outsider) or the vertical (leader versus rank-and-file members) dimension.
>
> (Offe, 1987: 70–1)

Ambiguous organisational strategies make the anti-capitalist movement difficult to pin down, as one might a political party with a published manifesto.

For Alex Callinicos 'the Seattle demonstrations at the end of November 1999 marked the beginning of a wave of anti-capitalist protests' (2001: 109), and Chris Harman sees 'the eruption of the anti-capitalist movement worldwide over the last two and a half years' (2002: 3). More usefully, George Monbiot views Seattle as the turning point, but indicates a prehistory of civic activism: 'Since the protests in Seattle, however, the thousands of people's movements confronting neo-liberalism have begun to recognise each other's existence' (2001: 6). Naomi Klein sees precursors to the movement in the 'culture jamming' of Canadian *Adbusters* editor Kalle Lasn, and Britain's 'Reclaim the Streets' campaign dating back to 1995 (Klein, 2000: 312). I remember 'Stop the City' demonstrations taking place as early as 1982, and anarchist protestors re-working the feminist slogan 'reclaim the streets' only later, in response to new road-building. But even recent history is subject to mythic reinvention, as activists in northern Europe and America prefer to see their movement arising out of peasant movements in the less-developed world, such as the Zapatistas (Kingsnorth, 2003: 2–9), Porto Alegre's 'citizens forums', or Indian farmers' movements.

The image of a movement appearing suddenly at the end of 1999 is not literally true, but it does capture the sense in which a tipping-point had been reached that lifted the previously disparate activists into view. The protests made the anti-globalisation movement into a recognisable, world-wide phenomenon. Seattle was a reference point for new layers of campaigners, for whom the prehistory of the movement was less important. In that sense, the anti-globalisation movement really did emerge in 1999. Its antecedents are less important than the movement today, as Noreena Hertz says 'these protestors are not the brown-rice-and-sandal-brigade of the 1960s and 1970s' (2001: 197).

To understand how that tipping-point was reached, we need to understand the importance of the context in which anti-capitalism became recognisable as the pre-eminent challenge to the 'Washington consensus'. In the first instance, the possibilities of the contemporary anti-capitalist movement arise because of the effective collapse of the other alternatives: the Eastern bloc of communist states, its allies in the mass communist parties of Western Europe, radical nationalism in the Third World, the left wing of the European Social Democratic parties, and the militant labour movement that re-emerged in the developed world in the 1960s and 1970s. For organised labour, the resurgence in militancy of the 1960s and early 1970s gave way to defensive skirmishes in the 1980s: the US airline strike in 1981, the reduction of the scala mobile in Italy in 1984, and the British miners' strike of 1984–85. Eventually these defeats took their toll on union membership and density, reducing the labour movement from favourite to also-ran. Parliamentary radicalism, such as the 'Bennite' left wing of the British Labour Party, Italy's PCI and France's Socialist Mitterand government, were defeated by the restraints that capital placed upon public spending, leaving the left administering public austerity, or losing all credibility in government (see Heartfield, 2003).

In Britain, millionaire Sir James Goldsmith founded the *Ecologist* magazine, edited by his brother Edward in 1970, and the organisation Friends of the Earth was founded in the same year. Three years later the Ecology Party – later the Green Party – was formed. These groups had supported the government's 'Save It' campaign, popularising austerity measures in 1974, but in the late 1970s they clashed with the establishment over the public enquiry into the Windscale nuclear plant. Conservation had made the transition from 'a fairly close and "gentlemanly" dialogue with the state' to a counter-cultural lifestyle 'comprising vegetarian diets, concern for animals, wholefood shops, open-air festivals, cycling, hiking and rallies' (Macnaghten and Urry, 1998: 51, 56). But it was only with the decline of the Labour left, following the party's 1983 election defeat, that environmentalism became widely accepted as an alternative to the status quo in the UK. The traditional left's nadir, 1989, coincides with the apex of environmental concerns, when eight per cent of Europeans voted for green parties (Macnaghten and Urry, 1998: 79).

The old left by no means welcomed the environmentalists' claim on radicalism. Tony Benn recorded his impressions of a Friends of the Earth Christmas Party in 1980: 'One felt that all this concern was the middle class expressing its dislike of the horrors of industrialisation – keeping Hampstead free from the whiff of diesel smoke, sort of thing' (Benn, 1996: 502–3). Rather than embrace ecology politics, the radical left were keen to differentiate their political outlooks. In the International Socialist Journal – which would embrace the anti-capitalist protests after Seattle – Mike Simons wrote: 'the key idea of the new environmental movement, "that the earth cannot cope with the strains inflicted upon it", is one of the oldest reactionary arguments around' (1988: 53). But already the old left was reaching out for a 'red-green alliance' to try to compensate for its declining influence – not something that held an immediate appeal for environmentalists. As the political agenda became more stridently anti-capitalist, though, the remnants of the old left found a home in the new anti-globalisation movement, doing the donkey-work of leafleting, placard-making and mobilising their supporters. Much of the movement was 'reds, pretending to be greens, pretending to be reds', one Trotskyist ruefully admitted to me.

Contemporary green activists have complex attitudes to the movement against capitalism represented by the old left. The re-branding of the anti-globalisation movement as an anti-capitalist movement means taking on some of the rhetorical force of the socialist slogans. Tony Juniper explains the evolution in their thinking:

> For the past 10 years we've been locating ourselves more in the bigger economic debate and less in the 'save the whales' type debate. Talking about rainforests led us into talking about Third World debt. Talking about climate change led us to talk about transnational corporations. The more you talk about these things, the more you realise the subject isn't the environment any more, it's the economy and the pressures on countries to do things that undercut any efforts they make to deal with environmental issues. By the time we got to Seattle, we were all campaigning on the same basic trend that was undermining everybody's efforts to achieve any progressive goals. That trend is the free market and privileges for big corporations and rich people at the expense of everything else.
>
> (*Observer*, 14 July 2002)

Paul Kingsnorth assimilates the Bolshevik revolution into the prehistory of today's movement, arguing that capitalism provoked 'a worldwide popular uprising which found its most forceful expression in Russia' (2003: 66). George Monbiot also has a kind word to say about the original anti-capitalist, Karl Marx, in an interview in *Socialist Worker*: 'certainly one of the thinkers whose work we should make good use of' (27 November 1999). At the same time, however, today's green activists come from a very different place than the original labour movement, and the strains show. Four years later Monbiot told the *Sunday Times* that Karl Marx's Communist Manifesto 'contains in theoretical form, all the oppressions which were later visited on the people of communist nations' (22 June 2003). The logical divide between contemporary anti-capitalism and the radical movements, both communist and social-democratic, of the past arises in the attitude to scarcity and mass society. Socialist oppositions saw mass society as a positive development, which would lead to the eradication of scarcity through new technologies. Environmentalists, by contrast, see scarcity as the unavoidable consequence of mass society. 'In the large industrialising countries (such as China, India and Brazil) such [population] growth compounds the burden caused by rising consumption' (Real World Coalition, 1996: 27).

The way that green activists negotiated between the competing ideological claims of capital and labour at the end of the twentieth century is captured in this rhetorical contrast drawn by Paul Kingsnorth: 'The rigid, utopian ideology of international communism was dead. In its place came another ideology: one equally utopian, equally rigid and equally immune to human suffering – the dream of a global free market' (2003: 67). How the environmentalists could write off communism is relatively easy to understand, but quite why it was that the free market could be decried in the same terms is less straightforward. After all, just 14 years earlier capitalism's triumph over its rivals appeared complete in the collapse of the Eastern bloc. How then did it come about that within a decade the anti-capitalists could be 'winning the battle of ideas'? The answer lies in the capitalists' own self-confidence in the claims of their system, or more pointedly their lack of such confidence.

From the perspective of today's environmental movement, it is difficult to recall the extent to which the emerging consciousness of natural limits was originally associated with the mainstream of elite thinking. And yet it is undeniably the case that conservationist policies and movements were once the preserve of the right. Think, for example, of the Club of Rome, founded in 1968. This was a 'non partisan' think-tank under Fiat CEO Aurelio Peccei and OECD scientific advisor Alexander King. They believed that 'the chief problems of the world today are not essentially problems of party politics and, being relevant to the survival of man, they even transcend current ideologies' (Peccei and King, 1975: 204). These former industrialists hoped to sidestep the class conflict of the 1960s and 70s by appealing to a larger 'problematique humaine'. MIT professor Jay Forrester created a computer model of the global economy for the Club, 'World 2', and, with Dennis and Donella Meadows, predicted that in the year 2100 collapse will occur 'because of non-renewable resource depletion' (Meadows *et al.*, 1972: 125).

Edward Goldsmith, brother to the financier Sir James, and a key figure in the ecological movement, clarified the substance of the anxiety over growth. Urbanisation, he told the Alternatives to Growth conference in 1975, 'is a particularly frightening prospect, since it is in the existing conurbations that the ills from which industrialized society is suffering are to be found in the most concentrated forms' (Meadows, 1977: 331). The misanthropic impulse of ecology is expressed also in Republican Senator Paul Ehrlich's overpopulation thesis: 'Too many cars, too many factories, too much pesticide ... too little water, too much carbon dioxide – all can easily be traced to too many people' (Ehrlich, 1971: 36). Similarly, British diplomat Crispin Tickell wrote a pioneering work; *Climate Change in World Affairs*, in 1978 that sought to remotivate Western domination of the Third World as a response to impending environmental disaster. The Malthusian sentiments of the ecological movement of the 1970s also found their realisation in National State Security Memo 200, the US State Department policy document that outlined the presumed danger of the burgeoning population of the Third World (Mumford, 1996: 455).

This early appearance of elite environmentalism in the 1970s was a defensive reaction to the challenge posed by its socialist opponents in the developed world, and by radical nationalists in the developing world. But by the end of the decade business and political elites had been reinvigorated by the resurgence of right-wing political parties, particularly in the US and Britain, with the elections of Ronald Reagan (1980) and Margaret Thatcher (1979). Throughout the 1980s, the New Right, so-called, had little need for environmental politics, appealing instead to a modified ideology of growth, now attained through liberalisation, rather than regulated capitalism. But the completion of its programme of liberalisation, welfare reduction and curbing union power had paradoxical results for right-wing governments and the business leaders who were its beneficiaries.

The programme of the New Right gave business and political leaders a strategy and purpose, along with a set of negatives – union power, 'outside agitators', tax-and-spend government. Fear of organised labour and the perceived threat it posed to their privileged status bound the middle classes to the New Right project. But as the challenge from organised labour was restrained, the middle classes came to resent big business even more. Middle class support for the parties of the right haemorrhaged at the end of the 1980s, leading to resurgence in fringe candidates and parties, such as Ross Perot in the US, Jean-Marie Le Pen in France and the Lega Lombardi in Italy. The leading recipients of the protest vote were the Green Parties of Europe and, to a lesser extent, of the US.

At the same time, environmentalism once again became an issue in international diplomacy. The ecological imperative has been an important sub-plot in international relations, especially for those nations that have difficulty in generalising their interests in traditional military-political terms. In 1980, German leader Willy Brandt led an independent commission that first questioned whether 'the whole world should copy the model of the highly industrialised countries' (Brandt Commission, 1980: 23).

Then, in 1987 the Ministerial Declaration of the Second Conference on the Protection of the North Sea adopted the *vorsorgeprinzip*, or 'precautionary principle', that technologies must be proved safe before application (this was first proposed by the German Federal Republic in 1976). Also in 1987, the World Commission on Environment and Development under Norway's Gro Harlem Brundtland popularised the concept of sustainable development (Heartfield, 2001: 98).

At the international level, Anglo-American diplomacy took its principle objective as security against the Soviet threat. But with President Gorbachev's application to join the Western club the Soviet bogeyman was tamed. Western international leadership needed new motivations. In 1988, Sir Crispin Tickell, by then British representative to the United Nations, persuaded Margaret Thatcher to address the issue of environment and climate change in a speech to the Royal Society. Thatcher joined other world leaders at the World Climate Conferences at Montreal in 1987 and Geneva in 1991, while her successor John Major took part in the Rio Earth Summit in 1992. In 1997, the Kyoto Summit on Climate Change agreed limits on greenhouse gases from industry. These international initiatives on the environment seemed to give world diplomacy a new sense of purpose, but in the process they added to the general problematisation of industrial growth, now cast less as development and more as pollutant.

Elite ambiguity about the advantages of industrial growth was reflected in the more strident anti-corporate mood. Middle-class families that lost out in the property crash of 1988 and struggled to secure incomes in the recession of the early 1990s were much less enamoured with 'popular capitalism'. The wider spread of asset ownership in the 1980s had raised false expectations on the part of small investors, who turned on the Boards of Directors at shareholders meetings. Shareholder activism demanded disinvestment from apartheid South Africa, punished 'fat-cat' pay awards to directors, and raised awkward questions over environmental degradation in the Third World. Having defended 'management's right to manage' against militant shop stewards, company directors were at a loss to defend it against their own shareholders.

Shocked to find themselves the target of criticism, corporations set about repairing their image – but in the process they only succeeded in confirming the view that they had something to hide. In Britain, the Greenbury (1992) and Cadbury (1995) commissions were set up to investigate the issue of top people's pay (see Hunt, 2003: 56). Corporations drafted mission statements underscoring their responsibility to the environment and the community. Thus in *There is no Alternative*, Shell makes 'a commitment to contribute to sustainable development' and 'achieving a more sustainable world' (2002: 22). BP also used its advertising budget to re-brand itself '*Beyond Petroleum*'. Arguably, BP's attempts to appeal to the environmental movement have not mollified their critics, but emboldened them. On 23 October 2003, 'Rising Tide', an umbrella organisation of green groups, protested at BP's AGM, heckling Chairman Lord Browne, and circulating a spoof Annual Report. Friends of the Earth, who had been drawn into consultation with BP, announced a re-think: 'We are not going to be cosy with them because they are doing bad things' (*Guardian*, 23 October 2003). BP's appeal to environmentalists may have worked at first, but in the long run it only raised expectations, as well as the status of its green critics.

Alongside the negative publicity they get, companies have positive examples of the rewards for corporate responsibility, like the phenomenal success of Anita Roddick's Bodyshop, which sold fair-traded goods earning profits of £6.8m and a book value of £300m at its height. In 2002, McDonald's, Rio Tinto, Nike, Nestlé, and British American Tobacco all produced 'sustainability reviews' – corporate social responsibility reports covering such issues as human rights, labour conditions and environmental impact (*Guardian*, 19 August 2002). Such activities are dismissed by activists as 'greenwashing', merely public relations exercises to disguise corporations' dirty dealings. But there is good reason to think that directors and managers of big corporations are also affected by the general disdain in which industry is held. At the second World Social Congress in Porto Alegre, economist Walden Bello argued that 'we are seeing a crisis of legitimacy for the global elite'. On 20 November 1998, then US President Bill Clinton gave voice to the inner doubts of the elite when he argued for a new regulatory approach to the international financial system to Japanese and American business leaders. Clinton's economic advisor, then chief economist at the World Bank, Joseph Stiglitz, warned of the 'massive failings of the market system, from massive inequality to unliveable [sic] cities marred by pollution and decay' (2002: 74).

The emergence of the anti-capitalist movement, then, was to a great extent shaped by the historical conjuncture. On the one hand, the decline of the old left created an opening for a different kind of criticism, with a distinctive social base. But more important was the inner crisis of belief being suffered by the international ruling elite itself. Indeed, we can say that the anti-capitalist movement is effectively an external reflection of the internal crisis of identity being experienced by the capitalist class. The activists give the inner doubts of the elite an external existence (see Heartfield, 2003).

The anti-capitalists

In the 1990s, road-protestors 'Swampy' (Daniel Hooper), 'Animal', 'Muppet Dave' or 14-year-old Christina Tugwell ('the female Swampy') briefly caught the attention of the media. These activists rose to prominence through their courage and willingness to lay themselves on the line. But they were less effective as spokespeople. Government, the academy, the Church and media sought a leadership they could talk to. Television researchers found the Exodus Collective and Camilla Behrens of Jubilee 2000 to beef up their studio debates. Crispin Tickell used his wardenship of Green College, Oxford, to provide a base for one rising star of the movement, George Monbiot. Educated at Stowe and Brasenose, Monbiot was headed for a career at the BBC until he threw in his lot with the Donga tribe at Twyford Down. Despite some suspicions about this 'careerist', he succeeded in making himself an accepted spokesman (Monbiot, 1998).

Indeed many of the emerging leaders of the developing anti-capitalist movement were drawn not from the have-nots, but from within the property-owning elite itself. Mark Brown (Radley School), heir to the Vestey fortune, was acquitted of leading the Carnival Against Capitalism of June 1999 – unlike one Etonian schoolmate to Prince William, too young to be named, who pleaded guilty to violent disorder and criminal damage (*Metro*, 4 August 2000). Lord Peter Melchett (Eton), former cabinet minister and grandson to Imperial Chemicals Industry's Lord Alfred Mond, was head of Greenpeace UK, as well as standing trial for wrecking genetically modified crops. Meanwhile, Zac Goldsmith (Eton), the son of Sir James and with a £300m fortune, is current editor of the *Ecologist*.

Indeed, it appears that those involved in direct action generally are not necessarily drawn from the lower rungs of society. According to the British Social Attitudes Survey, 'those in the professional and managerial class and those with O-level or equivalent qualifications or above, are much more likely than working class people or those with lower qualifications to have engaged in some form of activism'. Furthermore, they added 'we find that young people are less likely than older ones to undertake direct action, which is somewhat surprising' (Jowell *et al.*, 1998: 132). Charles Secrett (Cranleigh), executive director of Friends of the Earth, explains the appeal of environmentalism amongst the upper classes: 'Among the aristocrats there is a sense of noblesse oblige ... a feeling of stewardship towards the land' (*Guardian*, 5 May 2000).

The role of the NGOs

At Porto Alegre in Brazil in January 2001, the first World Social Forum attracted 'more than 10,000 activists' with around half from elsewhere in the world. The second conference drew 55,000 in January 2002, and the third 100,000 in January 2003. The conference is hosted by the Workers' Party, which, since the election of President Luiz Inacio Lula da Silva in 2002, has ruled Brazil. Porto Alegre, a Workers' Party stronghold, is the site of a novel experiment in direct democracy, with several rounds of public discussion preceding the allocation of the town's budget. In its international dimensions the World Social Forum (WSF) has become an opposing pole of attraction to the World Economic Forum at Davos, Switzerland, and the positive side of the anti-capitalist movement.

Attendees and organisers self-consciously contrast their conference to mainstream international cooperation between states and financial institutions. According to Hilary Wainwright, the WSF is the 'People's UN' (*Guardian*, 25 January 2003).

The core of the WSF is made up of non-governmental organisations, like the French-based Association for the Taxation of Financial Transactions for the Aid of Citizens (ATTAC), the Brazilian Association of Non Governmental Associations (ABONG), Oxfam, Vandana Shiva's Foundation for Science, Technology and Ecology, Corpwatch, the Economic Solidarity Group of Quebec, and so on. It is these that create the organisational continuity in the anti-capitalist movement. While the protests eschew organisational coherence the NGOs provide the support mechanisms that sustain the activists. They also influence the political outlook of the movement. Veteran Latin America solidarity worker James Petras complained that 'many of the participating European and US NGOs are paper organisations, and the majority of Third World NGOers are members of small groups of professionals with few if any organised supporters and little power of convocation' (2002: 60).

Making a virtue of informal and dispersed organisation, emerging in contrast to mass parties, environmental activists have tended to privilege small groups and sidestep traditional models of democratic accountability. The model in this respect is the campaigning group Greenpeace, formed in 1970 as a breakaway from the more mainstream Sierra Club which disapproved of its Canadian affiliate's direct action against nuclear testing in 1969 (Brown and May, 1991: 8). 'The organisation itself is unashamedly centralised and authoritarian: how else to be so secret and quick to respond?', wrote green activist turned critic Richard North in the *Independent* (18 October 1986). While actions are determined by a small group of full-timers, Greenpeace canvassers would go out and collect signatures on standing order forms. Greenpeace's subscribers reached their height in the 1980s at five million worldwide, but by 1994 the appeal of passive support was waning, and numbers dropped to four million, before slipping to 2.4 million in 1995. In 1995 its income was a staggering £101m, falling to £83m in 1998 (*Sunday Times*, 30 July 2000). The organisation suffered further difficulties when it was forced to apologise for its false claims over the hazard represented by the Brent Spar oil rig, and sought to reclaim the mantle of direct action by leading the destruction of GM crop testing in the UK.

The small-group character of the anti-capitalist movement is credited with enhancing the openness of the movement, though it can also tend to cliquishness. As journalist Andy Beckett reports, 'people who are prepared to take risks, or possess useful skills, can come to dominate, or even have contempt for, the more cautious and amateurish participants' (London Review of Books, 4 April 2002). This is closer to what Max Weber called 'charismatic leadership'. American labour researcher

Stephanie Ross argues that the 'uncompromising ideological rejection of leadership *tout court*, results in leadership unbound by structures of accountability' (2002: 294). From a rather different perspective, the Brussels-based public relations company Entente International Communication argues that 'pressure groups are exploiting the perceived democratic deficit in European society' to put pressure on business (in Balanyá *et al.*, 2000: 18).

One weakness of the professionalised leadership style of the ecologically-minded NGOs is that they are open to incorporation by big businesses that are determined to recruit high-profile green campaigners. In 2002, British Greenpeace Director and veteran activist Peter Melchett resigned to become an advisor to the PR firm Burson-Marsteller. Burson-Marsteller had become a byword for corporate manipulation in its promotion of GM food-producers Monsanto (*Guardian*, 12 January 2002). The problem of green activists being recruited by big business was highlighted by George Monbiot, who pointed to the environment group Forum for the Future, set up by Friends of the Earth's Jonathan Porrit and the Green Party's Sara Parkin. The Forum, Monbiot charged, 'takes money from BP, ICI, Tesco and Blue Circle', before laying out those companies' alleged crimes against the environment ('Sleeping with the Enemy', *Guardian*, 4 September 2001). Replying to Monbiot, former Friends of the Earth chair Des Wilson defended those environmentalists who were advising businesses on green policies, saying that 'these companies are at the forefront of a revolution in business behaviour', and accusing Monbiot of 'juvenile posturing' (*Guardian*, 16 January 2002). Much of the difference in style between the two generations of environmentalists was due to the different tenor of the grassroots anti-corporate movement that Monbiot stood for, compared to the gentler, lobbying organisations that Wilson and Porrit built up in the 1970s. Nonetheless, the corporations' success in recruiting environmental 'stars' to front up their Corporate Social Responsibility packages raises questions.

The dynamic between the anti-capitalists and the NGOs on the one hand and the business and political elites on the other, is less straightforward than it appears on first sight. Curiously, the more forthright the denunciations of the World Bank, IMF and the rest of the Washington consensus, the more solicitous these institutions are towards their critics. The World Bank's Development Report (2000) argues that: 'Global action can empower poor people and poor countries in national and global forums'. This is in effect an appeal to activists and NGOs to lobby and protest outside the World Bank. The Bank promises 'open, regular dialogue with civil society organisations, particularly those representing poor people'. Compellingly, Joseph Stiglitz goes so far as to argue that 'it is the trade unionists, students, environmentalists – ordinary citizens – marching in the streets of Prague, Seattle, Washington and Genoa who have put the need for reform on the agenda of the developed world' (2002: 9). When protestors demanded the cancellation of Third World debt at the June 1999 Cologne summit, British Prime Minister Tony Blair claimed credit for a debt-easing package (*Guardian*, 19 June 1999). After the rioting in Seattle outside the World Trade Organisation, President Clinton was careful to say that negotiators had to listen to the 'legitimate concerns of legitimate protesters' (*Guardian*, 2 December 1999). When protests were organised against US President Bush, the 'Toxic Texan', at a summit at Gothenburg, the Swedish authorities gave every indication of supporting at least peaceful protest. On the eve of the summit Prime Minister Goran Persson opened what he hoped would be a 'pre-emptive dialogue with the protestors, suggesting that the EU was well placed to help tame the forces of global capitalism' (*Guardian*, 16 June 2001).

A European Commission discussion paper makes it clear just how close relations are between the EU and NGOs:

> At present is it estimated that over €1,000 million a year is allocated to NGO projects directly by the Commission, the major part in the field of external relations for development co-operation, human rights, democracy programmes, and, in particular, humanitarian aid (on average €400 million). Other important allocations are in the social (approximately €70 million), educational (approximately €50 million), and environment sectors within the EU. Several hundred NGOs in Europe and world-wide are receiving funds from the EU.
>
> (Prodi and Kinnock, 2000: 4)

Of course, the EU does not only fund NGOs, but consults widely with them, entrenching the institutional lines of communication between Brussels and these 'non-governmental' organisations. Twice a year, for example, the biggest pan-European environmental NGOs ('Group of Eight') meet with the head of the commission's environment Directorate-General to discuss its work programme (Prodi and Kinnock, 2000: 11). The Group of Eight was formed in 1990 at the Commission's request and comprises Greenpeace Europe, WWF European Policy Unit, Birdlife International, Friends of the Earth, Climate Network Europe, European Environmental Bureau, European Federation for Transport and Environment, and International Friends of Nature (Peeters, 2003: 10). Not just the commission, but the European Parliament also solicits input from environmental lobbies. The Parliament's fictional engagement with civil society is summarised in the curious comic book *Troubled Waters*, presented by the Stalinist-sounding Directorate-General for Information and Public Relations. The storyline features a stylish reporter, Irina, risking her life to expose an oil company's pollution at Strasbourg.

The importance of the NGOs for the anti-globalisation movement is well-described by the analyst Marguerite Peeters, who points to the:

rapprochement between the anti globalization movement, which rejects any formal status, is not engaged in a dialogue but is just "against", and leftist NGOs, which do have a legal status and political influence. For the first time last January, Porto Alegre opened itself to NGOs, and most big NGOs were there. Lula's extreme left labor party and radical organizations such as ATTAC in France started realizing that they could not continue on their own if they wanted to have an impact, that they had to shift from an internal debate to political action and needed political go-betweens. NGOs and Brussels-based NGO consortia in particular may start acting as intermediaries between Porto Alegre and European social democrats. They seem willing to play that role.

(Peeters, 2003: 14)

Characteristically, the more that elite organisations like the European Commission support NGOs and flatter anti-capitalist protestors, the more strident their rhetorical demands become. But the importance of the NGOs is that they represent a moderate bridge between the protestors and those behind the barbed-wire defences.

The emergence of the Non-Governmental Organisations as the organ-isational form of anti-capitalism is the factor that ensures its coherence as a movement. Ultimately, though, the movement draws its momentum less from a popular base than it does from the specific features of this historical moment. Specifically, it is the coincidence of the disappearance of the class-based organisations of the old left with the crisis of confidence on the part of capitalist elites. Anti-capitalism, so to speak, is merely a summation of the inner doubts of the capitalist class, given an external existence in the corporate-watching NGOs.

References

Balanyá, B., Doherty, A., Hoedeman, O., Ma'nit, A. and Wesselius, E. (2000) *Europe Inc. Regional and Global Restructuring and the Rise of Corporate Power*, London: Pluto.

Benn, T. (1996) *The Benn Diaries*, London: Arrow.

Brandt Commission (1980) *North South: A Programme for Survival*, Foreign and Commonwealth Office, London.

Brown, M. and May, J. (1991) *The Greenpeace Story*, London: Dorling Kindersley.

Callinicos, A. (2001) *Against the Third Way*, London: Polity.

Ehrlich, P. (1971) *The Population Bomb*, London: Pan.

Harman, C. (2002) 'The workers of the world', *International Socialism* 96, Autumn.

Heartfield, J. (2001) 'The economics of sustainable development', in I. Abley and J. Heartfield, *Sustaining Architecture in the Anti-Machine Age*, London: Wiley.

Heartfield, J. (2003) 'Capitalism and anti-capitalism', *Interventions* 5, 2: 271–89.

Hertz, N. (2001) *The Silent Takeover: Global Capitalism and the Death of Democracy*, London: Heinemann.

Hunt, B. (2003) *The Timid Corporation: why business is terrified of taking risk*, London: John Wiley.

Jowell, R., Curtice, J., Park, A., Brook, L., Thomson, K. and Bryson, C. (eds) (1998) *British and European Social Attitudes: How Britain Differs: The 15th Report*, Aldershot: Ashgate Publishing.

Keegan, W. (2000) 'Free Trade: Battered Not Beaten', in B. Gunnell and D. Timms, *After Seattle: Globalisation and its Discontents*, London: Catalyst.

Kingsnorth, P. (2003) *One No, many Yeses*, London: Freepress.

Klein, N. (2000) *No Logo*, London: Flamingo.

Macnaghten, P. and Urry, J. (1998) *Contested Natures*, London: Sage.

Meadows, D., Randers, J. and Behrens, W. (1972) *Limits to Growth – A Report for the Club of Rome's Project on the Predicament of Mankind*, New York: Universe Books.

Meadows, D. L. (ed.) (1977) *Alternatives to Growth: A Search for Sustainable Futures*, Cambridge, Mass.: Ballinger.

Monbiot, G. (2000) *The Captive State*, London: Macmillan.

Monbiot, G. (2001) 'Introduction', in E. Bircham and J. Charlton (eds) *Anti Capitalism: A Guide To The Movement* (2nd Ed.), London: Bookmarks.

Mumford, S. (1996) *The Life and Death of NSSM 200: How the destruction of a political will doomed a US population policy*, North Carolina: Center for Research on Population and Security.

Offe, C. (1987) 'Challenging the Boundaries of Institutional Politics', in C. Maier (ed.) *Changing the Boundaries of the Political*, Cambridge: University Press.

Peccei, A. and King, A. (1975) 'Commentary', in M. Mesarovic and E. Pestel (eds) *Mankind at the Turning Point*, London: Hutchinson.

Peeters, M. (2003) 'The Principle Of Participatory Democracy In The New Europe: A Critical Analysis', paper given at American Enterprise Institute 11 June 2003 conference on *Nongovernmental organizations: the growing power of an unelected few*.

Petras, J. (2002) 'Porto Alegre 2002: A Tale Of Two Forums', *Monthly Review* 35, 11, April.

Prodi, R. and Kinnock, N. (*c*.2000) *The Commission And Non-Governmental Organisations: Building A Stronger Partnership*, European Commission.

Real World Coalition (1996) *The Politics of the Real World*, London: Earthscan.

Ross, S. (2002) 'Is this what democracy looks like?', *Socialist Register*, 2003: 281–304.

Shell (*c*.2002) *There is no Alternative: Shell on Sustainable Development*, London: Shell International Ltd.

Simons, M. (1988) 'The Red and the Green: The Socialists And The Ecology Movement', *International Socialism* 37, Winter.

Stiglitz, J. (2002) *Globalisation and its Discontents*, London: Penguin.

Tickell, C. (1978) 'Climatic Change and World Affairs', *Harvard Studies In International Affairs* 37.

Part 2

Global civil society – contesting future possibilities

6   The idea of global civil society

Mary Kaldor

I will argue in this chapter that the tradition of 'cosmopolitanism' or
Kantianism is much more realistic than it was 30 years ago because of the
profound changes that have occurred in the world in the interim – changes
we lump together under the rubric of 'globalisation'. It can be argued that
one cannot talk properly about international relations before the advent of
the state. What I think is happening today is that the growing interconnectedness of states, the emergence of a system of global governance, and
the explosion of the movements, groups, networks and organisations that
engage in a global or transnational public debate, have called into question
the primacy of states.

This does not mean the demise of states. On the contrary, I think that
states will continue to be the juridical repository of sovereignty, although
sovereignty will be much more conditional than before – increasingly
dependent on both domestic consent and international respect. Rather it
means that the global system (and I use the term 'global system' rather
than 'international relations') is increasingly composed of layers of political institutions, individuals, groups and even companies, as well as states
and international institutions.

The term 'global civil society' only really began to be used in the last
ten years – although Kant had referred to the possibility of a universal civil
society. My aim in this chapter is to explore the evolution of that idea and
how it challenges the concept of international relations. I will start with a
thumbnail sketch of the changing meaning of civil society. I will describe
the reinvention of civil society simultaneously in Latin America and
Eastern Europe, how its meaning at this juncture differed from earlier
meanings. I then want to say something about how the idea has changed
again in the 1990s and the competing versions of it that now exist. Finally,
I will ask whether September 11 and the war in Iraq represent a defeat for
the idea – a reversion to international relations.

Changing meanings of civil society

Civil society is a modern concept although, like all great political ideas, it
can be traced back to Aristotle. For early modern thinkers, there was no

distinction between civil society and the state. Civil society was a type of state characterised by a social contract. Civil society was a society governed by laws, based on the principle of equality before the law, in which everyone (including the ruler – at least in the Lockean conception) was subject to the law, in other words, a social contract agreed among the individual members of society. It was not until the nineteenth century that civil society became understood as something distinct from the state. It was Hegel who defined civil society as the intermediate realm between the family and the state where the individual becomes a public person and, through membership in various institutions, is able to reconcile the particular and the universal. For Hegel, civil society was 'the achievement of the modern world – the territory of mediation where there is free play for every idiosyncrasy, every talent, every accident of birth and fortune and where waves of passion gust forth, regulated only by reason glinting through them' (Comaroff and Comaroff, 1999: 3). Thus Hegel's definition of civil society included the economy and was to be taken up by Marx and Engels, who saw civil society as the 'theatre of history'.

The definition narrowed again in the twentieth century, when civil society came to be understood as the realm not just between the state and the family but occupying the space outside the market, state and family – in other words, the realm of culture, ideology, and political debate. The Italian Marxist, Antonio Gramsci, is the thinker most associated with this definition. He was preoccupied with the question of why it was so much easier to have a communist revolution in Russia than in Italy. His answer was civil society. In Italy, he said, 'there was a proper relation between state and society and, when the state trembled, a sturdy structure of civil society was at once revealed' (in Ehrenberg, 1999: 209). His strategy for the Italian Communist Party, which, in fact, was followed right up until the 1980s, was to gain positions in civil society – in universities, in the media and so on – so as to challenge the hegemony of the bourgeoisie. It was Gramsci who drew the distinction between hegemony, based on consent, and domination, based on coercion.

Despite the changing of the content of the term, I want to suggest that all these different definitions had a common core meaning. They were about a rule-governed society based on the consent of individuals; or, if you like, a society based on a social contract among individuals. The changing definitions of civil society expressed the different ways in which consent was generated in different periods, and the different issues that were important at different times. In other words, civil society, according to my definition, is the process through which individuals negotiate, argue, struggle against or agree with each other and with the centres of political and economic authority. Through voluntary associations, movements, parties, unions, the individual is able to act publicly. Thus in the early modern period, the main concern was civil rights – freedom from fear. Hence civil society was a society where laws replace physical coercion, arbitrary arrest, etc. In the nineteenth century, the issue was political rights, and the actors in civil society were the emerging bourgeoisie. In the twentieth century, it was the workers' movement that was challenging the state and the issue was economic and social emancipation – hence the further narrowing of the term.

Not only did all these definitions have this common core of meaning, but also they all conceived of civil society as territorially tied. Civil society was inextricably linked up with the territorial state. It was contrasted with other states characterised by coercion – the empires of the East. It was also contrasted with pre-modern societies, which lacked a state and lacked the concept of individualism – Highlanders, or American Indians. And, above all, it was contrasted with international relations, which was equated with the state of nature because it lacked a single authority. Many civil society theorists believed that civil society at home was linked to war abroad. It was the ability to unite against an external enemy that made possible civil society. Thus Adam Ferguson, the Scottish Enlightenment thinker whose book *An Essay on the History of Civil Society* is one of the core texts on civil society, was deeply concerned about modern individualism. Like the other Scottish Enlightenment thinkers, he wanted to develop a scientific approach to the study of social phenomena and believed this had to be done through empirical study of other societies. To understand the evolution of society, he studied the Highlanders and American Indians and became convinced that modern society had lost the spirit of community, natural empathy and affection among human beings. He believed, taking the example of Sparta, that the inclination of patriotism and the martial spirit was one way to overcome the dangers of individualism. An even stronger version of this argument was taken up by Hegel, who believed that war was necessary for the 'ethical health of peoples ... Just as the movement of the ocean prevents the corruption which would be the result of perpetual calm, so by war people escape the corruption which would be occasioned by a continuous or eternal peace' (Hegel, 1996: 331). Of course, not all civil society theorists took this view – Kant was the most important exception, believing that the perfect constitution of the state could be achieved only in the context of a universal civil society – but it was the dominant view.

The reinvention of civil society

The revival of the idea of civil society in the 1970s and 1980s, I believe, broke that link with the state. Interestingly, the idea was rediscovered simultaneously in Latin America and Eastern Europe. I was deeply involved in the East Europeans' discussions and always thought it was they who reinvented the term. However, subsequently, I discovered that it had been used earlier by the Latin Americans, notable among them Cardoso (until recently the President of Brazil). It is a fascinating task in the history of the ideas to explore the way in which this concept proved useful in two different continents at the same time but (so far as I am aware) with no communication between them – indeed, there seems on the contrary to have been widespread mistrust, since by and large the Latin Americans were Marxists and the East Europeans were anti-Marxists.

In both cases, the term 'civil society' proved a useful concept in opposing militarised regimes. Latin Americans were opposing military dictatorships; East Europeans were opposing totalitarianism – a sort of war society. Both came to the conclusion that overthrow of their regimes 'from above' was not feasible; rather it was necessary to change society. Michnik, in his classic article first published in 1978, 'The New Evolutionism', argued that attempts to bring change from above (Hungary 1956 or Czechoslovakia 1968) had failed, and that the only possible strategy was change from below, changing the relationship between state and society (Michnik, 1985). What he meant by civil society was autonomy and self-organisation. Thus the emphasis (and this was shared by the Latin Americans), was on withdrawal from the state. They talked about creating islands of civic engagement – a concept shared by both East Europeans and Latin Americans. East Europeans also used terms like 'anti-politics' and 'living in truth' – the notion of refusing the lies of the regime, or 'parallel polis' – of creating their own Aristotelian community based on the 'good', i.e. moral, life.

As well as the emphasis on autonomy and civil organisation, civil society also acquired a global meaning. This was a period of growing interconnectedness, increased travel and communication, even before the advent of the Internet. The emergence of 'islands of civic engagement' was made possible by two things:

1   Links with like-minded groups in other countries. The Latin Americans were supported by North American human rights groups. The East Europeans forged links with West European peace and human rights groups, which supported them materially and publicised their cases, and put pressure on governments and institutions.
2   The existence of international human rights legislation to which their governments subscribed and which could be used as a form of pressure. For Latin America, it was the human rights legislation that was important. For Eastern Europe, the Helsinki agreement of 1975, in which East European governments signed up to human rights norms, provided a platform for new groups like Charter 77 and KOR.

In other words, through international links and appeals to international authorities, these groups were able to create political space. Keck and Sikkink, in their book on transnational activism, talk about the 'boomerang effect', whereby instead of directly addressing your government, appeals to the international community bounce back, as it were, and put pressure on governments to tolerate certain activities (Keck and Sikkink, 1998).

This transnational or global aspect of the new understanding of civil society has been widely neglected by Western commentaries on the period, perhaps because they understood civil society within their own traditions of thought. Yet it was stressed by the new thinkers themselves, certainly in Eastern Europe. George Konrad, the Hungarian writer, and my favourite of these thinkers, used the word 'globalisation' in his book *Anti-Politics* written in 1982. Vaclav Havel talked about the 'global technological civilisation'. 'The post-totalitarian system', wrote Havel,

> is only one aspect – a particularly drastic aspect and thus all the more revealing of its real origins – of the general inability of modern humanity to be master of its own situation. The automatism of the post-totalitarian system is merely an extreme version of the global automatism of technological civilisation. The human failure that it mirrors is only one variant of the general failure of humanity. ... It would appear that the traditional parliamentary democracies can offer no fundamental opposition to the automatism of technological civilisation and the industrial-consumer society, for they, too, are being dragged helplessly along. People are manipulated in ways that are infinitely more subtle and refined than the brutal methods used in post-totalitarian societies. ... In a democracy, human beings may enjoy personal freedoms and securities that are unknown to us, but in the end they do them no good, for they too are ultimately victims of the same automatism, and are incapable of defending their concerns about their own identity or preventing their superficialisation or transcending concerns about their own personal survival to become proud and responsible members of the polis, making a genuine contribution to the creation of its destiny.
>
> (in Keane, 1985: 90–1)

Thus the new understanding of civil society represented both a withdrawal from the state and a move towards global rules and institutions. The groups who pioneered these ideas were central to the pressures for democratisation in Latin America and the 1989 revolutions in Eastern Europe. It is sometimes said that there were no new ideas in the 1989 revolutions – that the revolutionaries just wanted to be like the West. But I think this new understanding of civil society was the big new idea, an idea that was to contribute a new set of global arrangements in the 1990s.

Global civil society in the 1990s

In the aftermath of 1989, the idea of global civil society changed its meaning and was understood in very different ways. Below I describe three main paradigms:

First of all, the term was taken up all over the world by the so-called 'new social movements' – the movements that developed after 1968 concerned with new issues, like peace, women, human rights, the environment, and new forms of protest. The language of civil society seemed to express very well their brand of non-party politics. The concept was enthusiastically taken up in South Asia, Africa – especially South Africa – and Western Europe. During the 1990s, a new phenomenon of great importance was the emergence of transnational networks of activists who came together on particular issues – landmines, human rights, climate change, dams, AIDS/HIV, or corporate responsibility. I believe they had a significant impact on strengthening processes of global governance, especially in the humanitarian field. Notions of humanitarian norms that override sovereignty, the establishment of the International Criminal Court, the strengthening of human rights awareness – all these factors were very important in the construction of a new set of multilateral rules: what we might call a humanitarian regime. Towards the end of the 1990s, the emergence of a so-called anti-globalisation movement – concerned with global social justice – used the concept of civil society in the same way. I call this understanding the 'activist version'.

Second, the term was taken up by global institutions and by Western governments. It became part of the so-called 'new policy agenda'. Civil society was understood as what the West has; it is seen as a mechanism for facilitating market reform and the introduction of parliamentary democracy. I call this the 'neo-liberal version'. The key agents are not social movements but NGOs. I regard NGOs as tamed social movements. Social movements always rise and fall. And as they fall, they are either 'tamed' – institutionalised and professionalised – or they become marginal and disappear or turn to violence. Becoming 'tamed' means that you become the respectable opposition – the partner in negotiations. Historically, social movements were tamed within a national framework. Campaigners for the suffrage or for anti-slavery in the nineteenth century became absorbed into liberal parties. Labour movements were originally universalist and internationalist but became transformed into official trade unions and Labour and Social Democratic parties. What was significant in the 1990s was that the new social movements became tamed within a global framework. There have always been International NGOs like the Anti-Slavery Society or the International Committee of the Red Cross, but their numbers increased dramatically in the 1990s, often as a result of official funding (for details, see Anheier *et al.*, 2001, 2002). Indeed NGOs increasingly look both like quasi-governmental institutions, because of the way they substitute for state functions, and at the same time like a market, because of the way they compete with each other. The dominance of NGOs has led some activists to become disillusioned with the concept of civil society. Thus Neera Chandhoke, a civil society theorist from Delhi University, says civil society has become a 'hurrah word' and 'flattened out':

Witness the tragedy that has visited proponents of the concept: people struggling against authoritarian regimes demanded civil society, what they got were NGOs. If everyone from trade unions, social movements, the UN, the IMF, lending agencies, to states both chauvinistic and democratic hail civil society as the most recent elixir to the ills of the contemporary world, there must be something gone wrong.

(Chandhoke, 2001: 56)

And Mahmoud Mamdami, an African political scientist, says 'NGOs are killing civil society' (2002: 12).

Yet a third concept of global civil society is what I call the 'post-modern version'. Social anthropologists criticise the concept of civil society as Euro-centric, something born of the Western cultural context (according to this argument, Latin America and Eastern Europe are both culturally part of Europe). They argue that non-Western societies experience or have the potential to experience something similar to civil society, but not based on individualism. They argue, for example, that in Islamic societies institutions like religious orders, the bazaar or religious foundations represent a check on state power. Thus for post-modernists, new religions and ethnic movements that have also grown dramatically over the last decade are also part of global civil society. Global civil society cannot be just the 'nice, good movements'.

Civil society has always had both a normative and descriptive content. The definition that I gave at the beginning of this chapter was a normative definition. I said that civil society is the process through which consent is generated, the arena where the individual negotiates, struggles against, or debates with the centres of political and economic authority. Today, those centres include global institutions, both international bodies and companies. I think that all three versions have to be included in the concept. The neo-liberal version makes the term respectable, providing a platform via which more radical groups can gain access to power (both 'insiders' like NGOs and 'outsiders' like social movements). In normative terms, it might be argued that service-providing NGOs, especially those funded by states, should be excluded because they are not engaged in public debate and are not autonomous from the state. Likewise, it could also be argued that communalist groups should be excluded because central to the concept of civil society is individual emancipation; if communalist groups are compulsory, then they cannot be viewed as vehicles for individual emancipation. But in practice, in actually existing civil society, it is almost impossible to draw boundaries between who is included and who is excluded.

What has happened in the 1990s, I would argue, is that a system of global governance has emerged which involves both states and international institutions. It is not a single world state, but a system in which states are increasingly hemmed in by a set of agreements, treaties, and rules of a transnational character. Increasingly, these rules are based not just on agreement between states but on public support, generated through global civil society. Of particular importance, in my view, is a growing body of cosmopolitan law, by which I mean the combination of humanitarian law (laws of war) and human rights law. Cosmopolitan law is international law that applies not just to states but to individuals. This broadening and strengthening of cosmopolitan law, both immediately after the Second World War and in the 1990s, was largely a consequence of pressure from global civil society.

In other words, global civil society is a platform inhabited by activists (or post-Marxists), NGOs and neo-liberals, as well as national and religious groups, where they argue about, campaign for (or against), negotiate about, or lobby for the arrangements that shape global developments. There is not one global civil society but many, affecting a range of issues – human rights, environment and so on. It is not democratic – there are no processes of election, nor could there be at a global level, since that would require a world state. And such a state, even if democratically elected, would be totalitarian. It is also uneven and Northern dominated. Nevertheless, the emergence of this phenomenon does offer a potential for individuals – a potential for emancipation. It opens up closed societies, as happened in Eastern Europe and Latin America, and it offers the possibility to participate in debates about global issues. And it is my view that the emergence of this phenomenon – this new global system – makes the term 'international relations' much less appropriate.

After September 11

How have these trends, this activity, been affected by September 11 and the war on Iraq? Do terror and war on terror mark a reversal of the developments I describe? Both terror and war on terror are profoundly inimical to global civil society. Terror can be regarded as a direct attack on global civil society, a way of creating fear and insecurity that are the opposite of civil society. President Bush's response, I would argue, has been an attempt to re-impose international relations; that is to say, to put the threat of terrorism within a state framework. The US is the only country not hemmed in by globalisation, the only state able to continue to act as an autonomous nation-state: a 'global unilateralist' as Javier Solana puts it, or the last nation state. Bush declared the destruction of the World Trade Center towers as an attack on the United States, using the analogy of Pearl Harbor, and he identified the enemies as states which sponsor terrorism or which possess weapons of mass destruction – whether Afghanistan or Iraq or the 'axis of evil'. The term 'war' implies a traditional state conflagration. The language of war and war on terrorism closes down debate and narrows the space for different political positions. And the American determination to go to war with Iraq unilaterally has caused a profound crisis in the institutions of global governance.

But I do not think Bush can reverse the process of globalisation. The consequence of trying to do so will be still more uneven, anarchic, wild globalisation. If you like, it will be a situation in which the 'outside' of international relations, at least in a realist conception, comes 'inside'; in which we can no longer insulate civil society from what goes on outside. The distinction between war and domestic peace made by the classical theorists of civil society no longer holds. Global civil society offers the promise of bringing the 'inside' outside. The war on terror offers the opposite. The polarising effect of war is likely to increase rather than reduce terrorist attacks. It is the nature of war to discriminate among groups of human beings; however much the coalition forces insist on saving civilian lives, in practice their own lives are privileged over the lives of Iraqis, both military and civilian. The war has already generated tremendous anger and resentment, especially in the Middle East. Moreover, the difficulty of stabilising the region in the aftermath means that the kind of conditions that nurture terrorism – repression, sporadic violence, inequality, extreme ideologies – are likely to be reproduced for the foreseeable future.

Is there an alternative? Could we imagine domestic politics on the global scene? What I have been trying to argue is that this is exactly what has been happening over the last decade. Moreover, global civil society, especially the activist strand, has not gone away. The anti-globalisation movement is very active, especially in Latin America. There are new synergies between the anti-globalisation movement, the peace movement and Muslim communities, which have burst forth in a global anti-war movement, historically unprecedented in size and geographical spread. Many states, notably Germany and France, have followed public opinion and not the United States. On the one hand, this is the reason for the crisis in multilateral institutions. On the other hand, a new responsiveness to global civil society offers the possibility of a system of global institutions which act on the basis of deliberation, rather than, as in the past, on the basis of consent for American hegemony.

What happens depends on politics, on the agency of people who make history. The idea of global civil society is an emancipatory idea, which allows every individual the potential to engage in this debate. I do think we are living through a very dangerous moment – the war in the Middle East could spread, there could be a new war in South Asia, including the possible use of weapons of mass destruction, and we are likely to witness an increase in global terrorism. To what extent can global civil society convince states to adopt an alternative multilateralist framework for dealing with dictators, terrorism, and weapons of mass destruction, not to mention poverty, AIDS/HIV, the environment and other desperately important issues? Many commentators pointed out that the attacks of September 11 should have been dealt with in the framework of international law. They should have been treated as a crime against humanity; a war crimes tribunal should have been established by the Security Council; and efforts to catch and destroy terrorists, even if they involve the use of military means, should be considered not war but law enforcement (Howard, 2002). And the same argument can be made about the situation in Iraq. There were ways of dealing with Iraq, which might have been gleaned from the experience of Eastern Europe in the 1980s; United Nations Security Council resolutions, especially 687, emphasised human rights and democracy as well as weapons of mass destruction and could have been used in the same way as the Helsinki Agreement to put pressure on the regime; weapons inspectors could have been accompanied by human rights monitors; and the international community could have made it clear that it would protect Iraqis from Saddam Hussein's forces in the event of an uprising, as it did in Northern Iraq in 1991 and failed to do in the case of the Shiite uprising (see Kaldor, 2003).

I do not see any other way out of the current dangerous impasse than trying to establish a set of global rules based on consent. We have to find ways to minimise violence at a global level, in the same way that early modern thinkers envisaged civil society as a way of minimising violence at domestic levels. And this means opening up the conversation about what might be done.

I would like to end with a quotation from George Konrad. He was worried about the threat of nuclear war, the risk of a 'global Auschwitz' as he called it (he himself is a survivor of Auschwitz). That is the 'It' he refers to, although I think it could also apply to terror and the war on terror. Konrad (1984: 243) concludes his book by saying:

> Of course, I am small before the great, weak before the powerful, cowardly before the violent, wavering before the aggressive, expendable before It, which is so vast and durable that I sometimes think it is immortal. I don't turn the other cheek to it. I don't shoot with a slingshot; I look, and then I collect my words.

Acknowledgement

This chapter first appeared as an article in *International Affairs (London)*, 79, 4, July 2003 and is reproduced with permission.

References

Anheier, H., Glasius, M. and Kaldor, M. (2001, 2002) (eds) *Global Civil Society 2001* and *Global Civil Society 2002*, Oxford: Oxford University Press.

Chandhoke, N. (2001) 'A Cautionary Note on Civil Society', paper presented at the conference on *Civil Society in Different Cultural Contexts*, LSE, September.

Comaroff, J. L. and Comaroff, J. (1999) *Civil Society and the Political Imagination in Africa: Critical Perspectives*, Chicago and London: University of Chicago Press.

Ehrenberg, J. (1999) *Civil Society: The Critical History of an Idea*, New York and London: New York University Press.

Havel, V. (1985) 'The Power of the Powerless', in J. Keane (ed.) *The Power of the Powerless: Citizens Against the State in Central-Eastern Europe*, London: Hutchinson: 90–1.

Hegel, G. W. F. (1996) *The Philosophy of Right* [1820] Translated by S. W. Dyde, originally published in English in 1896, London: Prometheus Books.

Howard, M. (2002) 'What's in a Name?', *Foreign Affairs*, January/February.

Kaldor, M. (2003) 'In Place of War: Open Up Iraq', www.opendemocracy.net

Keane, J. (ed.) (1985) *The Power of the Powerless*, Armonk NY: M. E. Sharpe Inc.

Keck, M. E. and Sikkink, K. (1998) *Activists Beyond Borders*, Ithaca and London: Cornell University Press.

Konrad, G. (1984) *Anti-Politics: An Essay*, New York and London: Harcourt, Brace and Janovich.

Mamdami, M. (2002) Intervention at Expert Conference for *Human Development Report*, New York.

Michnik, A. (1985) 'The New Evolutionism', in *Letters from Prison and Other Essays*, California: California University Press.

7 Saying global civil society with rights[1]

Gideon Baker

Global civil society is widely celebrated for promising political action on a global scale and, by extension, for offering the best hope for the 'civilisation' of the world order. The key approaches all seek to move beyond 'Westphalia' (state sovereignty), and see global civil society as having a crucial part to play in this transformatory project. Richard Falk, for example, suggests that global civil society 'recasts our understanding of sovereignty' as 'the modernist stress on territorial sovereignty as the exclusive basis for political community and identity [is] displaced both by more local and distinct groupings and by association with the reality of a global civil society without boundaries' (1995: 100). Ronnie Lipschutz also sees the transnational political networks put in place by actors in civil society as 'challenging, from below, the nation-state system'. Indeed, 'the growth of global civil society represents an ongoing project of civil society to reconstruct, re-imagine, or re-map world politics' (1992: 391).

However, it is argued here that the now dominant vision of exactly *how* global civil society might achieve such a post-Westphalian order – what will be termed the 'globalisation from below' view – fails to re-imagine world politics in any substantive way, instead collapsing back into a familiar liberal discourse which valorises a rights-based approach to the political. This turn towards 'saying global civil society with rights' is problematic, it is suggested, for requiring fixed points of sovereignty from which to bestow such rights, which constitutes a return to Westphalia at precisely the moment when an alternative vision and practice of world politics is being attributed to global civil society.

Two models of global civil society

The architects of models of cosmopolitan democracy offered an early conception of a new role in world politics for global civil society. For David Held (1995), civil society provides for the public spheres which, taken together: offer a basis for dispersed sovereignty in a system of global governance; generate critical resources directed towards the institutional power required by such governance; and provide opportunities for voluntary association at the 'local' level. Civil society is constrained within a wider framework of cosmopolitan democratic law that 'delimits the form and scope of individual and collective action within the organisations of state *and* civil society. Certain standards are specified ... which no political regime or civil association can legitimately violate' (Held, 1995: 43). Of course, for this cosmopolitan democratic law to have any legitimacy and authority, global-level sovereign institutions are required, though Held imagines these also being constrained by such a law, particularly by the principle of subsidiarity (which disperses sovereignty), but also through ensuring that these are representative global institutions.

Held summarises his model as involving the call for a double-sided process of democratisation in both political and civil society. Thus although he sees civil society as one of the agents of democratic global governance, it is as much acted upon as actor, object as well as subject of his cosmopolitan democracy. Civil society is incorporated into the project of global democratisation from the 'top-down' as it were.

The second key approach to global civil society, and the particular focus of this chapter, can be termed the 'globalisation from below' model. 'Globalisation from below' theorists, contra Held, look to the agency of 'bottom up', 'solidarist' transnational social movements – to the struggle for a global ethic more than the construction of a global polity. What is meant by a 'global ethic' here? Simply that the growth of an increasingly norm-governed world system appears central to claims for an expanding role for global civil society. Thus Richard Falk (2000: 171), for example, writes of the need to build on Held's cosmopolitan democratic theory by emphasising 'the agency role of global civil society'. Falk also suggests that a 'normative' rather than a 'substantive' model of global democracy is preferable, since the former highlights 'ethical and legal norms, thereby reconnecting politics with moral purposes and values'.

This model, then, is focused more directly on nascent global civil society itself – on the potential for the 'civilisation' of world politics 'from below' via the moral advocacy of transnationally operational social movements focused on issues such as human rights and the environment. In this vein, Falk sees global civil society offering 'globalisation from below' as an alternative to the hegemonic 'globalisation from above' imposed by elites through a worldwide normative network premised not on human needs but on the needs of capital (neo-liberalism). For Falk, echoing cosmopolitans like Held, there *can* be a democratic global normative framework, a 'law of humanity'. Yet, unlike Held, Falk sees global civil society as the only means to this humane law – 'as the hopeful source of political agency need[ed] to free the minds of persons from an acceptance of state/ sovereignty identity ...' (Falk, 1995: 101). Furthermore, such global governance must be built 'from the ground up' and continue to be anchored in global civil society itself. This universalism 'from below' is also sought by

Paul Ghils, who wonders whether the 'universality of action in association' – a phrase reminiscent of Melucci's 'planetarization of action' (1989: 74) – makes 'civil society and its transnational networks of associations ... the *universum* which competing nations have never succeeded in creating' (Ghils, 1992: 429). The missing link in the cosmopolitan model that the 'globalisation from below' theorists seek to make good, then, is *agency*.

Such a focus on agency is also useful in exposing the ahistorical aspect of much cosmopolitan thinking, which seems to rest upon a neo-Kantian 'appeal to some supposedly already existing world politics or universal ethics, as if the grungy skin of modern statist politics can be cast off to reveal some essential or potential humanity beneath' (Walker, 1994: 673). Rob Walker is particularly critical of the cosmopolitical attempt to 'read off' social movements 'as agents of this revelation', and sees the focus on global civil society as an antidote to this:

> More interestingly, perhaps, it is possible to appeal to a rather less abstract and apparently more politically engaged account of an emerging global civil society. Indeed, much of the recent literature attempting to make sense of social movements/world politics has begun to draw quite heavily on the notion of a global civil society, not least so as to avoid falling back on some pre-political or even anti-political claim about an already existing ethics or world politics through which social movements can act without confronting the limits of modern politics in the modern state.
>
> (Walker, 1994: 674)

This critique of the absence of agency in the cosmopolitan account is persuasive. Cosmopolitical theorists, while they need global civil society normatively, say very little about global civil society as such. Andrew Linklater, for example, acknowledges that a post-Westphalian order requires 'post-Westphalian communities' that can 'promote a transnational citizenry with multiple political allegiances and without the need for submission to a central sovereign power' (Linklater, 1998: 181). However, Linklater's real concern is with setting out a normative defence of a· cosmopolitan ethic; indeed he summarises all recent work on cosmopolitan citizenship as defending 'the normative project of uncoupling citizenship from the sovereign state so that a strong sense of moral obligation is felt to all members of the species' (ibid.: 204). As to the *politics* of this project, however, only the following very general comments are made:

> Cosmopolitan citizenship requires international joint action to ameliorate the condition of the most vulnerable groups in world society and to ensure that they can defend their legitimate interests by participating in effective universal communicative frameworks ...

Cosmopolitan citizenship acquires its most profound praxeological significance when it is regarded as a guide to the moral principles which should be observed in these circumstances.

(ibid.: 206–7)

The problem here is that to stop at a normative critique of the conjunction between citizenship and the state is to fall short also of an assessment of political possibility in terms of identifying potential new forms of citizenship. Cosmopolitan theorists thereby face the problem of accounting for the transition to humane global governance. It also appears a quite anti-political view of praxis that so confidently sets out moral principles for practitioners to observe in advance of their practice.

The models converge

At first sight our two models appear to vary considerably on precisely these two points. Unlike the cosmopolitan model, which seeks to move beyond Westphalia almost by decree – by submitting states, along with all other forms of association, to a framework of democratic law and rights 'from above' – the 'globalisation from below' perspective works with a more organicist vision of how to replace state sovereignty. It sees it slowly being trumped by the ethical demands of global civil society (for example on behalf of human rights and the environment). With its focus on the actions of new social movements and other globally active organisations, *this* model, unlike the cosmopolitan approach, appears to offer an agency-rich account of how to civilise global politics. It also seems less prescriptive – apparently taking its ethics from the *practice* of global civil society rather than telling global civil society what ethics it should have.

However, the 'globalisation from below' approach is not in fact so different from the cosmopolitan model, nor is it a genuinely 'post-Westphalian' vision of the political, and for the following reasons. First, the overruling of sovereignty in the face of the ethical demands of global civil society may in practice be more tied up with inter-state politics than advocates of global society 'from below' would like to admit. Architects of cosmopolitics, given that their thinking is not so 'bottom up', are willing to concede this link between a global ethic and state action. Linklater (1998: 207), for example, argues that 'a post-Westphalian configuration of states committed to the … transformation of political community is the most involved system of joint rule which can be realised in the present era'. 'Globalisation from below' enthusiasts, however, are loath to attribute such ongoing agency to the state, though state action remains implicitly necessary. One enthusiast for a globally interventionist civil society unintentionally divulges as much when claiming that, 'given the right circumstances' – including, tellingly, 'a specific interest on the part of a major power capable of using force' – 'civil society might be able to play a role in getting rid of nasty dictatorships' (Kumar, 2000: 136). The sense here is that global civil society is the principle agent in riding the world of dictators, when in actual fact it is the nameless 'major power', no doubt with its own interests and agendas, that is the *sine qua non* (and the Iraq war to topple Saddam appears a very good example of this). Speaking more generally, we can observe that states and global civil society are mutually implicated in each other's affairs. States seek the backing of domestic civil societies for their foreign policies towards other states; they appeal to foreign civil societies for support in actions towards their states; and civil societies frequently call on the assistance of their own state in pursuing objectives in other states (Köhler, 1998: 245).

What stands out then is that even if global civil society is taken to be the 'ethical' driver behind the overriding of the principle of state sovereignty, in practice it is only states that are likely to have the capacity to enact these 'ethical' demands *vis-à-vis* other states. Martin Shaw, as one advocate of 'global society', lets this slip when stating that 'it is unavoidable that global state action will be undertaken largely by states, *ad hoc* coalitions of states and more permanent regional groupings of states' (1994a: 186). But which states have such a capability? For David Chandler, 'in practice, the prosecution of international justice turns out to be the prerogative of the West' (2000: 61).

In celebrating the ability of global civil society to make ethical demands on individual states, the 'globalisation from below' approach therefore misses the potentially deleterious effects of this on the right of equal sovereignty *between* states (which has been crucial in upholding the principle of self-determination since 1945). This ought to be of particular concern given that, on the basis of the uneven spread of power and resources, most 'global' civil society organisations are actually thoroughly Western (many based in, even resourced by, Western states) and the majority of 'world citizens' are more adequately conceptualised as objects rather than subjects of such organisations. Shaw unintentionally acknowledges this when he writes that 'the activities of globalist organisations, such as human rights, humanitarian and development agencies, make a reality of global civil society by bringing the most exposed victims among the world's population into contact with more resourceful groups in the West' (Shaw, 1994b: 655).

Such obliviousness to the implications for equal sovereignty – and by extension to the principle of self-determination – of providing *carte blanche* to global civil society is widespread in the literature. Falk, for example (1998: 327), advocates the 'emancipation' of the UN from the control of states in order to make it 'more responsive ... to pressure from transnational social forces expressive of global civil society'. What Falk does not consider is that his proposal could well lead to even further concentration of political influence in the Western societies once the principle of control of the UN by (all) states is supplanted by the principle of lobbying by (mainly Western) civil society organisations.

Second, the two models converge on the issue of rights. For cosmopolitan democrats, a truly global civil society would not only be dependent on such a rights-framework but would actually be partially constituted by it. The paradigmatic example here is Held's model, where all 'groups and associations are attributed rights of self-determination specified by a commitment to individual autonomy and a specific cluster of rights … Together, these rights constitute the basis of an empowering legal order – a democratic international law' (Held, 1993: 43). It is unsurprising that cosmopolitans take a rights-approach to global civil society, given their emphasis on a framework of global democratic law as the means to establishing a liberal-democratic ethic worldwide. Yet the same is true for 'globalisation from below' theorists in as much as they see the future of world politics in terms of ethical advocacy (regarding the environment and human rights, for example). Although by a different route, this aspiration to entrench 'ethical politics' from below is not so different from the desire to institutionalise a global ethic from above. Of course the former, we are told, comes from the ethics of an emergent civil society that is *building* normative consensus *politically* – as groups and movements construct alliances and align themselves behind a humane alternative to neo-liberalism – rather than dictating it from the academy. Yet 'ethical politics' leads to demands for rights every bit as much as cosmopolitan universalism. Thomas Risse (2000: 205), for example, contends that:

> transnational civil society needs the cooperation of states and national governments. To create robust and specific human rights standards [international nongovernmental organisations] must convince enough states that international law needs to be strengthened … Transnational civil society also needs states for the effective improvement of human rights conditions on the ground.

Mary Kaldor too sees 'the concept of global civil society' as 'equated with the notion of a human rights culture' and even writes that civil society issues 'such as peace, gender equality and the environment … can easily, and in some cases rather usefully, be reconceptualised as human rights issues'. Kaldor states it quite explicitly – global civil society is an adjunct to human rights; in her own words again: 'the language of civil society … adds to the human rights discourse the notion of individual responsibility for respect of human rights through public action' (Kaldor, 1999: 210–11).

It is not clear where exactly the *politics* – the building of global constituencies and alliances around shared values – of global civil society comes in here. Indeed, so sure are theorists such as Kaldor and Falk of what the ethics of global civil society are – Falk, for example, sees an 'embedded and emergent consensus' rising from global civil society around 'substantive democracy', human rights and non-violence (2000: 172–4) – that there is really very little difference between *their* confidence that such an ethical framework is being politically constructed 'on the ground', and the neo-Kantian cosmopolitan view that all reasonable, rational constituents of 'global society' could hypothetically agree to it:

> The transnational activity of [civil society organisations] is interpreted as evidence that an all-inclusive ethical base of world politics exists from which it is possible to appeal to governments as a supplementary element in the world community. In such a vision, the question of what exactly constitutes the political in the international system becomes unclear. Accountability is replaced by shared responsibility towards common ethical imperatives. The requirements of loyalty and conflict limitation are thus set a priori; they do not, that is, result from political discourse. Conflicting interests seem to disappear together with the political dimension of any transnational public sphere.
>
> (Köhler, 1998: 241–2)

The problem of the accountability of an ethically-driven global civil society is well raised by Köhler. In an account of transnational civil society from Risse, its growing influence is put down to 'the power of moral authority' and 'the accepted claim to authoritative knowledge'. The example used is that of the human rights area, where it is enthusiastically proclaimed that, 'today, Amnesty International, Human Rights Watch and the Lawyers Committee for Human Rights *define* what constitutes a human rights violation' (Risse, 2000: 186). This is a clear example, as Risse readily admits, of transnational civil society creating international norms, which must also mean, if true, that the norm-setting agenda for global politics is in no real sense under popular control (although Risse nowhere comments on *this* worrying, if unsurprising, feature). Taking a wider perspective, it is worth questioning how civil associations that assert moral authority can ever be held to account democratically, particularly when this is tied up, as it must be, with claims to special knowledge.

Global civil society and rights

The global spread of rights therefore plays just as central a role for 'globalisation from below' theorists as for cosmopolitans, since both effectively read a fully-fledged ethics *back* into the agency of global civil society, rather than vice versa. However, arguments for rights produce arguments for the state, not civil society; or, rather, arguments for the two understood as inseparable. Far from moving radically 'beyond' Westphalia, this brings us back to a more or less conventional account of the relationship between (global) civil society and the state.

Before rehearsing the ways in which rights require states, or more precisely statist politics, it is important to acknowledge that some 'globalisation from below' theorists are more cognisant of this than others. Falk is particularly frank here, noting that an emerging global ethic requires the 'reinstrumentalization' of the state. This would involve social forces represented by global civil society driving regional and global mechanisms of government towards an increasingly regulatory (presumably rights-based) approach to market forces, (de)militarization and public goods generally in world society. Indeed, Falk (2000: 177) is so bold as to say that 'such a process is likely to engender some type of global polity over the course of the next several decades'.

Falk, then, is one of the few celebrants of 'globalisation from below' who acknowledges that the telos of an increasingly rights-bound system of global governance, just as for the cosmopolitans, is something approximating a global polity. What Falk is less quick to acknowledge, given his emphasis on nascent 'global citizenry', is that such a polity would not only be constituted by the rights-based global public sphere he dreams of seeing, but also by *statist* institutions at the global level without which these rights could not be instantiated. Thus we need at this point to rehearse in more detail exactly why rights are locked into *statist* forms of governance.

This is, first, because the discourse of sovereignty central to the state's monopoly of the political can absorb all challenges to its authority posed by strategic rights-claims given their articulation in terms of interest and identity, terms that implicitly seek *recognition* from the state (Schecter, 2000: 135). Action in civil society, even before the adjunct 'global' was added, has always involved the struggle to 'win back' power from states – struggles which, when successful, came to be expressed in the form of rights setting out limits to state power (Blaug, 1999: 120). But the state has always been the addressee where struggles for rights are concerned.

Second, structures of rights are compromises secured through legal contract and valid contracts presuppose a sovereign state, or joint action on the part of sovereign states (Schecter, 2000: 134). The response that 'while the state is the agency of the legalization of rights, it is neither their source nor the basis of their validity' misses the point here (Cohen and Arato, 1992: 441). For although the state is undoubtedly not the source of rights or of their legitimacy, it remains the agent without which rights cannot be instantiated. The state is therefore *functionally indispensable* to a rights-agenda.

Third, once rights become the measure of things politically, then, in addition to the monopoly of the use of coercion required for their enforcement, it is even more fundamentally the case that, if my conception of rights clashes with yours, we need the state to adjudicate between our claims; we are now in need of protection from one another by the state (Schecter, 2000: 130). Thus (global) rights necessitate but also *stimulate* the growth of the (global) state. Yet few, if any, theorists of global civil society actually want a world state or think that such an institution would ever be desirable (given seemingly insurmountable problems of popular control and accountability at such a level of remove from individual citizens).

Fourth, once in place, rights represent a crystallised configuration of ethical learning, which is a completely different moment of the political from the fluid forms of critical practice characteristic of movements in global civil society. These movements, on the contrary, *challenge* existing ethical patterning, for example in the name of the environment. As we have seen, this isn't a problem just for the cosmopolitan approach, with its 'top-down' approach to global law and rights, but for the 'globalisation from below' school, too. Their pre-commitment to closely defined ethical values (western, liberal) is equally susceptible to closing down the political moment by which these norms might be contested. To imply that this problem can be overcome by global civil society stimulating a worldwide process of ethical learning – leading to an agreed upon set of truly universal values – is not only Eurocentric (since such 'learning' is always implicitly understood as other cultures 'catching up' with western liberal values), but also misses the ways in which such a process could only be imposed by means of power, not agreed upon by equal participants in a discursive process. There cannot be a global political community in a world whose inhabitants do not have political equality; we cannot have global political equality without first having global-level political institutions; and in the absence of such institutions there can be no worldwide democratic deliberation. Once again, therefore, we see that we cannot have the spread of rights across the world without the spread of statist institutions of governance accompanying, even preceding, them.

Critiquing 'globalisation from below'

From the 'globalisation from below' perspective there is justified scepticism of the cosmopolitan attempt to structure humane global governance from the 'top down'. Yet the attempt to 'say global civil society with rights' implies much the same arrangement of law and overarching sovereignty as in the cosmopolitan model. This is still statist global governance, if only by a different route and called by a different name. The 'globalisation from below' model thus moves far less 'beyond' Westphalia than its proponents would like to think.

There is another sense in which 'Westphalia' continues to cast its long shadow over such a global-governance-dependent vision of world politics. This is that, based on current evidence, burgeoning global governance seems to be further entrenching the longstanding power of the North over the South. Indeed, one reading of the emergence of global civil society suggests that it is much more a response to the transformation of state power, rather than simply its erosion. Along these lines, Shaw argues that the appearance of global civil society is at once a reaction to *and* a source of pressure for the globalisation of state power, which exists *de facto* in the 'complex of global state institutions [that] is coming into existence through the fusion of Western state power and the legitimation framework of the

United Nations' (Shaw, 1994b: 650). Köhler also suggests that 'the transnationalization of civil society activities is intrinsically related to the state's increasing commitment to intergovernmental cooperation' (1998: 233). Of course, this very process also undermines the traditional West-phalian order of state sovereignty in that 'once legitimacy and recognition are granted to transnational coalitions, interest aggregation and policy formulation ... cease to be *national* affairs, subject to the indivisible loyalty requested by the state' (Köhler, 1998: 246). So 'Westphalia' is transformed, but not surpassed. To put the point another way: extant global civil society appears to be both an outcome of, and a stimulus for, the transformation of the states' system.

To the extent that there is an emerging *de facto* global state, this is arguably the Western state writ large – with all the problems that this poses for the representativeness of the transnational civil society organisa-tions that can hope to influence it:

> From the viewpoint of many groups in non-Western society ... being involved in global civil society is in fact a way of connecting to Western civil society and hence of securing some leverage with the Western state which is at the core of global power ... The question that arises is whose voices are heard and how? If Western civil society is the core of global civil society, just as the Western state is the core of the global state, how do non-Western voices become heard? ... How far can non-Western voices makes themselves heard directly? In what ways are they filtered by Western civil society, and how is their representation affected by the specific characteristics of Western civil institutions?
>
> (Shaw, 1999: 223)

There are additional problems with the 'globalisation from below' approach to global civil society. First, this model does violence to the self-understanding of many of the movements that it is supposed to be celeb-rating, which often seek to contest structures of global governance rather than strengthen them. The agenda of *these* movements is an 'autonomy' rather than a 'recognition' one (see, for example, the Zapatista's on civil society in Baker, 2002 and 2003).

Second, specifying the ethical ends of global civil society in advance (human rights, environmentalism, etc.) is somewhat tautologous – civil society becomes what we say it is, namely those groups which pursue the programmes already identified as concerns of global civil society. The attribution of a particular *telos* to action in global civil society also fails to capture its fluid, movement aspect and its agonistic, contestatory charac-ter. Of course, many visions of 'globalisation from below' do speak of a global civil society that contests an enemy from without – neo-liberalism – but there is little sense of competition *within* and between its groups and movements. Here, the problem becomes one of a homogenised, de-politicised version of global civil society, as when Falk (2000: 165), for example, talks of 'normative convergence' around visions of a more sustainable, compassionate and democratic future world order. Does global civil society really have such a coherent ethical agenda even at this particular historical moment, quite apart from some transhistorical unity of purpose? To claim that 'the historic role of globalization-from-below is to challenge and transform the negative features of globalization-from-above' (Falk, 2000: 164) cannot be deduced from its practice but from nothing less than a philosophy of history with civil society cast in the role of principal agent.

Alternatives to 'globalisation from below'

A liberal-republican model

As we have seen, statist institutions of global governance constitute the ghost in the machine of 'globalisation from below' teleologies. We have also noted that there is some tension between the impulse to subaltern politics which animates visions of 'globalisation from below' and the reality of an attendant globalisation of statism. The question remains, then, of whether there is any way to ameliorate this tension.

In this regard, a recent piece by Michael Kenny (2003) may prove instructive. Kenny seeks to provide a liberal-republican lens through which to view the role of global civil society in a re-imagined world politics. Kenny (2003: 25–6) suggests that republican thought is capable of conceiving ethical and political relations beyond modern states due to its roots in a pre-nation state world. Thus the ongoing republican concern with the 'optimal framework for political community', although it has historically been resolved mostly in the direction of small city-states, actually involves posing a larger question about the preconditions for political communities to flourish as 'free states'. Republican answers to this question focus on the institutions and constitutional mechanisms necessary in order to foster individual liberty, which is at once to promote a citizenry committed to public duty. Put another way, there is an emphasis in republican thought, as Quentin Skinner and others have long reminded us, on the political preconditions of liberty – freedom is understood to be premised on the institutionalisation of citizenship in a free polity.

Visions of 'globalisation from below', in pointing up that the conditions of liberty at the local level are today intertwined with – and dependent on the transformation of – global politics, could thus be seen as continuing in the republican tradition. Here we have a hoped-for (global) 'citizenry' that is alive to the (global) political context underpinning the (un)freedom of the (global) community of which it is part. However, 'globalisation from below' departs from the republican tradition with its failure to attend to how this project might be *institutionalised*. Thus we have the attempt to 'say global civil society with rights' without consideration of just how much this involves falling back on an unreconstructed statism. A liberal-republican perspective, on the other hand, alive as this would be to 'the dynamics of interdependence *and* separation that shape the state-society relationship' in a free polity (Kenny, 2003: 29), is more likely to address itself to the institutions necessary, not only to the entrenchment of rights at the global level, but also to political freedom expressed through citizenship. While the former focus (rights) is more or less compatible with global governance evolved piecemeal from extant institutions and practices, global citizenship requires a much more thoroughgoing – and politically willed – revolution in global-level institutions of governance. It might require a global constitution, no less.

What then can we say about the conditions of possibility attaching to this process of institutionalisation? Kenny (2003: 28–9) makes an important point in observing that a sense of obligation between citizens, particularly in multicultural settings, will require sufficiently dense forms of interdependence emerging from the social roles that citizens occupy. In other words, a liberal-republican agenda is not as dependent as a 'globalisation from below' one on the (remote) possibility of worldwide ethical agreement. An ethic of *citizenship* is built instead on 'social and civic sources of mutuality', and in fact it is *this* 'thin' form of mutuality, not the 'thick' ethical variety, upon which rights-entitlements depend in contemporary democratic political communities (pluralist liberal democracies).

Despite its seeming advantages in enumerating the possibilities of a global civil society, however, it remains the case that the liberal-republican approach is underdeveloped on precisely the terrain that it sells itself – that of institutionalisation. For his part, Kenny can only claim 'the centrality of institutional and constitutional considerations' and signal 'the importance of the development of international law and accompanying institutions' (2003: 35). Indeed, for 'programmatic suggestions', he ends up volunteering Held's cosmopolitan democracy as a 'continuation of liberal-republican ambitions' (2003: 35), when, as we have seen, there is no sense in which Held's global framework of law can be said to have authorship in political community.

A neo-Gramscian model

Another model which appears to offer a more guarded, though certainly not cynical, account of the transformatory potential of global civil society is neo-Gramscian in origin. The particular attraction of the neo-Gramscian approach – both in light of the weaknesses of 'globalisation from below' and here bettering the liberal-republican model also – lies in its ability to describe a *politics* of global civil society. Global civil society itself is seen as a space for political and normative contestation. By extension, the teleological aspect of 'globalisation from below' is refused, as the space of global civil society itself becomes a battle ground in the undecided war of 'globalisation from above' versus 'globalisation from below'.

Prominent here is the work of Robert Cox. Cox internationalises Gramsci in the sense of seeing civil society *itself* as a field of global power relations – involved, that is, in the reproduction of global capitalist hegemony but as also containing the potential to organise *counter*-hegemonically at this level. Thus in the first instance states – as agencies of the global economy – and corporate interests seek to use civil society in order to stabilise the social and political status quo that is globalised capital, for example through state subsidies to NGO's which orientate them towards operations in conformity with neo-liberalism (Cox, 1999: 11). Yet in the second dimension, and Cox is another to use the phrase 'bottom up' to describe this,

> civil society is the realm in which those who are disadvantaged by globalization of the world economy can mount their protests and seek alternatives. This can happen through local community groups that reflect diversity of cultures and evolving social practices world wide ... More ambitious still is the vision of a 'global civil society' in which these social movements together constitute a basis for an alternative world order.
>
> (Cox, 1999: 10–11)

Cox sees 'something moving' in this direction across the globe as a counterweight to hegemonic power (global capital) and ideology (neo-liberalism), but is also quick to admit that such movement is still relatively weak and uncoordinated. 'It may contain some of the elements but has certainly not attained the status of a counterhegemonic alliance of forces on the world scale' (Cox, 1999: 13). Stephen Gill, whose work is close to Cox's, also sees counterhegemonic action through transnational links in civil society as more promissory than actual:

> [E]merging global civil society ... might then provide the political space and social possibility to begin to mobilize for the solution to deep-seated problems of social inequality, intolerance, environmental degradation and the militarization of the planet.
>
> (Gill, 1991: 311)

Such counterhegemonic elements as are found in the world system occur when, following the resurgence of civil society, there is transnational coordination of popular movements. Crucially for Cox, the forces of a transformatory civil society *must* operate globally since this is the level at which hegemony prevails (Cox, 1983: 171). In resisting this hegemony, however, the goal of civil society-based global action – and here Cox again follows Gramsci – is to effectively challenge and replace political authority in the system of states (Cox, 1999: 16, 27–8). Nevertheless, neo-Gramscian visions of global civil society resist Gramsci's more orthodox vanguardism – seeking a non-hierarchical mode of coordination in global civil society as a 'postmodern' alternative to the steering role allocated by Gramsci to his modern Prince – the Communist Party (Cox, 1999: 15).

Despite its strengths in analysing the operations of power *within* global civil society, the weaknesses of the neo-Gramscian model are to be found, once again, on the issue of institutionalisation. It is not at all clear what a non-hierarchical mode of organisation in global civil society would look like, but, if it is supposed to be pre-figured in 'institutions' such as the World Social Fora, then the problem remains that pluralism appears to be as much an outcome of these processes as it is a starting point (at least this is the rhetoric of many of the participants). But neo-Gramscians want co-ordination for a specific purpose and that purpose is clear: Cox's 'alternative world order' is very specifically an alternative to neo-liberalism. As with 'globalisation from below', then, neo-Gramscian analysis of global civil society takes place through an ethical lens which pre-identifies a particular enemy and which therefore valorises certain forms of 'subaltern' practice over others. Unlike the 'globalisation from below' model, with its largely unreflected liberal universalism, the justification for this selective reading of global civil society at least rests in a self-consciously neo-Marxist world view, the merits of which cannot be considered here. But what is clear is that the nature and significance of global civil society in neo-Gramscian analysis is identified in accordance with an already established view of the political. Though perhaps with good reason, we are not really seeing world politics anew here.

Conclusion

There is a strong suspicion that neither 'globalisation from below' nor its alternatives really tell us what is going on in the world at present outside of international relations, or at least only very partially. The versions of global civil society considered here share a tendency to identify the activities of global civil society in accordance with their extant view of the political. And of course this is how it must be; how else to go submarining in the vast sea of facts that is global politics other than armed with sonar that pick out some forms rather than others? The attempt to understand such an immense and complex set of processes as world politics, which is at once to impose a rather rudimentary order on these processes, must go on. And the category of global civil society has proved helpful, at the very least, in stimulating debate, as this book attests.

Be this as it may, the predominant 'globalisation from below' perspective, with its attempt to 'say global civil society with rights', is particularly guilty – of all the models considered – of conceptual distortion. For it subsumes *analysis* of the political possibilities of global civil society to projections of moral agency onto its groups and movements. This then blinds 'globalisation from below' accounts to the ways in which the institutionalisation of the putative moral project of global civil society – through the global spread of rights – is necessarily tied into statist politics, to a continuation of business as usual in terms of the predominance of statist forms. Thus we have a concept of global civil society that does the most to celebrate its capacity to move us 'beyond' Westphalia while doing the least to suggest a real alternative.

Note

1 I here adapt the phrase 'saying civil society with rights' as used in Blaug, 1999: 120–1.

References

Baker, G. (2002) *Civil Society and Democratic Theory: Alternative Voices*, London: Routledge.

Baker, G. (2003) ' "Civil Society that so Perturbs": Zapatismo and the Democracy of Civil Society', *Space and Polity* 7, 3: 293–312.

Blaug, R. (1999) *Democracy, Real and Ideal: Discourse Ethics and Radical Politics*, Albany, NY: State University of New York Press.

Chandler, D. (2000) 'International Justice', *New Left Review* 6, Nov/Dec: 55–60.

Cohen, J. A. and Arato, A. (1992) *Civil Society and Political Theory*, Cambridge, MA: MIT Press.

Cox, R. (1983) 'Gramsci, Hegemony and International Relations: An Essay in Method', *Millennium* 12, 2: 162–75.

Cox, R. (1999) 'Civil Society at the Turn of the Millennium: Prospects for an Alternative World Order', *Review of International Studies* 25: 1–28.

Falk, R. (1995) *On Humane Governance: Towards a New Global Politics*, Pennsylvania: Pennsylvania University Press.

Falk, R. (1998) 'The UN and Cosmopolitan Democracy', in D. Archibugi, D. Held and M. Köhler (eds) *Reimagining Political Community*, Cambridge: Polity.

Falk, R. (2000) 'Global Civil Society and the Democratic Project', in B. Holden (ed.) *Global Democracy: Key Debates*, London: Routledge.

Ghils, P. (1992) 'International Civil Society: International Non-Governmental Organizations in the International System', *International Social Science Journal* 133: 417–31.

Gill, S. (1991) 'Reflections on Global Order and Sociohistorical Time', *Alternatives* 16, 3: 305–20.

Held, D. (1993) 'Democracy: From City-states to a Cosmopolitan Order?', in D. Held (ed.) *Prospects for Democracy*, Cambridge: Polity Press, 13–52.

Held, D. (1995) *Democracy and the Global Order: From the Modern State to Cosmopolitan Governance*, Cambridge: Polity Press.

Kaldor, M. (1999) 'Transnational Civil Society', in T. Dunne and N. J. Wheeler (eds) *Human Rights in Global Politics*, Cambridge: Cambridge University Press, 195–213.

Kenny, M. (2003) 'Global Civil Society: A Liberal-Republican Argument', *Review of International Studies*, 29 December: 119–44.

Köhler, M. (1998) 'From the National to the Cosmopolitan Public Sphere', in D. Archibugi, D. Held and M. Köhler (eds) *Reimagining Political Community*, Cambridge: Polity, 231–51.

Kumar, C. (2000) 'Transnational Networks and Campaigns for Democracy', in A. M. Florini (ed.) *The Third Force: The Rise of Transnational Civil Society*, Washington, D.C.: Carnegie Endowment for International Peace, 115–42.

Linklater, A. (1998) *The Transformation of Political Community*, Cambridge: Polity.

Lipschutz, R. D. (1992) 'Reconstructing World Politics: The Emergence of Global Civil Society', *Millennium* 21, 3: 389–420.

Melucci, A. (1989) 'Nomads of the Present: Social Movements and Individual Needs in Contemporary Society', J. Keane and P. Mier (eds), London: Hutchinson Radius.

Risse, T. (2000) 'The Power of Norms versus the Norms of Power: Transnational Civil Society and Human Rights', in A. M. Florini (ed.) *The Third Force: The Rise of Transnational Civil Society*, Washington, D.C.: Carnegie Endowment for International Peace, 177–209.

Schecter, D. (2000) *Sovereign States or Political Communities? Civil Society and Contemporary Politics*, Manchester: Manchester University Press.

Shaw, M. (1994a) *Global Society and International Relations*, Cambridge: Polity.

Shaw, M. (1994b) 'Civil Society and Global Politics: Beyond a Social Movements Approach', *Millennium* 23, 3: 647–67.

Shaw, M. (1999) 'Global Voices: Civil Society and the Media in Global Crises', in T. Dunne and N. J. Wheeler (eds) *Human Rights in Global Politics*, Cambridge: Cambridge University Press, 214–32.

Walker, R. B. J. (1994) 'Social Movements/World Politics', *Millennium* 23, 3: 669–700.

8 Global civil society

Thinking politics and progress

Kimberly Hutchings

Since 1989, a number of counter-narratives to the realist accounts of international politics, which dominated academic theorizations of international relations in the 1945–89 period, have proliferated. A common, central thread in these counter-narratives is the reconceptualization of international political time in terms which admit the possibility of transnational or global historical progress. Examples include the revival of versions of liberal internationalism, cosmopolitanism and historical materialism. Within certain of these arguments the idea, variously specified, of 'global civil society' plays a prominent role. The issues raised by this re-opening of the question of political time at the international level are complex, but the attempts to theorize the 'new' phenomenon of global civil society provide a possible way into addressing the question of how political time in the context of world politics should be thought, especially from the perspective of those who are critical of statist accounts of world politics. The idea of global civil society has become, as this book testifies, a terrain in which not only realist and anti-realist conceptions of politics and progress, but also alternative anti-realist understandings of politics and progress, clash. The idea of global civil society potentially can be subsumed under a variety of metanarratives of world political time, but there is as yet no consensus. The aim of this chapter is to raise critical questions about ways of thinking the political temporality of global civil society which rely on modernist philosophies of history.

The chapter falls into four main sections. In the first section, I will look briefly at the fall and rise of speculative philosophy of history in the understanding of international politics. In the second and third sections of the chapter, I will sketch out two influential counter-narratives to realist international political time, which each make a claim to capture the meaning and promise of global civil society. These are the theories of *cosmopolitanism*, exemplified here by the work of Andrew Linklater, and *post-Marxist postmodernism*, exemplified in Hardt's and Negri's notion of empire/counter-empire (Linklater, 1998; Hardt and Negri, 2001). I see Linklater's work as embedded in a reading of history characteristic of the liberal enlightenment, most obviously derived from Kant.

Hardt and Negri, on the other hand, offer an explicitly post-Marxist interpretation, but one which is heavily informed by a Foucauldian account of power and subjectivity.[1] In both cases I will show how these theories frame particular interpretations of global civil society, both analytic and normative. In the fourth section of the chapter, I will suggest that neither cosmopolitanism nor empire provide adequate frameworks for the analysis and judgement of global civil society, and that this is to do with the specific kinds of closure inherent in the modernist philosophies of history on which those frameworks rely. In conclusion, it will be suggested instead that global civil society requires a mode of theorization which keeps its distance from both the temporality of realism and the progressivist temporalities of cosmopolitanism and empire/counter-empire. The challenge is to find a way to think the time of global civil society as world political time, without either denying the possibility of progress or occluding the colonizing logic of unitary philosophies of world history.

Section one: the fall and rise of the philosophy of world history

> Our concept of history, though essentially a concept of the modern age, owes its existence to the transition period when religious confidence in immortal life had lost its influence upon the secular and the new indifference toward the question of immortality had not yet been born.
>
> (Arendt, 1961: 74)

Arendt's account of the emergence of the modern conception of history (which she argues culminates in Marx's historical materialism) is a familiar one, and chimes in with most standard accounts of the distinctiveness of modernist conceptions of political time, in comparison to classical and Christian ideas. Koselleck draws the contrast between three understandings of history as political time, drawn from the early modern to the enlightenment periods in Europe: first, the cyclical view of secular history found in thinkers such as Machiavelli in which history is infinitely repeatable and political life is therefore always the same; second, the powerfully eschatological vision of early Protestantism, in which prophecies of an imminent end to secular politics were crucial (Luther); and third, the 'history' of modernity, characterized by a future-oriented conception of the present, which defines itself as both 'new' (not repetition) and secular (with no imminent or certain end) and in which political action can change its own conditions of possibility (Koselleck, 1985: 7–17). Philosophical history (or the speculative philosophy of history) emerges in the later eighteenth century as a response to this new appreciation of political time.

In the absence of the certainties of either secular repetition or other-worldly end, philosophers began to tell new stories about how the past, present and future of humanity could be understood in universal terms. The extent to which philosophical history is simply the secularisation of a Christian millenarian vision is debatable, but Koselleck suggests that enlightenment philosophical history should be read, not as an attempt to straightforwardly replace God's plan by the workings of 'providence', but rather to deal with the uncertainties as well as possibilities of having both embraced the demand for future good and abandoned its guarantor. In one sense, modern conceptions of history mean that the last judgement is infinitely postponed, in another sense the crisis of that judgement is always already upon us, a philosophical conception which is taken as confirmed politically by the French Revolution as the archetypal modern experience, in which history is taken into human hands and a new calendar is instituted.

> The dynamic of the modern is established as an element sui generis. This involves a process of production whose subject or subjects are only to be investigated through reflection on this process, without this reflection leading, however, to a final determination of this process. A previously divine teleology thus encounters the ambiguity of human design, as can be shown in the ambivalence of the concept of progress, which must continually prove itself both finite and infinite if it is to escape.
>
> (Koselleck, 1985: 103–4)

The philosophies of history that we find in the work of thinkers such as Kant and Marx are very different. But there are certain features which they have in common and which, I would argue, are distinguishing characteristics of the modernist understanding of political time.[2] Three features are of particular importance: first, the idea that modernity, the 'new' time of the present, is *revolutionary* time, that is to say the time in which progress through human intervention is possible, if not inevitable. Second, the *telos* of this revolutionary present is understood in terms of an ideal of freedom. The meaning of this freedom in both principle and practice, and therefore of the implicit 'end of history', clearly differs between different thinkers, but it always refers back to an ideal of self-determination in which human beings, individually and/or collectively control their own destiny. Third, modernist philosophy of history assumes that the political time of modernity has a world-wide destiny. This means that Europe, as the cradle of modernity, is also, as it were, the 'carrier' of world-political time. The mechanisms through which the telos of world history will be achieved, as with the form that the 'end of history' will take, are understood differently between different thinkers. Nevertheless, in all cases, the argument involves a complex interrelation between material and ideal forces, and a constant shifting on the philosopher's part between the realms, to borrow Kant's terminology, of 'empirical' (events in the world) and 'philosophical' (theorizations of world events) history (Kant, 1991: 51–3).

The idea of Europe as 'ahead' of other parts of the world in the end of history stakes came to be a taken for granted premise of theorizations of world politics in the nineteenth century. Thus, we find thinkers such as J. S. Mill happily combining liberal and colonialist arguments in his work. For Mill the non-contemporaneity of the contemporaneous nations of Britain and India is an obvious fact, which straightforwardly justifies paternalist imperialism in India (Mill, 2002: 488). The same kind of thinking helps to legitimise liberal internationalist principles enshrined in the post-1918 international order, with its promise of a future time in which all nations could grow up and join the adults already at the table. Whether explicitly or implicitly, modernist philosophy of history haunts the ways in which international politics are understood into the early part of the twentieth century. And even after the ascendancy of historicism in both philosophy and social science is radically challenged in the aftermath of the interwar years and the 1939–45 conflict, its influence is by no means entirely excised from the western academy's accounts of politics both within and between states.

For example, in the context of intra-state politics, in its dominant Anglo-American mode, political theory presents itself as both practised in and concerned with the present as such (as an intellectual pursuit it distinguishes itself firmly from activities such as the history of political thought). However, even when it initially presents itself as universal in scope, the 'present' of political theory turns out to be spatially delimited and to mean the present of liberal democratic or of liberal multicultural states. Political theory can contemplate liberalism's present as 'the' present because it is implicitly assumed that this is the direction in which all states are (and ought to be) developing, it is what *matters* in the present. Similarly, and even more obviously, there are the discourses applied in the field of international political economy, of 'modernization' or 'development' on the one hand, and of 'world system' and 'core/periphery' on the other. Underpinning these discourses we again find progressivist theories of history, in which both empirical analysis and policy prescriptions are premised on an idea of what the end of history will be and ought to be.[3]

Having said this, however, it is important to distinguish between the modernist narratives which have never ceased to mark the dominant understandings of politics within states from those which dominated the understanding of politics (as opposed to economics) between or across states in the latter half of the twentieth century. During this time, the most powerful voices offering accounts of international or world politics in the Western academy insisted on a deep distinction between politics internal to states and politics external to states. The former could be understood in terms of progress and/or regress according to a modernist measure, whereas the latter occupied a distinct temporal dynamic that had more in common with the early modern, proto-classical Machiavellian notions of political time than the revolutionary time of Kant and Marx. For the dominant political realist or neo-realist conception of international politics, states might or might not change for the better, but regardless of this, the ways in which they operated internationally would remain the same, reflecting a primordial political temporality of ongoing struggle, victory and defeat, which admitted of no end or escape.[4] This way of thinking world-political time excludes the notion of world political progress by definition. It is also resistant to taking seriously any internationalist or globalist movements or ideologies which aim to put world political progress on the international agenda. Such movements and ideologies, from a realist point of view, are either irrelevant or else can only be understood as masking the *real* power interests of which the stuff of international politics is made. The progressivist narratives I am going on to discuss explicitly contest the understanding of the political temporality of the international realm on which political realism/neo-realism relies and hark back to the earlier modes of thinking international politics in which world-historical progress is a taken for granted possibility, and one to which the theorist holds the key.

Section two: global civil society and cosmopolitan time

Over the past ten years a rapidly expanding literature in international political theory and ethics has argued for the development of cosmopolitan democracy and citizenship as both a normative ideal and an immanent potential of world-historical development. This literature clearly offers a counter to the realist conception of international political time. In its place, it puts forward an analysis of international, transnational and global politics in terms of the progressive transformation of the political temporality of inter-state relations into the global political temporality of humanity as a whole. My exemplary figure for this kind of counter-narrative is Andrew Linklater and his 1998 book, *The Transformation of Political Community*. Linklater draws explicitly on the legacies of Kant and Marx in his work, mediated through Habermasian critical theory. Unsurprisingly, therefore, he offers a narrative strongly reminiscent of the distinctive features, outlined above, of a modernist account of the historical meaning of the present.

In Linklater's argument, modernity is revolutionary time, in the sense that it is defined by a principle of universalizability which successively challenges limits to the moral and political progress of humanity. In a more specific sense, the present is revolutionary as the Westphalian international order is in the process of transformation into a new form of political community in which citizenship is no longer confined by the boundaries of states. The telos towards which the transformations analysed by Linklater are leading is that of self-determination, understood along the lines of Kantian autonomy in which individuals become self-legislating. For Linklater, this means that the end of history takes the form of a cosmopolitan, egalitarian, dialogic democracy. The mechanisms through which progress happens are not assured. Linklater essentially relies on two such mechanisms, both of which reflect the importance of Europe as the carrier of world-political time. First, there are the material mechanisms of globalization which lead to the increase of economic inter-dependency, abetted by advanced communicative technologies with global reach, and which necessitate the development of increasing inter- and trans-state co-operation in global governance and regulation. However, these material processes are by no means straightforwardly progressive. On the one hand, they facilitate the recognition of the commonality of the situation of humans across the globe; on the other hand, they exert frag-menting as well as unifying pressures, alienating those at the sharp end of global inequalities and deepening rifts between rich and poor, dominant and subaltern cultures (Linklater, 1998: 30–2). It is therefore the second mechanism which is much more important for Linklater's theory of history, this is the non-material process of moral learning, in which both individuals and collectivities absorb and proselytize the universalizing lessons of enlightenment reason (Linklater, 1998: 118–19). Linklater borrows strongly from Habermas here, for whom progress at the 'phyloge-netic' level is tied to the emergence of reflexive modernity, first instanti-ated in Europe and in the liberal capitalist West. Linklater's most powerful example of moral learning draws on Marshall's theory of the development of citizenship rights, in which the logic of universality implicit in liberal citizenship pushes forward an increasingly inclusive understanding of both who is included as a citizen and the kind of rights that he or she bears (Linklater, 1998: 184–9). Although progress cannot be guaranteed, the theorist's analysis confirms that it is moral learning which is the *sine qua non* of progress. In so far, therefore, as the theorist points out and reinforces the moral lessons of modernity, he is acting as a good global citizen. The demand to read history as if it were progress becomes a categorical imperative.

> Promoting the Kantian vision of a universal kingdom of ends, and the parallel enterprise of realising the neo-Marxist ideal of overcoming asymmetries of power and wealth, form the essence of cosmopolitan citizenship.
>
> (Linklater, 1998: 212)

In Linklater's analysis, civil society is the arena in which political actors challenge the unjustifiable exclusions inherent within states and in inter-state relations. Feminist and multiculturalist movements are taken to exemplify the way that Habermasian performative contradictions within liberal states, in which states act in contradiction with their own grounding principles, provide revolutionary opportunities for social and political transformation. The same logic which pushes the extension of rights within states challenges the validity of the distinctions drawn between those within and those without state borders. The development of global civil society is therefore a logical development of enlightenment reason, as is the European Union (Linklater, 1998: 189–211). On Linklater's interpretation the analysis of global civil society is necessarily linked to his broader progressivist narrative, in which liberal enlightenment reason plays the crucial role. This does not mean that Linklater is claiming that all activity in global civil society is necessarily progressive. But he is providing a way of distinguishing between the progressive and reactionary within civil society movements, and putting the emphasis on the positive logical weight carried by progressive developments. It is therefore also the case that an idealized version of global civil society itself, as a public sphere of open and inclusive dialogue, becomes an integral part of the historical telos of modernity.

Given the degree to which the most high profile developments within global civil society are non-governmental organizations (NGOs) and social movements which espouse egalitarian and universal rights based programmes, it is not surprising to find that cosmopolitanism has been the most significant framework of analysis in the burgeoning literature on global civil society (Falk, 1995; Kaldor, 1999; Archibugi, 2003). An example of this influence can be seen in the work of Mary Kaldor, who has been one of the foremost theorists of the 'new' time of global civil society, and who is also one of the editors of the *Global Civil Society Yearbook*.[5] In her recent book, *Global Civil Society: An Answer to War*, Kaldor begins by laying out five different interpretations of what global civil society means, all of which, she claims, contain both analytic and normative dimensions. These five conceptions draw on competing traditions of thought about the meaning of civil society in general. In the list are: *societas civilis*, in which civil society is identified with the rule of law; 'bourgeois society' in which civil society is the space between the state and the private sphere; 'activist version' in which civil society is defined as a public sphere in which different groups can participate in uncoerced dialogue; 'neo-liberal version' in which civil society is the space for market and non-governmental organizations to operate; and 'postmodern version', in which civil society is defined in fundamentally pluralist terms and is suspicious of enlightenment universalism (Kaldor, 2003: 7–12). Although she argues that her definition encompasses elements of all five, her emphasis is on what she calls the 'activist' version. According to this version, global civil society is primarily about 'civilizing' globalization by enabling the free and rational dialogue between different civil society actors and interests to take place, and thereby encouraging global legality, justice and the empowerment of global citizens (Kaldor, 2003: 12). Kaldor, like Linklater, links the idea of civil society to the ideal of a Habermasian, dialogic public sphere and sees enlightenment reason as carrying the transformative potential of the present of global civil society. Like Linklater again, Kaldor is not suggesting that progress is inevitable, but she is tying her own analysis to the interpretation of civil society in emancipatory terms. As an activist theorist, Kaldor is being a good global citizen in so far as she highlights and reinforces the ways in which global civil society is, and might become more, progressive. The key to progress is the emancipatory force of ideas, which are inherently universal. One of these ideas is the idea of civil society itself.

> the argument that civil society was invented in Europe and that its development was associated with conquest, domination and exploitation still does not negate the emancipatory potential of the term. Ideas have no borders and the evolution of human knowledge is characterized by an endless borrowing and mixing of concepts and insights.
>
> (Kaldor, 2003: 44)

What then are the implications of Kaldor's emphasis on the 'activist version' for the analysis and normative judgement of global civil society? Analytically, there are obvious constraints on what can count, by definition, as global civil society activity, so that, for instance, violent activity of any kind is excluded. For Kaldor, the most basic aspect of any view of civil society is that it is literally the realm of 'civility', beyond the state of nature. In addition, by defining global civil society in terms of voluntary and participatory activity, Kaldor puts into question the civil society status of certain kinds of groups or movements, notably those she labels as 'new' nationalist or fundamentalist movements (Kaldor, 2003: 97–101). There are also more subtle implications for what is foregrounded and what is under-emphasized in Kaldor's analysis. A very wide range of actors and developments are acknowledged as part of global civil society, but in general it is movements in which the goal of emancipation is explicit which are highlighted as core to the meaning of global civil society. The normative parameters of Kaldor's account are made very clear, and they provide definite criteria for judging what is to count as progressive civil society activity – that is to say activity which preserves civil society itself. The crucial criterion here is universality, organizations and movements which are in any way exclusive and closed to open debate with other civil society actors act contrary to the 'civility' which is central to Kaldor's ideal. Kaldor's moral clarity also underpins her willingness to support a framework of law, governance and policing, based on principles of universal human rights, to sustain the operations of global civil society. Although Kaldor is explicitly sceptical of global democracy, her account of what global civil society needs to sustain it clearly invokes the traditional liberal state/civil society distinction and relation. And it suggests a global order which is modelled in terms of a liberal constitution, in which key moral principles are enshrined and may be enforced (Kaldor, 1999: 210; 2003: 128–41).

Section three: global civil society and imperial time

The account of global politics in Hardt and Negri's *Empire* appears radically different to that of Linklater and other cosmopolitan theorists and owes significantly more to Marx than to Kant or Habermas. It also draws heavily on a certain interpretation of Foucault's conception of power, in particular his notions of 'disciplinary' and 'bio-power'. Nevertheless, like the cosmopolitan theories of Linklater and Kaldor, it presents a clear challenge to realist political temporality and locates international relations firmly within modernist political time. In this case, the present is revolutionary as the unprecedented time of 'empire', which as the decentred accumulation of global economic and political power (as 'bio-power') nourishes and harbours the revolutionary forces of counter-empire. Empire, although it is to be transcended, is understood as a progressive force because of the ways in which it has dismantled the mediations (such as those of nation-states and the civil societies of nation-states) of earlier capitalist eras and brings the population of the globe (in Hardt and Negri's terms, the 'multitude') face to face with imperial power as such (Hardt and Negri, 2001: 8–13, 392). The telos of Hardt and Negri's account of history harks back to the communist ideal of a world in which freedom is grasped by humanity in and for itself. The meaning of this telos in practice is not spelled out, though by implication this will be a holistic, undifferentiated social condition in which the breaking down of boundaries initiated by empire will be carried further. This is gestured towards in two of the immediate aims suggested by Hardt and Negri for the multitude, that of the right to free mobility for labour and a global minimum wage (Hardt and Negri, 2001: 396–403). The means by which the telos is attained, as with Linklater's argument, are twofold. First, Hardt and Negri suggest that internal tensions or contradictions within the mechanisms of empire will push forward revolutionary change, for instance through the forced globalization of labour. This is clearly a re-working of the Marxist notion of capital harbouring the seeds of its own destruction. Second, change will come about through the political demands and resistance of the 'multitude', as its consciousness is politicized (Hardt and Negri, 2001: 394–6). In contrast to Linklater's emphasis, typical of cosmopolitanism, on the power of reason, here the emphasis is on resistant action, in which the generative power of desire which empire has both relied on and exploited is turned in novel directions (Hardt and Negri, 2001: 406). This means that on this model the ideal of a discursive politics, common to the cosmopolitan view of global civil society, is replaced by an ideal of revolutionary practice.

Hardt and Negri claim that models of post-Westphalian world politics which treat it as analogous to, or as an extension of, the politics of the modern capitalist state are mistaken. For this reason they reject cosmopolitan narratives in which global civil society mediates between global governance and humanity, as civil society had traditionally been seen to mediate between the state and the private sphere (Hardt and Negri, 2001: 7). In addition, they argue that the category of 'global civil society' is far too broad and encompasses developments that are both pro and counter empire. For instance, they argue that global civil society in the form of humanitarian NGOs sustains rather than subverts imperial bio-power (Hardt and Negri, 2001: 313–14).

> These NGOs are completely immersed in the bio-political context of the constitution of Empire; they anticipate the power of its pacifying and productive intervention of justice. It should thus come as no surprise that honest juridical theorists of the old international school (such as Richard Falk) should be drawn in by the fascination of these NGOs. The NGOs' demonstration of the new order as a peaceful bio-political context seems to have blinded these theorists to the brutal effects that moral intervention produces as a prefiguration of world order.
>
> (Hardt and Negri, 2001: 36–7)

It is clear, therefore, that Hardt and Negri are suspicious of the kind of links which Linklater and Kaldor draw between moral universalism and historical progress. Nevertheless, this moral universalism, manifested in the development of humanitarian NGOs in global civil society, *is* linked to progress for Hardt and Negri, because it represents the breakdown of the mediating role played by the civil societies of nation-states, which in the past protected certain populations against the full consequences of global imperial power. This breakdown is a stage on the way to a different kind of change, in which 'the multitude' directly confronts empire. Exemplary cases of the latter kind of revolutionary practice on Hardt and Negri's account take the form of some manifestations of anti-globalization politics and some cases of indigenous revolutionary movements (Hardt and Negri, 2001: 54–7).

The difference between the 'imperial' and 'counter-imperial' aspects of global civil society, for Hardt and Negri, is reminiscent of the traditional Marxist distinction between a class 'in-itself' and a class 'for-itself', in which a transformation in political consciousness makes an objectively existing socio-economic group into a revolutionary subject (Hardt and Negri, 2001: 60–1).[6] Whilst humanitarian NGOs confirm 'the multitude' as a global entity, in acting on behalf of humanity as such they also confirm the passivity of the multitude. Whereas anti-globalization protests and indigenous revolutionary politics are the multitude acting in- and for-itself, albeit in a fragmentary and uncoordinated way. In the final section of the book, Hardt and Negri address the question of what the politicization of the multitude, in which its revolutionary energies would become genuinely global, would mean. Perhaps somewhat surprisingly, this revolutionary change is associated with the demand for global citizenship as the right to free immigration and a social wage, as well as with the expropriation of property, an odd mixture of traditional class based politics and the kind of language spoken by contemporary global civil society activists of the more radical sort (Hardt and Negri, 2001: 393–413).

Although cosmopolitan frameworks have tended to dominate work on global civil society, there is a counter-trend which reflects something of the mix of post-Marxism and postmodernism in Hardt's and Negri's position.[7] This approach to global civil society is sceptical of cosmopolitan enlightenment, and of the universalizing claims of dominant Western-based NGOs, and looks instead to more particular modes of resistance in the non-state sphere to exemplify the genuinely radical potential of global civil society. At the same time, however, it holds on to a universalizing commitment to an ideal of freedom and is as suspicious of the 'new' nationalisms and fundamentalisms as cosmopolitan theorists such as Kaldor (Walker, 1994; 1999; Baker, 2002; Mignolo, 2002; Calhoun, 2003). This is the kind of argument made in Gideon Baker's book, *Civil Society and Democratic Theory: Alternative Voices*, which claims that cosmopolitan arguments, whether they explicitly invoke the notion of a global democratic structure or not, are inherently blind to the meaning of the political embedded in the practice of actual global civil society activists:

> Whether from the standpoint of cosmopolitan democracy or global civil society theory, then, transnational civic action loses its self-determining character and, with this, its ability to reshape our understanding of the political. This is a particularly regrettable failure in theory since it is precisely this re-enacting of the political that many groups in global civil society identify as their practice.
>
> (Baker, 2002: 129)

The emphasis in Baker's account, as with Hardt and Negri, is on the ideal of revolutionary practice as the distinctive mark of genuine civil society activism. On this account there is an agonism built into the politics of global civil society, in which movements have to hold onto the radicalism by which they were initially inspired, and which is threatened by any form of institutionalization within the current world order. For instance, Baker is critical of the hegemony of rights language as the way to articulate the goals of global civil society actors, because he sees it as confirming a top-down, sovereignty-based approach to politics. Underpinning this distrust of the cosmopolitan position is a particular account of the meaning of freedom. The normative commitment of post-Marxist postmodernists is to a freedom which cannot be identified with any particular content and which, whenever it does take on a fixed meaning, inevitably betrays its own ideal. This means that the criterion by which progressive and regressive dimensions of global civil society are identified is as much a matter of form as of content. All global civil society actors may be challenging the status quo, but only those which embody the goal of freedom within their own praxis as political actors provide the appropriate vision for what global civil society should mean.

The implications for the analysis and judgement of global civil society of approaches such as that of Hardt and Negri are similar to those of cosmopolitanism in some ways, but also clearly differ in important respects. The link between global civil society and a universal ideal of self-determination remains, as does the rejection of new fundamentalisms and nationalisms. However, post-Marxist postmodernist arguments are less sure about the exclusion of violence from genuine civil society activity, given that revolutionary movements such as that of the Zaptistas have exemplary status within their discussion (Hardt and Negri, 2001: 55; Baker, 2002: 130–44). In addition, on this kind of account, grassroots political action becomes the exemplar for global civil society activity, and larger scale, more formally organized movements, which reflect universal liberal norms and interact with state and inter-state institutions, are seen as increasingly co-opted by that system and as falling outside of the genuinely non-state sphere. Unlike theorists such as Kaldor, Hardt and Negri are in principle opposed to the idea of humanitarian intervention, and see the governance of global civil society as an aspect of empire, rather than as a counter-imperial strategy. Above all, the vision of the 'end of history' implicit in the analysis is different. In place of a rule governed world order, which frames the ongoing dialogue of diverse civil society actors, we are presented, in John Keane's terms with:

> A future social order unmarked by the division between government and civil society, an order in which the "irrepressible lightness of joy of being communist" – living hard by the revolutionary values of love, cooperation, simplicity and innocence – will triumph, this time on a global scale.
>
> (Keane, 2003: 65)

Section four: critical reflections on the time of global civil society

The theories of Linklater and Hardt and Negri are examples of counter-narratives to realist accounts of world politics, which reclaim the international onto the ground of modernist political time, in principle the time of humanity as a whole as opposed to that of discrete political communities. In doing this, they offer certain tools for understanding and interpreting the phenomenon of global civil society. In both cases, political action, of certain kinds, within the non-state sphere of voluntary association and resistance to global power is identified with the transformative potential of the present. In both cases also, we are given ways of discriminating between those political actions which are genuinely progressive and those which essentially preserve the status-quo or are more profoundly reactionary. In the discussion so far, I have treated the meaning of 'global civil society' in the terms of the thinkers whose work has been under review. As has been demonstrated, these terms inevitably foreground some aspects of global civil society and under-emphasize or occlude others. If we take global civil society, in the most general terms, to mean the full range of non-state organizations, movements and activities which are transnational in their operations and aims, what are the problems inherent in examining global civil society in terms of either cosmopolitanism or empire? The problems, I suggest, can be labelled under three headings: *exclusivity*; *hubris*; and *either/or*. I will go on to explain each of these headings and to show how these problems are bound up with assumptions about the relation between past and future which characterize modernist philosophies of history.

Let us begin with the problem of *exclusivity*. Why is the exclusivity of these approaches to understanding global civil society a problem, given that all conceptualizations will set up stipulative definitional criteria which are exclusive? The answer to this, in my view, lies in the ways in which the lines are drawn between what is to count as genuine civil society activity and what is not. In the case of both cosmopolitan and empire arguments there is a peculiar, ongoing trade-off between the empirical and the normative which fixes the parameters of analysis. Because of this, the ideals of rational dialogue and of revolutionary practice, respectively, exert unnecessary closure on the concept of global civil society and therefore on the ways in which it can be analysed or understood. The effect of this closure is to occlude both interconnections between what is counted as inside civil society and what is excluded, and to occlude the possibility of recognizing ambivalences internal to that which is counted as inside. Thus, following the cosmopolitan path, we are diverted from theorizing the connection between civility and violence, even when it is acknowledged that coercion plays a necessary role in sustaining civil society. We are also encouraged to see the distinction between violence and civility as clear cut, so that identifying 'goodies' and 'baddies' within global civil society is relatively unproblematic. In the case of empire, although they reject the terminology of 'global civil society', Hardt and Negri similarly divert us from considering the link between the moral humanitarianism of the NGOs, which they see as implicated in empire, and the resistant practices of anti-globalization protestors or indigenous social movements. We are only permitted to see the former as an aspect of the material conditions for the latter, but not the actual and ongoing interplay between grass-roots movements and transnational organizations. At the same time, the 'multitude' is presented as necessarily pure in its generative power in sharp distinction to the corruption and crisis of empire, and we are encouraged to think that the distinction between empire and counter-empire is somehow straight-forward.

In the yearbook *Global Civil Society 2002*, Neera Chandhoke asks the question: 'To put it bluntly, should our *normative* expectations of civil society blind us to the nature of *real* civil societies whether national or global?' (Chandhoke, 2002: 37). Like Chandhoke, I would answer that they should not, but that one of the reasons that they are able to is because of the way in which the relation between the normative and the empirical is configured in the modernist philosophy of history. The exclusions in both post-Kantian and post-Marxist accounts of global civil society are particularly powerful because they are not simply reducible to wishful thinking. Instead, they reflect a way of thinking about the world in which the theorist is doubly invested in reading history as progress. The theorists of cosmopolitanism and empire have normative standards which the world fails to live up to, but they also understand history in such a way that they are obliged to read the world as if it were developing in accordance with their normative telos, because, even if they don't see progress in world history as inevitable, they know that one of the ways in which progress will happen is through the intervention of the theorist, insistent that this progress is visible and that he or she knows how it works. This respons-ibility of the theorist derives from the modernist assumption that self-determination is the key to progress, and that to the extent that this isn't apparent to social and political actors, it must be foregrounded by the the-orist him or herself. Thus, Linklater is himself part of the rational dialogue which pushes moral learning forward, and Hardt and Negri are part of the transformation of the multitude from a class in-itself to a class for-itself.

The *hubris* implicit in theorizing global civil society within a modernist framework, is not only apparent in the way in which modernist theorists take on the mantle of the revolutionary for themselves. It is also apparent in the unselfconscious way in which their normative criteria are presented as a global telos. I call the former 'unselfconscious', because it is so quick to ignore or sidestep the question of the identification of what progress means with Western modernity. This is only possible, in my view, because of the implicit reliance on an interpretation of the present in which the non-contemporeneity of the contemporaneous is taken for granted. Such an interpretation only makes sense because a modernist philosophy of history is presumed, and it works to disguise the fact both that this is a normative stance *and* that it is a stance which implies not just the inferiority but the outmoded nature of the ways of life which most of the world's population are living. As with Mill, the commitment to freedom becomes easily com-patible with the paternalist condemnation of non-modern ways of life. It is much easier for the theorists not to take seriously ways of thinking or political goals which do not fit with their own normative agenda, if those ways of thinking or political goals are understood as essentially past.

The combination of the assumption of normative standards at work in history and the supposedly demonstrable (but rarely demonstrated) superiority of those normative standards presents us with a pattern typical of modernist philosophy of history. It invariably works on a twin-track approach in which the analysis constantly shifts from a claim about morality (the ideal) to a claim about politics (the real) and *vice versa*. The mechanisms through which global civil society develops are identified with enlightenment reason or revolutionary action respectively, but this is presumed rather than demonstrated through empirical investigation. The fact that the explanation for progress is always already known clearly has strong prescriptive implications, but it also has implications for the description and explanation of events, closing off possibilities which don't fit with the criteria. It is this point which lies behind Chandhoke's argument as to the dangers of neglecting important aspects of global civil society in contemporary theorizing (Chandhoke, 2002).[8]

The latter point brings us to the final set of problems, which I have labelled under the heading of *either/or*. In the cases of both post-Kantian and post-Marxist approaches, global civil society comes to be interpreted in essentially Manichaean terms. I have already suggested above that this has negative implications for the analysis of global civil society, since it blocks the possibility of reading the interconnections between the inside and outside of global civil society, and also puts paid to a 'both and' (ambivalent) reading of the normative implications of particular civil society developments. It also encourages sectarianism in analysis, in which cosmopolitan and empire theorists compete unhelpfully over claims as to who has identified the *genuine* heart of global civil society activity and the *genuine* key to progress. Most importantly of all, however, it pre-empts arguments *either* for a less purist understanding of both morality and politics *or* for moral pluralism. Modernist philosophy of history precludes anything other than an essentially linear account of global historical development. This linearity lines history up to either succeed or fail according to a singular understanding of what success and failure mean. But it is only if one has bought into this framework of interpretation in the first place (whether consciously or not) that this is the choice with which those trying to analyse and judge global civil society are faced.

Conclusion

I have argued above that frameworks for understanding global civil society which depend on modernist philosophy of history pose a variety of problems. This is important because so much of the theoretical work on global civil society replicates assumptions embedded in post-Kantian and post-Marxist approaches to the interpretation of the present and the future. The problem is that, from the standpoint of Western modernity, Kant and Marx provide ways in which it is possible to think the present in terms of at least the possibility of progress, not just in the sense of the short-term peaks of a Machiavellian cycle, but as a lasting and reliable improvement of the human condition. The alternative to cosmopolitanism or empire would appear to be a lapse back into realism, in which notions of progress are a priori discredited, and many of the actors and organizations in global civil society can therefore only be understood as victims of false consciousness in their struggles for positive political and economic change. However, I would argue that this is misleading. The problem does not lie in the invocation of progress *per se*, but in the tying of the idea of progress to a unifying temporality, which is posited as universal and is therefore able to ignore (de-historicize and de-politicize) its own particular historicity and politics.[9]

The terms of the choice between Machiavelli and Marx or Kant themselves reflect an essentially modernist understanding of history and progress, in which world politics and progress can only be thought together through a particular unifying strategy in which a purist understanding of the mechanisms of progress is somehow embedded in the world as a whole (Spivak, 1998: 333). Refusing this choice does not close off debates either about 'world' or 'progress', but it does demand a reconceptualization of both and of their relation to one another. A first step in this task would be a greater degree of self-consciousness in theorists of world politics as progress of the origins and political effects (intended and unintended) of the vocabularies in which their analysis is conducted. A second step would be to be more open to the possibility that not only is the notion of *progress* highly contested, but that even where there is agreement on its meaning, the question of *how* it comes about should not be short-circuited by the presumption that we already know how progress happens and therefore what the end of history could be. Perhaps most importantly of all, however, a third step would be to pay more attention to the philosophical problem of how to conceptualize 'world' politics simultaneously in both holist and pluralist terms. Modernist philosophies of history and their realist counterparts both impede forms of thinking which are not binary and reductive. In their place, we need a form of thinking adequate to the complexity, inter-connection, division, plurality and hierarchy by which global civil society is characterized.

Notes

1 Hardt and Negri are unusual in that they formulate a systematic post-Marxist postmodernist theory of globalization, which is explicitly grounded in a theory of history. Few theorists of global civil society would subscribe to Hardt's and Negri's theory *in toto*. However, as I will argue below, work on global civil society which is influenced by Marxism and postmodernism implicitly relies on features of the modernist philosophy of history which we find at work in Hardt

and Negri, and this has similarly occlusive effects on the analysis and judgement of global civil society.

2 Within the space of this chapter, it isn't possible to provide a full justification for my account of the distinctive features of modernist philosophy of history, though I would argue that they are in keeping with Koselleck's account discussed above. I am also clearly being selective in picking out Kant and Marx as the key exemplars, rather than, for instance, Hegel or Herder. The reason for this is that it is the legacies of Kant and Marx that are most clearly reflected in contemporary work on global civil society. See: Kant 'Idea for Universal History with a Cosmopolitan Purpose' and 'Perpetual Peace: A Philosophical Sketch' (Kant, 1991); Marx and Engels *The German Ideology* (Marx and Engels, 1970), 'The Communist Manifesto' (Cowling, 1998) and Marx 'Preface to a Contribution to the Critique of Political Economy' (Marx, 1975).

3 See, for example, in the case of political theory introductory texts such as Kymlicka (2002) and Mulhall and Swift (1996). For an overview of theories of international economic development, see Brown (2001: 194–217) and Thomas (2001).

4 See Morgenthau (1985) and Waltz (1979) for exemplars of realism and neo-realism respectively.

5 This is a recently inaugurated series of volumes (beginning 2001) which seeks to analyse, chart and measure the development of global civil society in successive years. References in this chapter are to the 2002 volume (Glasius, Kaldor and Anheier, 2002).

6 It's important to note that the distinction cannot be the *same* as the 'in-itself'/ 'for-itself' distinction in Marx, since Hardt and Negri presuppose a Foucauldian account of subjectivity which is at odds with Marx's account of the revolutionary subject. Nevertheless, the Hardt/Negri distinction is clearly analogous to Marx's, both in its meaning and its function within the argument.

7 It's important to stress, see Note 1 above, that I am not suggesting that any of the theorists mentioned below endorse Hardt's and Negri's argument as such. However, I am suggesting that the leftist critique of cosmopolitanism, which we find in the work of theorists such as Walker and Baker, shares elements of the post-Marxist legacy in Hardt and Negri's thought, most notably an implicit philosophy of history which then exerts a particular influence on how global civil society is analysed and judged.

8 It is interesting to note that empirical analysis of global civil society often gives a much more complex and interesting picture than we find in theoretical work. One of the most important developments in global civil society organizations and movements in recent years has been the ways in which conceptions of progress, and problems of the Western domination of political agendas, have become contested within those organizations and movements (Edwards and Gaventa, 2001).

9 One attempt to refuse the choice between realism or cosmopolitanism/empire can be found in John Keane's theorizing of global civil society as 'cosmocracy' (Keane, 2003; Chapter 2 of this collection). Keane aims for a more inclusive and normatively pluralist account of global civil society than that provided by either Linklater or Hardt and Negri. I am in sympathy with much of his account and it goes a considerable way to addressing the shortcomings I have identified in post-Kantian and post-Marxist approaches. It is interesting, however, that he succumbs to the typically modernist temptation of identifying 'cosmocracy' as 'new' time (Keane, 2003: 97).

References

Archibugi, D. (ed.) (2003) *Debating Cosmopolitics*, London: Verso.

Arendt, H. (1961) *Between Past and Future: Six Exercises in Political Thought*, London: Faber and Faber.

Baker, G. (2002) *Civil Society and Democratic Theory: Alternative Voices*, London: Routledge.

Brown, C. (2001) *Understanding International Relations*, Basingstoke: Palgrave.

Calhoun, C. (2003) 'The Class Consciousness of Frequent Travellers: Towards a Critique of Actually Existing Cosmopolitanism', in D. Archibugi (ed.) *Debating Cosmopolitics*, London: Verso.

Chandhoke, N. (2002) 'The Limits of Global Civil Society', in M. Glasius, M. Kaldor and H. Anheier (eds) *Global Civil Society 2002*, Oxford: Oxford University Press.

Cowling, M. (ed.) (1998) *The Communist Manifesto: New Interpretations*, Edinburgh: Edinburgh University Press.

Edwards, M. and Gaventa, J. (eds) (2001) *Global Citizen Action*, London: Earthscan.

Falk, R. (1995) *On Humane Governance*, Cambridge: Polity Press.

Glasius, M., Kaldor, M. and Anheier, H. (eds) (2002) *Global Civil Society 2002*, Oxford: Oxford University Press.

Hardt, M. and Negri, A. (2001) *Empire*, Cambridge MA: Harvard University Press.

Kaldor, M. (1999) 'Transnational Civil Society', in T. Dunne and N. Wheeler (eds) *Human Rights in Global Politics*, Cambridge: Cambridge University Press.

Kaldor, M. (2003) *Global Civil Society: An Answer to War*, Cambridge: Polity Press.

Kant, I. (1991) *Kant's Political Writings* (ed.) H. Saner, Cambridge: Cambridge University Press.

Keane, J. (2003) *Global Civil Society?*, Cambridge: Cambridge University Press.

Koselleck, R. (1985) *Futures Past: On The Semantics of Historical Time*, Cambridge MA: MIT Press.

Kymlicka, W. (2002) *Contemporary Political Philosophy: An Introduction*, Oxford: Oxford University Press.

Linklater, A. (1998) *The Transformation of Political Community: Ethical Foundations of the Post-Westphalian Era*, Cambridge: Polity Press.

Marx, K. (1975) *Early Writings* (ed.) L. Colletti, Harmondsworth: Penguin.

Marx, K. and Engels, F. (1970) *The German Ideology* (ed.) C. Arthur, London: Lawrence and Wishart.

Mignolo, W. D. (2002) 'The Many Faces of Cosmo-polis: Border Thinking and Critical Cosmopolitanism', in C. A. Beckenbridge *et al.* (eds) *Cosmopolitanism*, Durham and London: Duke University Press.

Mill, J. S. (2002) 'A Few Words on Non-Intervention', excerpted in C. Brown, T. Nardin and N. Rengger (eds) *International Relations in Political Thought*, Cambridge: Cambridge University Press.

Morgenthau, H. (1985) *Politics Among Nations: The Struggle for Power and Peace*, New York: Arnold Knopf.

Mulhall, S. and Swift, A. (1996) *Liberals and Communitarians*, Oxford: Blackwell.

Spivak, G. (1998) 'Cultural Talks in the Hot Peace: Revisiting the "Global

Village" ', in P. Cheah and B. Robbins (eds) *Cosmopolitics: Thinking and Feeling Beyond Nations*, Minneapolis: University of Minnesota Press.

Thomas, C. (2001) 'Poverty, Development and Hunger', in J. Baylis and S. Smith (eds) *The Globalization of World Politics: An Introduction to International Relations*, Oxford: Oxford University Press.

Walker, R. B. J. (1994) 'Social Movements/World Politics', *Millennium: Journal of International Studies* 23, 3: 669–700.

Walker, R. B. J. (1999) 'Citizenship After the Modern Subject', in K. Hutchings and R. Dannreuther (eds) *Cosmopolitan Citizenship*, London: Macmillan.

Waltz, K. (1979) *The Theory of International Politics*, Reading MA: Addison-Wesley.

9 Constructing global civil society

David Chandler

In international relations theorising, constructivist theories have been central to the revival of interest in global civil society. This theoretical approach, which developed in the early 1990s, challenged the central assumptions of the academic discipline of international relations, particularly the research focus on states and power relations. During the Cold War and most of the history of international relations, the research agenda was dominated by rationalist approaches which subordinated morality to the interests of power. The constructivist framework challenges this emphasis on power and seeks to demonstrate that rather than power it is norms and values which shape the behaviour of the majority of states. States may still wield power in terms of military and coercive might but the use of this power is not guided solely by state interests of security and self-protection. Rather, in the constructivist framework, power is constrained and state interests reshaped through international normative structures created by the multiple interactions of states and non-states actors operating in global civil society.

This chapter focuses on constructivist theory as it relates to empirical studies of global civil society rather than attempting to engage with constructivist thinking per se. The following sections outline briefly the developments leading to a shift away from more traditional international relations concerns of liberal institutionalism and towards transnational networks operating in global civil society, it then considers the explanatory strength of the constructivist approach in this area and finally raises some of the limitations.

A new research agenda

Until the end of the Cold War, the dominant theoretical perspectives in international relations assumed the nation-state was the key actor and that it acted in the pursuit of pre-given national interests. There were a number of disagreements between commentators and theoreticians, regarding the nature of these interests and whether cooperation or conflict were the predominant means of attaining them, but whichever perspective was followed the assumption was that these 'self-interested' interests were themselves pre-given. The main debate in international relations was between neo-realists who focused on the limits of cooperation and the possibility of conflict and the neo-liberals who focused on the possibilities for cooperation and the limits to conflict (for surveys see Keohane, 1986; Nye, 1988; Baldwin, 1993). For both sides, states were theorised as rational actors pursing self-interested goals.

These approaches had three core assumptions. First, that states were the key subjects, i.e. the main actors in international relations. Second, that the interest of states as rational actors was to maximise their power and influence by pursuing their self-interests. Third, that in the context of international anarchy, i.e. the lack of a world government, states had to pursue self-help strategies, limiting the nature of international cooperation and making the international sphere one of strategic interaction in which security concerns were paramount. The development of constructivist approaches challenged all three of these core assumptions.

De-centring the state

Constructivist theory de-centres both the subject, or active agent, of international relations, the nation-state, and simultaneously the structural constraints of neo-realism. Rather than the structure of anarchy creating states and state interests, in which case the needs of 'power' constitute ideas and ideological constructions which further these interests, constructivists assert that understanding international relations in purely structural or 'instrumental' or 'rationalist' terms is inadequate. The structure of self-guided egoistic state-subjects operating in a world of self-help power politics is questioned. The relationship between the individual state and the society of the international sphere of relations is transformed. Rather than the immutable framework of anarchy creating the conditions of possibility and structural limitations for state interaction and state interests, constructivists hold that state interaction creates society. States have mutually-constituted themselves as self-interested power-seekers and in so doing have created and reproduced this particular form of international anarchy as a central feature of international political life (see further, Wendt, 1999: 246–312).

Alexander Wendt was one of the first influential international relations theorists to take up a constructivist approach (however, see also Kratochwil, 1991; Onuf, 1989; Katzenstein, 1996). Wendt argues:

> states do not have conceptions of self and other, and thus security interests, apart from or prior to interaction ... [Rationalist] claims presuppose a history of interaction in which actors have acquired "selfish" identities and interests; before interaction ... they would have no experience upon which to base such definitions of self and

other. To assume otherwise is to attribute to states in the state of nature qualities that they can only possess in society.

(Wendt, 1992: 401–2)

Wendt is still starting the analysis with nation-states as the subject of inter-national relations, the central actor, but the subject is transformed in two contradictory directions. On the one hand, the state is freed from the structural constraints of neo-realism. As Andrew Linklater argues, con-structionist thought highlights the importance of agency at the basis of normative international theorising, as the dominance of norms and values would be impossible without the presupposition that states and other actors have the capacity to overcome structural limitations on ethical action (Linklater, 1998: 19). However, the agency which constructivist frameworks give with one hand they take away with the other. The auton-omy or subjective agency of the state is 'hollowed-out'. The subject is no longer a self-determining, self-interested actor but rather is constituted through interaction. It is 'inter-subjective knowledge' which constitutes the interest or identity of the subject rather than self-determined or struc-turally determined interests. It is this inter-subjective focus which distin-guishes constructivism from the English School focus on the shared norms of 'international society' (see Bull, 1995). Wendt explains the importance of this shift in perspective:

This may all seem very arcane, but there is an important issue at stake: are the foreign policy identities and interests of states exogenous or endogenous to the state system? The former is the answer of an indi-vidualistic or undersociologized systemic theory for which rationalism is appropriate; the latter is the answer of a fully socialized systemic theory.

(Wendt, 1992: 402)

Constructivism is a theory of change. Rather than seeing states as having pre-given interests or 'being exogenously constituted', i.e. having identi-ties established outside of the international sphere, states and their iden-tities and interests are understood to be constructed through the process of international interaction (Wendt, 1992: 392). In Alexander Wendt's famous phrase, 'anarchy is what state's make of it' (Wendt, 1992). If identity and interests are not pre-given but shaped through social inter-action, identities and interests can change. For Wendt, the nation-state is still the subject of analysis but the focus has shifted towards the sphere of interaction rather than that of rational interests. Wendt saw this as an extension of neo-liberal theorising, freeing the study of the process of interaction, highlighted in regime theory, from the structuralist frame-work of fixed identities (Wendt, 1992: 393, 417; see also Kratochwil and Ruggie, 1986; Finnemore, 1996a; 1996b; Ruggie, 1998; Haas, 1999;

Wendt, 1999: 36). Some critics have questioned whether Wendt's work does in fact break with rationalist approaches (see Smith, 2001: 247; Smith, 2000: 15). Nevertheless, the logic of de-centring the state as the primary subject and prioritising regulative norms, established through interaction and ideas, laid the foundation upon which international relations theories of the importance of global civil society were constructed. Once state actors were seen to intersubjectively constitute their interests and identities, the focus shifted to the role of transnational and international network activity in establishing and internalising these new norms.

Identities and interests

Writing in the aftermath of the end of the Cold War, constructivist theorising which challenged the structural fixity of neo-liberal and neo-realist thought found a ready audience. As Christian Reus-Smit notes: 'the end of the Cold War undermined the explanatory pretensions of neo-realists and neo-liberals, neither of which had predicted, nor could adequately comprehend, the systematic transformations reshaping the global order' (Reus-Smit, 2001: 216). It appeared that the study of states and state interests could no longer adequately explain international politics. Instead, the research focus shifted away from fixed identities and narrow material interests to one which emphasised the power of norms and ideas. As Jack Donnelly argues in his comprehensive study of realist approaches:

> Neorealism ... cannot comprehend change. During the Cold War, this theoretical gap seemed acceptable to many. But when the Cold War order collapsed seemingly overnight, even many otherwise sympathetic observers began to look elsewhere – especially because the collapse was intimately tied to ideas ... and processes ... that were excluded by neorealist structuralism.
>
> (Donnelly, 2000: 31)

Wendt argued that it was not just the distribution of power that was important but also the 'distribution of knowledge', the intersubjective understandings which constitute the state's conception of its self and its interests. As an example, he states that having a powerful neighbour in the United States means something different to Canada than its does for Cuba, or that British missiles would have seemed more of a threat to the Soviet Union than to America (Wendt, 1992: 397). It was the interaction between states that shaped their identities and interests. Rather than power it was subjective conceptions that were important. The collapse of the Soviet Union, through implosion rather than military defeat, fundamentally challenged realist perspectives of state interests and the importance of military power and thereby facilitated the revival of more idealist perspectives of change – based on social interaction rather than material interests. As Wendt stated, inversing the rationalist framework: 'Identities are the basis of interests' (Wendt, 1992: 398).

Where rationalist approaches were based on the assumption that states pursued (relatively fixed) national interests, constructivist theorists argue that national interests should be seen as flexible and indeterminate. Thomas Risse and Kathryn Sikkink write:

> Actors' interests and preferences are not given outside social inter-action or deduced from structural constraints in the international or domestic environment. Social constructivism does not take the inter-ests of actors for granted, but problematizes and relates them to the identities of actors.
>
> (Risse and Sikkink, 1999: 8–9)

As Risse and Sikkink note: 'This new emphasis has resulted from the empirical failure of approaches emphasizing material structures as the primary determinants of state identities, interests and preferences' (Risse and Sikkink, 1999: 6). They continue:

> We do not mean to ignore material conditions. Rather, the causal rela-tionship between material and ideational factors is at stake. While materialist theories emphasize economic or military conditions or interests as determining the impact of ideas in international and domestic politics, social constructivists emphasize that ideas and com-municative processes define in the first place which material factors are perceived as relevant and how they influence understandings of interests, preferences, and political decisions.
>
> (Risse and Sikkink, 1999: 6–7)

In a fluid context where identities and interests are no longer constrained by material divisions, ideas become more important. If identities are much more flexible then, by implication, there is no inherent barrier to a global moral outlook. Constructivists assert that the abstract theorising of a Rawlsian 'veil of ignorance' is then not so abstract after all. If ideas are more important than military or economic power then moral agencies and actors such as international NGOs will be able to have a major influence merely through 'the power of persuasion' (Korey, 1999).

The global as a constitutive sphere

Wendt's view of ideas overcoming structures and material interests was a liberating one for a discipline in a state of crisis, but his narrow confine-ment of constructive methodology to the traditional field of international relations – the relations between states – was seen to be too restrictive. Instead, other strands of neo-liberalism were drawn upon, particularly the pluralist focus on the growing influence of non-state actors. Once it was established that old-fashioned instrumental politics, based on territorially restricted states, was the outcome of territorially-tied communicative processes, leading to the construction of competing interests, then the addition of non-state actors changed the picture. It was now argued that the growth of non-state actors in international affairs could be constituting a new type of non-instrumental dialogue and discussion where values and norms rather than instrumentality prevailed. This focus of attention on non-state actors tied in with the concerns of civil society theorists which emphasised the generation of ideas and norms in the non-governmental sphere (Diamond, 1994; Seligman, 1992; Cohen and Arato, 1992; Keane, 1998).

Rather than Wendt's focus on the interactions between states, constructivist theory was extended to give a central role to non-state actors. It is at this point that the concept of transnational or global relations comes in, in distinction to international relations, i.e. relations between states. The international sphere is no longer seen as one in which states project their national interests, instead the process is reversed – through participation in international and transnational relations the national interests of states are constituted and reconstituted.

In this way, the end of the Cold War could be held not just to discredit realist approaches but also to provide compelling evidence of the role of non-state actors in the development of state 'identities' and interests. As Risse and Ropp argue:

> the turnaround of Soviet foreign policy as an enabling condition for the peaceful revolutions of 1989 resulted at least partly from the fact that the Gorbachev leadership was itself heavily influenced by Western liberal ideas spread through transnational actors and coalitions ... the peaceful transformation [in Eastern Europe] was brought about by dissident groups in Poland and Czechoslovakia with the transnational human rights networks empowering and strengthening their claims.
>
> (Risse and Ropp, 1999: 268)

Over the last decade, the growth of international human rights norms is the leading example, held to demonstrate the strength of constructivist approaches: 'because international human rights norms challenge state rule over society and national sovereignty, any impact on domestic change would be counter-intuitive' (Risse and Sikkink, 1999: 4). The assertion that human rights norms challenge nation-state interests therefore assumes that norm changes cannot come solely from state agency but must also stem from the influence of transnational non-state actors. Even where states may use normative rhetoric, such as human rights concerns, it is the influence of non-state actors in global civil society which serves to prevent these from being used in a purely instrumental way.

Thomas Risse and Kathryn Sikkink argue that the 'process by which international norms are internalised and implemented domestically can be understood as a process of *socialization*' (Risse and Sikkink, 1999: 5). One example given by Risse and Sikkink is that of US foreign policy. They argue that the Reagan administration took a principled position in favour of democratisation but used it instrumentally as a vehicle for an aggressive assertion of US interests against left regimes, such as the USSR, Nicaragua and Cuba. However, the US establishment could not use the principled issue purely instrumentally because it was obliged to a minimal consistency and eventually actively encouraged democracy in authoritarian regimes which were loyal allies to the US, such as Chile and Uruguay. US interests changed as the 'principled issue' won out over the state's attempt to use the issue instrumentally (Risse and Sikkink, 1999: 10). In this way, constructivist theorists write about the 'power of principles' to overcome the instrumentalist purposes behind their initial adoption (Risse and Sikkink, 1999: 9).

The articulation of certain principled norms potentially changes the identity of the state itself. In *The Power of Human Rights*, edited by Risse, Ropp and Sikkink (1999), the authors analyse 'the process through which principled ideas (beliefs about right and wrong held by individuals) become norms (collective expectations about proper behaviour for a given identity), which in turn influence the behaviour and domestic structure of states' (Risse and Sikkink, 1999: 7). The constructivist argument is that global civil society plays a powerful role in turning ideas (held by individuals) into norms (collective guidelines) and establishing norms as state practice. International society, rather than inter-state competition is crucial because: 'While ideas are usually individualistic, norms have an explicit intersubjective quality because they are *collective* expectations. The very idea of "proper" behaviour presupposes a community able to pass judgments on appropriateness' (Risse and Sikkink, 1999: 7).

The constructivist 'turn' in international relations fundamentally lays open the previous assumptions of the discipline. The relationship between power and morality is inversed; no longer does Carr's dictum hold true that: 'Theories of international morality are ... the product of dominant nations or groups of nations' (Carr, 2001: 74). In today's globalised world, with the emergence of transnational linkages, committed transnational ethical campaigners are held to be capable of changing the identity, and thereby the interests, of leading states. What is crucial to this thesis is the socially constructed identity of the state actor rather than the alleged structural constraints overturning the realist understanding of 'identities' as merely a reflection of pre-given material interests:

What I am depends to a large degree on who I am. Identities then define the range of interests of actors considered as both possible and appropriate. Identities also provide a measure of inclusion and exclusion by defining a social "we" and delineating the boundaries against the "others".

(Risse and Sikkink, 1999: 9)

The non-instrumentalist assumptions made for global civil society rest heavily on the constructivist framework that assumes a connection between moral or ethical discourse and a power to shape identities and interests:

Moral discourses in particular not only challenge and seek justifications of norms, they also entail identity-related arguments. What I find morally appropriate depends to some degree on who I am and how I see myself ... The logic of discursive behaviour and of processes of argumentation and persuasion rather than instrumental bargaining and the exchange of fixed interests prevails when actors develop collective understandings that form part of their identities and lead them to determine their interests ... People become convinced and persuaded to change their instrumental interests, or to see their interests in new ways, following the principled ideas.

(Risse and Sikkink, 1999: 13–14)

The constitution of an international community 'able to pass judgements on appropriateness' and therefore establish principled international norms does not depend on free-floating norms and ideas but the impact of 'transnationally operating non-state actors', specifically the impact of 'principled-issue' or 'transnational advocacy networks' which diffuse 'principled ideas' and new 'international norms' (Risse and Sikkink, 1999: 4). Rather than states and inter-state arrangements being key to international change it is the action and linkages of non-state actors:

the diffusion of international norms in the human rights area crucially depends on the establishment and the sustainability of networks among domestic and transnational actors ... these advocacy networks serve three purposes ... They put norm-violating states on the international agenda in terms of moral consciousness-raising ... They empower and legitimate the claims of domestic opposition groups against norm-violating governments ... They challenge norm-violating governments by creating a transnational structure pressuring such regimes simultaneously "from above" and "from below".

(Risse and Sikkink, 1999: 5)

Where power and instrumentality are acknowledged to dominate the world of traditional inter-state politics, 'the power of principles' is king in the extended international sphere of global civil society where identity creation is driven by developing international norms and values (Risse and Sikkink, 1999: 9). Constructivist theorists posit the existence of a virtuous circle whereby global interconnectedness establishes a new sphere or new space for non-instrumental politics which potentially transforms the actors engaged in it. As Martha Finnemore states:

> [S]tates are embedded in dense networks of transnational and international social relations that shape their perceptions of the world and their role in that world. States are socialized to want certain things by the international society in which they and the people in them live.
>
> (Finnemore, 1996a: 2)

This new sphere, which includes both states and non-state actors engaged in communicative action, is often termed global civil society. For leading global civil society theorist, Mary Kaldor, global civil society is less a definition of which organisations or institutions are included or excluded but 'the global process through which individuals debate, influence and negotiate' with centres of power (Kaldor, 2003: 79). The presumptions of constructivist constructions of global civil society turn those of rationalism on their head. Rather than self-interested and self-directed subjects, states now become bearers of international values and socialised by international society. An instrumentalist power-seeking government, institution, association or individual engaging in norm-orientated debate in the global civic space will eventually emerge with a new and better identity and a broader, less exclusive view of their 'interests'.

The explanatory framework of constructivism

The area where most theoretical analysis has been undertaken to substantiate constructivist claims about the nature of global civil society has been in the impact of new international norms in changing policy in non-Western states. Network theory has been one of the most important developments in linking change in state policy to the activity of non-state actors in global civil society. Keck and Sikkink argue: 'network theory links the constructivist belief that international identities are constructed to empirical research tracing the paths through which this process occurs' (Keck and Sikkink, 1998: 214–15). Network theory builds on the work of theorists, like Paul Wapner, who have emphasised the new nature of non-state campaigning groups, seeing them not as traditional lobby or pressure groups, organised around changing state policies, but as 'political actors in their own right' (Wapner, 1995: 312). He argues:

> [T]he best way to think about transnational activist societal efforts is through the concept of "world civic politics." When activists work to

change conditions without directly pressurising states, their activities take place in the civil dimension of world collective life or what is sometimes called global civil society.

(Wapner, 1995: 312)

Rather than pressurising the state through traditional means, new social movements and activist networks rely on the power of information and ideas. They are engaged with transnational society beyond the boundaries of the state as well as lobbying states (see further Melucci, 1985; Habermas, 1981; Offe, 1987).

The 'boomerang' approach

Probably the most cited example of constructivist explanations is the boomerang theory where non-state actors are credited with achieving change through mobilising international pressure (see e.g. Kaldor, this collection: 106–7). Margaret Keck and Kathryn Sikkink in their path-breaking work *Activists beyond Borders* (1998) argue that the shift to international concerns with human rights practices can be explained by studying the emergence of transnational advocacy networks which instigated and sustained this international value shift (Keck and Sikkink, 1998: ix). According to these writers: 'The new networks have depended on the creation of a new kind of global public (or civil society), which grew as a cultural legacy of the 1960s' (Keck and Sikkink, 1998: 14).

In the view of Keck and Sikkink, transnational advocacy campaigns have shifted the balance between states and individuals in need of support through the 'redistribution of knowledge':

[I]n a world where the voices of states have predominated, networks open channels for bringing alternative visions and information into international debate. Political scientists have tended to ignore such nongovernmental actors because they are not "powerful" in the classic sense of the term. At the core of the network activity is the production, exchange, and strategic use of information ... When they succeed, advocacy networks are among the most important sources of new ideas, norms, and identities in the international system.

(Keck and Sikkink 1998: x)

Keck and Sikkink argue that the space for alternative voices to be heard, provided by transnational networks challenges the domination and control of states. The 'boomerang process' occurs through these non-state channels of information: 'Voices that are suppressed in their own societies may find that networks can project and amplify their concerns into an international arena, which in turn can echo back into their own countries' (Keck and Sikkink, 1998: x). This boomerang effect blurs the boundaries tying nation-states and their citizens as these citizens can now join trans-national networks which give them a voice and capacity to alter state policy. As Ann Florini asserts:

> For a large number of people whose governments are less than fully democratic (or less than fully responsive to the needs of those citizens unable to make large campaign donations), transnational civil society may provide the only meaningful way to participate in decision-making.
>
> (Florini, 2001: 39)

Keck and Sikkink emphasise the non-rationalist aspect of transnational advocacy networks, the key agents of global civil society:

> Advocacy captures what is unique about these transnational networks: they are organized to promote causes, principled ideas, and norms, and they often involve individuals advocating policy changes that cannot be easily linked to a rationalist understanding of their "interests".
>
> (Keck and Sikkink, 1998: 9)

They also stress the importance of the strategic use of information in mobilising international allies which can bring pressure on their states from outside. They term this 'leverage politics' and argue: 'By leveraging more powerful institutions, weak groups gain influence far beyond their ability to influence state practices directly' (Keck and Sikkink, 1998: 23). The most important international allies are, of course, other states. In dia-grammatic shorthand, they describe the boomerang pattern: 'State A blocks redress to organizations within it; they activate network, whose members pressure their own states and (if relevant) a third-party organ-ization, which in turn pressure State A' (Keck and Sikkink, 1998: 13). As Risse outlines, the constructivist thesis is focused on the development and implantation of international norms. The relationship of global civil society to state power is an ambivalent one though, and relies on some states to impose norms on other states: 'transnational civil society needs the cooperation of states and national governments. To create robust and specific human rights standards [and] ... also needs states for the effective improvement of human rights conditions on the ground' (Risse, 2000: 205).

Clearly, the constructivist analysis does not ignore the role played by states in international change. In fact, the role of the Western state is central to the success of the work of non-state actors. 'Bypassing the state' and mobilising in the international arena only works if other states or international institutions are willing to take up the call. The new space which is created and the new possibilities depend as much, if not more, on the activity of states than they do on non-state actors. The key to the success of the boomerang is the relative power of the states involved in the equation. Power is crucial to the success of principled-issue campaigns, as Keck and Sikkink state: 'The human rights issue became negotiable because governments or financial institutions connected human rights practices to military and economic aid, or to bilateral diplomatic relations' (Keck and Sikkink, 1998: 23). Ideas and values may be necessary but they are by no means sufficient:

> In the United States, human rights groups got leverage by providing policy-makers with information that convinced them to cut off military and economic aid. To make the issue negotiable, NGOs first had to raise its profile or salience, using information and symbolic politics. The more powerful members of the network had to link cooperation to something else of value: money, trade, or prestige.
>
> (Keck and Sikkink, 1998: 23)

The imbalance of power would appear to be essential to the 'boomerang' theoretical approach. American citizens concerned about the death penalty, for example, would probably have little success persuading principled-issue networks to get governments to cut off military and economic links. This would appear to be a one-way process which can only work where target states are 'sensitive to leverage' and dependent on economic or military assistance (Keck and Sikkink, 1998: 29; see also Burgerman, 1998). The 'boomerang' can only work against non-Western states. As Chetan Kumar notes the 'right circumstances' for the likely success of global civil activism in effecting the removal of 'nasty dictatorships' necessarily include 'a specific interest on the part of a major power capable of using force' (Kumar, 2000: 136). As Martin Shaw argues: 'the activists of globalist organisations, such as human rights, humanitarian and development agencies, make a reality of global civil society, by bringing the most exposed victims among the world's population into contact with more resourceful groups in the West' (Shaw, 1994: 655). However, rather than emphasise the power side of the equation, constructivists choose to emphasise the role of global civic actors. Some, such as Susan Burgerman, explicitly shift the focus away from states, she argues:

> The research program on transnational issue networks is designed to capture the increasingly complex webs of nonstate actors who participate in other people's politics without resorting to the power base of either their own government or that of the target state.
>
> (Burgerman 1998: 908)

The implication is that this intervention 'in other people's politics' is not based on power but morality, the power that some states wield over others merely demonstrates the influence of network activists in lobbying states other than their own. The implicit assumption appears to be that because some states are more moral than others small groups which are too weak to influence their own states can influence other (more morally aware) states and persuade these states to 'leverage' their own one. The boomerang perspective assumes first, that it is principled non-state actors that set the agenda and, second, that they can do this because the states with the most leverage are also the most open to moral appeals. Burgerman terms network activists 'moral entrepreneurs' to highlight the fact that their strength and influence stem from the content of their ideas rather than the political or economic weight of their supporters (Burgerman, 1998: 909).

Keck and Sikkink argue that 'perhaps the best example' of transnational advocacy politics was the ability of the human rights network to use the human rights provisions of the 1975 Helsinki Accords to pressure the Soviet Union and the governments of Eastern Europe to reform (Keck and Sikkink, 1998: 24). The weakness of East European dissident groups and state restrictions on political activity meant that they were forced to rely on external institutions to legitimise them and strengthen them domestically. Kaldor also notes, the turning point in the creation of the current concept of global civil society was the Helsinki Accords which established the Conference on Security and Cooperation in Europe (CSCE), later formalised as an organisation, the OSCE, under whose auspices the domestic policies of East European states came under international monitoring arrangements. The Helsinki Accords established a process whereby in exchange for recognition and economic aid from the West, East European states were pressurised on human rights questions. This process encouraged the formation of small dissident groups of intellectuals such as Charter 77 in Czechoslovakia, KOR (the defence of workers) in Poland and the Democratic Opposition in Hungary (Kaldor, 2003: 54–5).

However, this example could also be read to demonstrate the centrality of state action, and many would argue the instrumental rational interests of Western states in pressing for 'regime change'. The mechanisms set up under the CSCE were a direct reflection of Cold War rivalries. For example, the human rights monitoring forum, the Human Dimension Mechanism, was used overwhelmingly by Western states against Eastern Bloc states, with only one example where intra-bloc concerns were raised (see Chandler, 1999: 62–3). Human rights concerns would appear to have been used instrumentally by Western powers, in fact, this process continued in the OSCE's double-standards of intervention in East European states over minority rights, while ignoring concerns of recognition of minorities in Western states (see Heraclides, 1992; Barcz, 1992; Zaagman and Zaal, 1994). While there may have been a concurrence of interests between powerful groups of Western states and weak opposition groups in Eastern Europe, there seems little evidence that the Western states involved went through any change in their 'identities' and their interests seemed relatively fixed.

The limits of constructivism

The empirical focus of constructivism is on why non-Western states follow the principled-issue agenda, but there is a prior assumption that the 'principled-issue' agenda is established by non-state actors rather than states. The key empirical evidence which constructivists use to justify the argument of the influence of global civil society is the increase in numbers of NGOs and campaign groups in parallel with the shift in foreign policy and development of ethical norms in international relations. John Keane scathingly describes this methodological approach as the 'numerical theory of global politics', whereby a quantitative model, derived from counting up the number of non-state institutions and rates of growth, is alleged to demonstrate their influence (Keane, 2003: 95). We learn from the statistics that the linkages between international NGOs has increased 35 per cent from 1990 to 2000 and that while there were 13,000 international NGOs in existence in 1981, there were 23,000 in 1991 and 47,000 in 2001 (Anheier, Glasius and Kaldor, 2001a: 5; Anheier and Themudo, 2002: 194–5). One study of global civil society provides 90 pages of statistical tables charting the growth, density and participation in global civil society (Anheier, Glasius and Kaldor, 2001b: 231–322).

Since 1989, the collapse of traditional foreign policy concerns which shaped international institutions around the Cold War has led to a new language and new methods of doing international relations. Mary Kaldor notes that states and international institutions are 'more receptive to individuals and citizen groups outside the corridors of power' (Kaldor, 2003: 79). This is undoubtedly the case. However, the correlation between NGOs and non-state actors' international engagement with states and international institutions and specific policy-changes is hard to quantify (Burgerman, 1998: 913–14; Keck and Sikkink, 1998: 202; Forsythe, 2000: 168–78). First, it is difficult to establish criteria by which policy-success can be measured, for example at the level of statements, written policy or substantial outcome changes. Second, as with all cases of lobby groups or interest campaigns it is difficult to specify their impact in a particular foreign policy case, bearing in mind the wide range of interests and concerns government policy needs to take account of, let alone to generalise from a particular case (Hubert, 1998). The constructivist approach generally uses empirical case studies rather than the study of overall policy changes but even in a particular case study multiple factors are at play in the development of government policy, let alone the success or failure of its implementation. For example, commonly referred to interests in US politics such as the 'tobacco lobby', the 'Israeli lobby' or the 'China lobby' have all seen their influence wax and wane in different periods with no obvious connection to their own campaigning (Forsythe, 2000: 173).

In the early 1990s, few NGO analysts saw the increasing links between NGOs and states and international institutions as part of a shift towards a more ethical, normative agenda. While constructivist theory gives primary importance to non-state actors many empirical studies suggest that the impact of NGOs and non-state actors on the policy choices of international institutions and Western states is minimal. Until recently, NGO activists rarely saw themselves as occupying positions of power or influence and NGO-based analysts were often bemused by the idea that they could be dictating terms in the relationship and counselled against the exaggeration of their success and influence (Hulme and Edwards, 1995; 1997).

In fact, there was concern that NGOs were being incorporated and losing their distinctive moral authority under the late 1980s 'neo-liberal agenda'. Leading authorities saw the shift towards the voluntary sector as potentially problematic and one which could see NGOs lose their moral legitimacy, derived from their independence and connections with those most in need, and become tools of international financial institutions promoting the 'new policy agenda' (Edwards and Hulme, 1995; 1996; Clayton, 1996). For many commentators, neo-liberalism and structural adjustment policies were creating a welfare crisis that necessitated further Western engagement in welfare through non-state agencies in the late 1980s and early 1990s (de Waal, 1997: 49–64; Van Rooy and Robinson, 1998).

Much of the critical work on global civil society argued that institutions imposing the neo-liberal agenda promoted civil society as an apolitical form of welfare administration independent of and opposed to the state. This process undermined state authority and contributed to a 'crisis of governance' in many non-Western states (de Waal, 1997: 55; Duffield, 1996; 2001; Onishi, 2002; White, 1999: 319). The global civil society realm was one of regulation, 'of stability rather than struggle, of service provision rather than advocacy, of trust and responsibility rather than emancipation' (Kaldor, 2003: 22; see also Hearn, 2000). Critical analysts, such as John Clark, argued that official agency funding had resulted in the 'puppetisation' of NGOs (Clark, 1991). However, in the late-1990s, the shift away from a narrow emphasis on economic development and towards more comprehensive forms of external regulation highlighting poverty reduction and social capital, the 'post-Washington consensus', led some theorists to see that NGOs could potentially have a limiting effect on international financial institutions (Edwards, 2001: 2; Brown and Fox, 2001).

The empirical studies suggest that the vast majority of NGOs have to operate on the terms of states and international institutions and that where there is engagement in policy-making this is on highly unequal and selective terms (see for example, Scholte, 2001; Lister, 2000; Najam, 1996;

Hudock, 1999). Paul Cammack's work on the World Bank concludes that the bank has created a set of discursive devices and channels of consultation which aim to promote local input – 'country ownership' in the bank's terminology – from developing countries, but which are, in reality, highly coercive (Cammack, 2002). The World Bank's own internal publications make clear the hierarchy involved, stating that 'consultations' with civil society should not be confused with 'negotiations' or with 'a shared control over outcomes' (World Bank, 2000: 8). The fact that the World Bank is actively involved in establishing NGOs and community-based organisations (CBOs) in order to assist in pushing through its projects, that Western government are increasingly using NGOs as conduits for overseas aid and development funds, and that non-Western governments are setting up their own NGOs to access these funds, suggests that if any empirical correlation exists between NGOs and power hierarchies it is just as likely to be a positive one (Alkire *et al.*, 2001: 4, 29; Tusie and Tuozzo, 2001: 112; White, 1999: 313; *The Economist*, 2000).

Traditional political theorising would suggest that NGO lobby groups would have less influence on state policy-making than that of traditional interest groups such as mass membership organisations, like trade unions, or business interests (Forsythe, 2000: 169). As Mary Kaldor notes: 'The weakness of both "new" social movements and NGOs is that although they have widespread moral authority, they are largely composed of an educated minority and they lack the capacity for popular mobilization' (Kaldor, 2003: 100). Without a large or concentrated membership, which could threaten the electoral chances of political candidates or the financial resources to affect party financial contributions, it would seem that small groups of NGO lobbyists are in a weak position either to influence the policy of their own government or that of foreign governments.

However, constructivist case studies nearly always correlate the numbers and activities of non-state actors with the success of certain policies which have been lobbied for. It is easy to do case studies which retrospectively study a certain policy adoption, for example, the Ottawa land mines treaty, but even then few analysts focus on the role played by governments or actually study the impact and implementation of their select example (for a useful study of the landmines campaign see Scott, 2001; also Florini, 2001: 34). The focus is on the success stories and history is then read backwards to substantiate how global civil society works; for example, how the environmental lobbyists managed to influence the World Bank over certain projects in the developing world, rather than why they failed to influence US policy and prevent the US rejection of the Koyoto accords, or how the human rights movement managed to influence US foreign policy on Latin America, rather than how they failed to influence it regarding Turkey, Saudi Arabia and Indonesia. Figures and estimations for the success of global civil society vary widely, but few would argue that success goes beyond selective concerns and issues.

The advocates of a constructivist approach argue that the selective approach to the empirical information is implicitly valid because they are identifying an emerging context in which decision-making takes place. For critical theorists, anxious to accentuate the positive and 'encourage confidence' in popular initiatives, a one-sidedness in analysis is not problematic. Richard Falk, for example, argues: 'In this spirit, an emphasis is placed on positing the reality of "global civil society" and of accentuating transnational extensions of democratic and non-violent forms of governance' (Falk, 1995: 44). However, there is a danger that the normative theorising of critical theorists can undermine the pretence to objectivity and 'explanation' of constructivists. Ronen Palan, for example, argues that the claims of constructivists are inevitably exaggerated by their normative aspirations:

> [Constructivism] effectively conflates a methodology with a theory ... general theories of interactionist order cannot provide an explanation for the specificity of an *order* ... Theirs is a phlegmatic society – a harmonious society based on laws and norms ... [W]hy are there variations in social constructions? ... When ... constructivism ... is used as a theory of international relations, it exorci[ses] any form of social critique from the narrative. It tells us that while neorealists think that world politics are "mean and nasty", in fact it is not.
>
> (Palan, 2000: 592–3)

Attempting to force the empirical facts into the constructivist framework has meant that an increasingly flexible methodology is often employed. Starting from the assumption that new social movements and 'principled-issue' NGOs are shaping the moral and political agenda means that traditional methods of doing and theorising politics come under question (see, for example, Wapner, 1995: 318–20). The lack of clear material influence of NGOs is held to demonstrate that it is their ideas which are crucial and that the methods of influencing state policy must be much more mediated. As Paul Wapner notes: 'one must focus on the political action per se of these organizations and trace its world significance and interpret its meaning independently of the argument about relative causal weight' (Wapner, 1995: 320). Rob Walker similarly argues that: 'It is futile to gauge the importance of social movements without considering the possibility that it is precisely the criteria of significance by which they are to be judged that may be in contention' (Walker, 1994: 672). This increasingly 'post-modern' methodological approach has led to an exaggeration of the power and influence of global civic actors and a downplaying of power relations. In the words of Alejandro Colás:

> Such primarily descriptive accounts tend to conflate the self-proclaimed aspirations and objectives of international social movements with their

actual impact, thereby falling into the trap of an excessively subjectivist and therefore one-sided view of the ... international social world.

(Colás, 2002: 65)

Conclusion

In international relations theorising the case for the existence of global civil society is still an open one. The constructivist framework puts the strongest case for the influence and power of non-state actors, operating through the distribution of information and their skills as 'moral entrepreneurs', and thereby capable of influencing and changing the policies, interests and even the 'identities' of nation states. There is little doubt that the international agenda has been transformed since the end of the Cold War and that non-state actors have become increasingly involved in policy-making at the state and inter-state level. However, to date, constructivist approaches to global civil society seem to be driven more by a normative desire to support the 'principled-issues' advocated by non-state actors than by any clear analysis of the complex relationship between state and non-state actors (see further Chandler, 2004).

References

Alkire, S., Bebbington, A., Esmail, T., Ostrom, E., Polski, M., Ryan, A., Van Domelen, J., Wakeman, W. and Dongier, P. (2001) *Community Driven Development*, available from: http://www.worldbank.org/poverty/strategies/chapters/cdd/cdd0427.pdf

Anheier, H. and Themudo, N. (2002) 'Organisational Forms of Global Civil Society: Implications of Going Global', in M. Glasius, M. Kaldor and H. Anheier (eds) *Global Civil Society 2002*, Oxford: Oxford University Press.

Anheier, H., Glasius, M. and Kaldor, M. (eds) (2001a) *Global Civil Society 2001*, Oxford: Oxford University Press.

Anheier, H., Glasius, M. and Kaldor, M. (2001b) 'Introducing Global Civil Society', in H. Anheier, M. Glasius and M. Kaldor (eds) *Global Civil Society 2001*, Oxford: Oxford University Press.

Baldwin, D. A. (1993) *Neorealism and Neoliberalism: The Contemporary Debate*, New York: Columbia University Press.

Barcz, J. (1992) 'European Standards for the Protection of National Minorities with Special Regard to the OSCE – Present State and Conditions of Development', in A. Bloed and A. de Jonge (eds) *Legal Aspects of a New European Infrastructure*, Utrecht: Europa Instituut and Netherlands Helsinki Committee.

Brown, L. D. and Fox, J. (2001) 'Transnational Civil Society Coalitions and the World Bank: Lessons from Project and Policy Influence Campaigns', in M. Edwards and J. Gaventa (eds) *Global Citizen Action*, London: Earthscan.

Bull, H. (1995) *The Anarchical Society: A Study of Order in World Politics* (2nd ed.), Basingstoke: Palgrave-Macmillan.

Burgerman, S. D. (1998) 'Mobilizing Principles: The Role of Transnational

Activists in Promoting Human Rights Principles', *Human Rights Quarterly* 20: 905–23.

Cammack, P. (2002) 'The Mother of all Governments: The World Bank's Matrix for Global Government', in R. Wilkinson and S. Hughes (eds) *Global Governance: Critical Perspectives*, London: Routledge.

Carr, E. H. (2001) *The Twenty Years Crisis, 1919–1939: An Introduction to the Study of International Relations* (new ed.), Basingstoke: Palgrave-Macmillan.

Chandler, D. (1999) 'The OSCE and the Internationalisation of National Minority Rights', in K. Cordell (ed.) *Ethnicity and Democratisation in the New Europe*, London: Routledge.

Chandler, D. (2004) *Constructing Global Civil Society: Morality and Power in International Relations*, London: Palgrave-Macmillan.

Clark, J. (1991) *Democratizing Development: The Role of Volunteer Organizations*, Basingstoke: Earthscan.

Clayton, A. (ed.) (1996) *NGOs, Civil Society and the State: Building Democracy in Transitional Societies*, Oxford: INTRAC.

Cohen, J. L. and Arato, A. (1992) *Civil Society and Political Theory*, Cambridge, MA: The MIT Press.

Colás, A. (2002) *International Civil Society: Social Movements in World Politics*, Cambridge: Polity.

De Waal, A. (1997) *Famine Crimes: Politics and the Disaster Relief Industry in Africa*, London: Africa Rights/James Currey.

Diamond, L. (1994) 'Rethinking Civil Society: Toward Democratic Consolidation', *Journal of Democracy* 5, 3: 4–17.

Donnelly, J. (2000) *Realism and International Relations*, Cambridge: Cambridge University Press.

Duffield, M. (1996) 'The Symphony of the Damned: Racial Discourse, Complex Political Emergencies and Humanitarian Aid', *Disasters* 20, 3: 173–93.

Duffield, M. (2001) 'Governing the Borderlands: Decoding the Power of Aid', *Disasters* 25, 4: 308–20.

The Economist (2000) 'Sins of the Secular Missionaries', *The Economist*, 29 January: 25–8.

Edwards, M. (2001) 'Introduction', in M. Edwards and J. Gaventa (eds) *Global Citizen Action*, London: Earthscan.

Edwards, M. and Hulme, D. (1995) 'NGO Performance and Accountability in the Post-Cold War World', *Journal of International Development* 7, 6: 849–56.

Edwards, M. and Hulme, D. (1996) 'Too Close for Comfort? The Impact of Official Aid on Nongovernmental Organizations', *World Development* 24, 6: 961–73.

Falk, R. A. (1995) *On Humane Governance: Toward a New Global Politics*, Cambridge: Polity.

Finnemore, M. (1996a) *National Interests in International Society*, Ithaca: Cornell University Press.

Finnemore, M. (1996b) 'Norms, Culture, and World Politics: Insights from Sociology's Institutionalism', *International Organization* 50: 325–47.

Florini, A. M. (2001) 'Transnational Civil Society', in M. Edwards and J. Gaventa (eds) *Global Citizen Action*, London: Earthscan.

Forsythe, D. P. (2000) *Human Rights in International Relations*, Cambridge: Cambridge University Press.

Haas, P. M. (1999) 'Social Constructivism and the Evolution of Multilateral Environmental Governance', in A. Prakash and J. Hart (eds) *Globalization and Governance*, London: Routledge.

Habermas, J. (1981) 'New Social Movements', *Telos* 49, Fall: 33–7.

Hearn, J. (2000) 'Aiding Democracy? Donors and Civil Society in South Africa', *Third World Quarterly* 21, 5: 815–30.

Heraclides, A. (1992) 'The CSCE and Minorities: The Negotiations behind the Commitments, 1972–1992', *Helsinki Monitor* 3, 3: 5–18.

Hubert, D. (1998) 'Inferring Influence: Gauging the Impact of NGOs', in C. Ku and T. G. Weiss (eds) *Toward Understanding Global Governance: The International Law and International Relations Toolbox*, Providence, RI: ACUNS Reports and Papers, No. 2.

Hudock, A. C. (1999) *NGOs and Civil Society: Democracy by Proxy?*, Cambridge: Polity Press.

Hulme, D. and Edwards, M. (eds) (1995) *Non-Governmental Organisations – Performance and Accountability: Beyond the Magic Bullet*, London: Earthscan/Save the Children Fund.

Hulme, D. and Edwards, M. (eds) (1997) *NGOs, States and Donors: Too Close for Comfort?*, London: Macmillan/Save the Children Fund.

Kaldor, M. (2003) *Global Civil Society: An Answer to War*, Cambridge: Polity.

Katzenstein, P. (ed.) (1996) *The Culture of National Security: Norms and Identity in World Politics*, New York: Columbia University Press.

Keane, J. (1998) *Democracy and Civil Society: on the Predicaments of European Socialism, the Prospects of Democracy, and the Problem of Controlling Social and Political Power*, London: Verso.

Keane, J. (2003) *Global Civil Society?*, Cambridge: Cambridge University Press.

Keck, M. E. and Sikkink, K. (1998) *Activists beyond Borders: Advocacy Networks in International Politics*, Ithaca: Cornell University Press.

Keohane, R. O. (ed.) (1986) *Neorealism and Its Critics*, New York: Columbia University Press.

Korey, W. (1999) 'Human Rights NGOs: The Power of Persuasion', *Ethics and International Affairs* 13: 151–74.

Kratochwil, F. (1991) *Rules, Norms and Decisions*, Cambridge: Cambridge University Press.

Kratochwil, F. and Ruggie, J. (1986) 'International Organization: A State of the Art on an Art of the State', *International Organization* 40: 753–75.

Kumar, C. (2000) 'Transnational Networks and Campaigns for Democracy', in A. M. Florini (ed.) *The Third Force: The Rise of Transnational Civil Society*, Washington, D.C.: Carnegie Endowment for International Peace.

Linklater, A. (1998) *The Transformation of Political Community*, Cambridge: Polity.

Lister, S. (2000) 'Power in Partnership? An Analysis of an NGO's Relationships with its Partners', *Journal of International Development* 12: 227–39.

Melucci, A. (1985) 'The Symbolic Challenge of Contemporary Movements', *Social Research* 52, 4: 789–816.

Najam, A. (1996) 'NGO Accountability: A Conceptual Framework', *Development Policy Review* 14: 339–53.

Nye, J. S. (1988) 'Neorealism and Neoliberalism', *World Politics* 40, 2: 235–51.

Offe, C. (1987) 'Challenging the Boundaries of Institutional Politics: Social

Movements since the 1960s', in C. Maier (ed.) *Changing Boundaries of the Political*, Cambridge: Cambridge University Press.

Onishi, N. (2002) 'Nongovernmental Organizations Show Their Growing Power', *New York Times*, 22 March.

Onuf, N. (1989) *A World of our Making: Rules and Rule in Social Theory and International Relations*, Columbia: University of South Carolina Press.

Palan, R. (2000) 'A World of their Making: An Evaluation of the Constructivist Critique in International Relations', *Review of International Studies* 26: 575–98.

Reus-Smit, C. (2001) 'Constructivism', in S. Burchill *et al.* (eds) *Theories of International Relations* (2nd ed.), Basingstoke: Palgrave-Macmillan.

Risse, T. (2000) 'The Power of Norms Versus the Norms of Power: Transnational Civil Society and Human Rights', in A. M. Florini (ed.) *The Third Force: The Rise of Transnational Civil Society*, Washington, D.C.: Carnegie Endowment for International Peace.

Risse, T. and Ropp, S. C. (1999) 'International Human Rights Norms and Domestic Change: Conclusion', in T. Risse, S. C. Ropp and K. Sikkink (eds) *The Power of Human Rights: International Norms and Domestic Change*, Cambridge: Cambridge University Press.

Risse, T. and Sikkink, K. (1999) 'The Socialization of International Human Rights Norms into Domestic Practices: Introduction', in T. Risse, S. C. Ropp and K. Sikkink (eds) *The Power of Human Rights: International Norms and Domestic Change*, Cambridge: Cambridge University Press.

Risse, T., Ropp, S. C. and Sikkink, K. (eds) (1999) *The Power of Human Rights: International Norms and Domestic Change*, Cambridge: Cambridge University Press.

Ruggie, J. G. (1998) *Constructing the World Polity*, London: Routledge.

Scholte, J. A. (2001) 'The IMF and Civil Society: An Interim Progress Report', in M. Edwards and J. Gaventa (eds) *Global Citizen Action*, London: Earthscan.

Scott, M. J. O. (2001) 'Danger – Landmines! NGO-Government Collaboration in the Ottawa Process', in M. Edwards and J. Gaventa (eds) *Global Citizen Action*, London: Earthscan.

Seligman, A. (1992) *The Idea of Civil Society*, New York: Free Press.

Shaw, M. (1994) 'Civil Society and Global Politics: Beyond a Social Movements Approach', *Millennium: Journal of International Studies* 23, 3: 647–67.

Smith, H. (2000) 'Why is There no International Democratic Theory?', in H. Smith (ed.) *Democracy and International Relations: Critical Theories/Problematic Practices*, Basingstoke: Palgrave-Macmillan.

Smith, S. (2001) 'Reflectivist and Constructivist Approaches to International Theory', in J. Baylis and S. Smith (eds) *The Globalization of World Politics: An Introduction to International Relations* (2nd Edn), Oxford: Oxford University Press.

Tussie, D. and Tuozzo, M. F. (2001) 'Opportunities and Constraints for Civil Society Participation in Multilateral Lending Operations: Lessons from Latin America', in M. Edwards and J. Gaventa (eds) *Global Citizen Action*, London: Earthscan.

van Rooy, A. and Robinson, M. (1998) 'Out of the Ivory Tower: Civil Society and the Aid System', in A. van Rooy (ed.) *Civil Society and the Aid Industry*, London: Earthscan.

Walker, R. B. J. (1994) 'Social Movements/World Politics', *Millennium: Journal of International Studies* 23, 3: 669–700.

Wapner, P. (1995) 'Politics Beyond the State: Environmental Activism and World Civic Politics', *World Politics* 47: 311–40.

Wendt, A. (1992) 'Anarchy is what States Make of it: The Social Construction of Power Politics', *International Organization* 46, 2: 391–425.

Wendt, A. (1999) *Social Theory of International Politics*, Cambridge: Cambridge University Press.

White, S. C. (1999) 'NGOs, Civil Society, and the State in Bangladesh: The Politics of Representing the Poor', *Development and Change* 30: 307–26.

World Bank (2000) *Consultations with Civil Society Organizations: General Guidelines for World Bank Staff*, Washington, D.C.: World Bank.

Zaagman, R. and Zaal, H. (1994) 'The CSCE High Commissioner on National Minorities: Prehistory and Negotiations', in A. Bloed (ed.) *The Challenges of Change: The Helsinki Summit of the CSCE and its Aftermath*, London: Martinus Nijhoff.

10 Global civil society and global governmentality

Resistance, reform or resignation?[1]

Ronnie D. Lipschutz

How should we regard 'global civil society' and the practices attributed to its agents? Is it really 'global', as is often argued (Anheier *et al.*, 2001), or merely 'international', as some might have it (Colás, 2002)? Are its agents independent or prisoners of states, elements of global governance or hand-maidens of markets? And what are the consequences of their activities? Do they have an effect on the world's serious problems? Does global civil society help promote a 'better' world or merely 'more of the same'? Over the past decade, most who have written about global civil society have taken one or another of these positions, and the result has been something of an epistemological free-for-all. Even the classical theorists of civil society – Locke, Ferguson, Marx, Tocqueville, and Hegel – could not agree on what it was, and they had states with which to work. It is not surprising, then, that there should be so much disagreement when the concept of civil society is globalized.

As I have asked elsewhere (Lipschutz, 1999), if there is a global civil society then where is the global state to which it corresponds? Colás (2002) argues that this civil society is international and corresponds to the state system and its national states, while Martin Shaw (2000) posits the emergence of a 'global state' encompassing the industrial heartland of the West, which may offer the political framework within which global civil society has been able to develop. But these analyses, while useful, are incomplete. In this chapter, I draw on the work of Michel Foucault (1991) and situate global civil society (GCS) in 'global governmentality'. Governmentality is to be understood here as a system of management, regulation, and normalization. I argue that much of GCS is one element in the globalization of governmentality. It is deeply imbricated with the market and is political only in a rather impoverished sense.

I begin the chapter with a discussion of Foucault's concept of 'governmentality' and the ways in which it has become globalized under a neo-liberal regime of discipline and control. I then turn to GCS and separately problematize its relationship to both state and market under neo-liberal globalization. In the third part of the chapter, I describe an empirical case of social activism articulated by GCS through market mechanisms and offer a critique of these activities. I conclude with an argument that GCS must seek to incorporate *politics* into its activism in order to present genuine challenges to global governmentality and its political economy.

Governmentality

The global unevenness of social regulation – indeed, its absence in many instances – has led to a transnational version of a phenomenon observed during the nineteenth and early twentieth centuries in most industrial countries: the emergence of populist and social efforts to impose political constraints over the 'self-regulating' markets that have arisen out of the globalization of neo-liberalism (Polanyi, 2001; Lipschutz, 2003). These projects take a number of forms, the most visible of which are campaigns to boycott the products of certain highly-visible companies, such as Nike, and to coerce or cajole manufacturers to adopt 'codes of conduct'. Capital has responded with the 'corporate social responsibility' movement, the best known example being the Global Compact sponsored by the UN Secretary General. All of these campaigns and projects seek to smooth out the rougher edges of globalized capitalism, to manage its externalities, as it were (Lipschutz, 2003; 2004c). While 'global governance' is the term commonly applied to such regulatory projects (Lipschutz, 1999), I see them in a rather different way: as elements of what Michel Foucault called 'governmentality'.

Governmentality is about management, about ensuring and maintaining the 'right disposition of things' of that which is being governed or ruled. As Foucault put it, governmentality is:

> the ensemble formed by institutions, procedures, analyses and reflections, the calculations and tactics that allow the exercise of this very specific albeit complex form of power, which has as its target populations, as its principal form of knowledge, political economy, and as its essential technical means apparatuses of security.
>
> (Foucault, 1991: 102)

This 'right disposition' has as its purpose not the action of government itself, but the welfare of the population, the improvement of its condition, the increase of its wealth, longevity, health, etc. (ibid. 1991: 100; see also Dean, 1999). Governmentality is effected through 'bio-politics'. According to Mitchell Dean (1999: 99), this 'is concerned with matters of life and death, with birth and propagation, with health and illness, both physical and mental, and with the processes that sustain or retard the optimization of the life of a population'. He writes that:

Bio-politics must then also concern the social, cultural, environmental, economic and geographic conditions under which humans live, procreate, become ill, maintain health or become healthy, and die. From this perspective bio-politics is concerned with the family, with housing, living and working conditions, with what we call 'lifestyle', with public health issues, patterns of migration, levels of economic growth and the standards of living. It is concerned with the bio-sphere in which humans dwell.

(Dean, 1999: 99)

Populations, as conceived here, are not composed of sovereign or autonomous individuals, as pictured by liberalism. Rather, they are analysed and treated as homogenous collections of people to be moulded (or normalized) into particular categories and forms, who regard themselves as belonging to these categories and forms, and who behave in ways ascribed to and by those categories and forms.

Who or what, then, are the actors and agents in a system of governmentality? The biopolitical management of human populations and their environments is the task of both the agencies of 'government' and the populations themselves. The former includes the myriad of governmental and international agencies, public and private associations, and even non-governmental organizations and corporations that populate the globe, each of which has its own instrumental function as well as normative goals. This is not to suggest that all of these actors behave in coherence with one another in either their activities or objectives; they all are interested, however, in 'managing Planet Earth' (Scientific American, 1990).

Populations are both the products of the system of governmentality and, through their normalized actions, (re)producers of that system. Individuals comport themselves according to the standards of 'normality' of their specific population. The right disposition of things is maintained through the standardization of populations within certain defined parameters, the self-disciplining of their own behaviour through conformity to these parameters, and the disciplining function of surveillance and law which seeks to prevent any straying outside of those parameters. Taken together, these constrain individuals' practices to a 'zone of normality'. Power is then embedded within the hegemonic discourses that naturalize normality and reproduce themselves through associated practices. Resistance is possible, of course, but that risks losing the benefits of governmentality and biopolitics and, indeed, being marginalized completely. It is in this sense, as Foucault puts it (1980: 109–33), that we are the products of power circulating through society in capillary fashion.

Foucault never wrote about 'global' governmentality – indeed, it is not even clear that he would have accepted such a notion. Within states there are political, social, and economic mechanisms that are part and parcel of management; among states, only the economic mechanisms are well-developed. One consequence is that global governmentality relies heavily on markets for its effects; as Dean argues:

> Neo-liberalism ceases to be a government of society in that it no longer conceives its task in terms of a division between state and society or of a public sector opposed to a private one.... The market has ceased to be a kind of fenced-off nature reserve kept at arm's length from the sphere of public service; instead, the contrivance of markets becomes the technical means for the reformation of all types of provision.... The point of doing this is ... to reform institutional and individual conduct so that both come to embody the values and orientations of the market, expressed in notions of the enterprise and the consumer.
>
> (Dean, 1999: 172)

Others have described this process as the instantiation of a global 'economic constitutionalism' associated with neo-liberal globalization (Gill, 1995; 2002; Jayasuriya, 2001). As Jayasuriya puts it, 'Economic constitutionalism refers to the attempt to treat the market as a constitutional order with its own rules, procedures and institutions that operate to protect the market order from political interference' (2001: 452).

The world's riot of global civil society organizations (CSOs) and social movements, international organizations and associations, transnational corporations and business associations, and even democratic market governments, all constitute agents of a global biopolitics seeking to further human progress and welfare. Global governmentality is, however, more than the sum of national governmentalities, it is more than the state system and its associated regimes, and more than the standard definitions of global governance. It is the product of a complex network of institutions, organizations, and actions associated with contemporary globalization. Global governmentality is an empirical phenomenon whose specific features are determined by contingency and context, and which may fit one or more of the conventional theoretical framings of international relations that, themselves, are the products of power as deployed in particular spaces at particular times. The global governmentality of the Cold War addressed primarily the management of differences between East and West; the global governmentality of today addresses primarily the attempt to transform populations into consumers and practitioners of neo-liberal discourses and practices; the global governmentality of tomorrow is likely to represent a fusion of military and police-state practices with high rates of accumulation and consumption (Lipschutz, 2002a).

Foucault's concepts of governmentality and biopolitics help to highlight several other critical points. First, they suggest that those CSOs of greatest interest to IR theorists (Lipschutz and Mayer, 1996; Wapner, 1996; Smith and Johnston, 2002) are internalized within a system of governmentality that constitutes and subjectifies them. Moreover, the institutions and arrangements of rules, regulations, and practices characteristic of contemporary capitalist states, operating under and through global neo-liberalism, do not and cannot address more than a fraction of the 'welfare of populations'. Within states, many matters are dealt with through and by civil society, whose groups and organizations are often drawn into exist-ence in order to address such lacunae. That is to say, the projects of civil society are directed ultimately to the reorganization, stabilization, and normalization of conditions that are seen as threats or disturbances to the welfare of those human populations and the 'order of things'. The precise methods of accomplishing these ends, as well as the specific parameters of the ends themselves, may be the focus of intense contestation, but the overall objective is the same: improvement in the social welfare of popula-tions and management of the neo-liberal system. No one is in favour of impoverishment, hunger, violence, and so on, while everyone wants popu-lations to be 'better off' (civil society is never interested only in the welfare of specific populations). Thus, although many civil society organ-izations are often thought to be opposed to states and corporations, their activities are better understood as integral to governmentality.

Politics, markets and governmentality

What, then, is the nature of politics under a regime of neo-liberal govern-mentality and conditions of economic constitutionalism? Although Ulrich Beck (2000) does not use the term governmentality in his work, his concept of 'sub-politics' captures much the same point. Today, most polit-ical matters are treated as technical and managerial problems, to be addressed by non-elected experts such as economists, biologists, public health authorities, and planners through non-political means, rather than by those who are either directly affected or elected as political representa-tives. The organization and structure of decision-making is established through economic constitutionalism. I argue that politics is relegated largely to distribution and, to a growing degree, reliant on 'decisions' taken through the market.

Here, I make a distinction between 'constitutive' and 'distributive' poli-tics (Lipschutz, 1989: 17–20). Constitutive politics has to do with the 'rules of the game'. Constitutive politics are about 'constitutions', that is, the processes of decision-making as well as the construction of those dis-courses that constitute and structure social and political life. Constitutive politics involve deciding and acting on the shared goals of a polity, of exer-cising the power to 'do' (Arendt, 1958). Distributive politics is about how points are scored, about the 'what, when, and where' of governing (Laswell, 1936). Most, if not all, of what today passes for 'politics' in liberal systems has to do with the distributive aspects of social life rather than with its constitution. After all, in Lasswell's definition, and as it is generally understood and practised, the end of distributive politics within a liberal polity is the determination of how much is to be received by each party to a social contract and whether newcomers will be granted or denied a share of that pie. Politics, in this respect, becomes the struggle for entitlements and the protection of what one already has. The fairness of the distribution comes to be judged, rather simply, on the basis of income, efficiency, or utility rather than other, deontological considerations such as justice, recognition, and capacity (Sen, 1999). Under these circumstances, the constitutive basis for such decisions remains unexamined, and the 'good life' comes to be defined by consumption and the market. The very discourse associated with 'living the good life' – the traditional concern of politics and political theory and, it could even be said, republican democracy – has been transformed into 'living life with goods'.

The particular organization of market societies, with public and private constituted as distinct realms of activity, is hardly a 'natural' one (Rosenberg, 1994; Wood, 2002). In further marking the line between constitutive and distributive politics, the liberal state comes to depend on civil society to maintain and reproduce that boundary. To wit, the decentralized nature of such societies mandates limits to the number of activities construed as 'political' (Mouffe, 2000), and civil society comes to be the realm within which collective activities can take place without impinging on or threatening institutionalized politics (i.e. voting, lobbying, etc.). Civil society also helps to instantiate the line between the political and the economic, the public and the private (Colás, 2002; Rosenberg, 1994). Because the distributive shortcomings and disruptive impacts of capitalist markets and social reorganization always threaten to unravel the social contract and spill over into the political (Polanyi, 2001), it is incumbent upon civil society and the state to continually regulate the market so that it appears to be 'natural'. This division is a function of the discursive power of liberalism, which seeks to prevent the state from intruding on all areas of daily life, especially those involving private property rights. Nonetheless, the state returns through the back door, getting involved in all aspects of private life, from what constitutes a 'legally-recognized' family to regulation of what goes on in the bedroom.

Under neo-liberal governmentality, the state has become more intent on providing attractive and stable conditions for capital than in addressing externalities or market failures. Given such conditions, it seems to fall to civil society to become more politicized and, through its own regulatory activities, to reinforce the separation between the public (politics) and the private (markets). But permitted forms of action available to civil society for this purpose are relatively limited: constitutive politics has been largely removed from the agenda through mobilization bias and discursive power, while protests and violence are rejected by both state and capital as destabilizing and undermining of confidence in the system. Under neo-liberal conditions, the only accepted means of *regulating* markets are based on the *methods* of the market and, as we shall see below, this is the path being taken by many CSOs. Consequently, what appear to be the sovereign agents of civil society become, instead, an effect of neo-liberal governmentality, of an ontology of reason and logic, cause and consequences, separable institutions and 'issue areas'. In the international realm, where there is no state as such, the market as a mechanism of decision-making and distribution is dominant. It is not that there are no international politics but, rather, that such politically-based constitutional arrangements as do exist – within the UN system, for example – have been largely superseded by the economic constitutionalism described above.

Activism and governmentality

Let us examine an empirical case and its implications more closely. Paradoxically, perhaps, the vast majority of the campaigns and projects alluded to earlier have focused not on politics, but on markets. By this, I mean that most of them attempt, through an elucidation of 'real' interests, to leverage both consumer and corporate behaviours as a means of improving labour conditions in factories, reducing environmental externalities from industry, and boycotting or managing international trade in various kinds of goods, such as clothing and coffee (Lipschutz, 2002b; 2003). Many of these campaigns have been successful in terms of their instrumental goals, but they also suffer from serious *political* limitations. These limitations become very evident in apparel industry campaigns. For example, there are at least a dozen civic action and social activism campaigns aimed at the Nike Corporation (Connor, 2001; Lipschutz, 2002b; 2003; forthcoming). All focus on distributive strategies designed to improve health and safety conditions, and to provide minimum wages to workers in Nike's 600-odd subcontractors' plants scattered around the world. These campaigns have generated considerable public attention (although it is not clear that they have affected the company's financial performance; see Lipschutz, 2003), and Nike has responded energetically, concerned about its market share, its competitiveness, and its image.

The company has adopted codes of conduct, contracted out audits of its subcontractors' factories, and permitted independent monitors either to accompany auditors or conduct their own inspections. It has joined the Fair Labour Association and co-established the Workers' and Communities' Association, as well as taken a number of other steps to improve both conditions of production and its own reputation. And, while there apparently remain significant problems in many, if not all, of its subcontractors' operations, there has been a not inconsiderable amount of ratcheting upwards of conditions within the Nike subsystem of global apparel production (Lipschutz, 2002b; 2003). But what have been the *constitutive* effects of these campaigns? How have these campaigns altered either corporation or capitalism in structural terms? Nike offers improved conditions and higher wages to the workers in its subcontractors' factories, but both workers and consumers remain fully-integrated into the regime of consumption that constitutes contemporary globalization and objectifies both workers and consumers. Workers still have no power to make political decisions and there are no changes either in the position of waged labour or in the structures of capitalism.

Campaigns against other apparel companies have had similar impacts. In the host societies as a whole there has been little in the way of political reform, of stronger state regulation, or greater exercise of labour's right to unionize (Lipschutz, 2002; 2004c). The structures might have received a paint job, so to speak, but underneath the ironwork is the same. In other words, amidst all of these efforts, almost no attention has been paid to the constitutive political conditions that led to the demand for social regulation in the first place, namely that Northern capital makes substantial profits on the backs of relatively powerless, badly-paid, mostly female workers. It is the very fact that labour is badly-paid and powerless that makes the host countries so attractive in the first place (and has even led to the reappearance of sweatshops in Los Angeles and New York; see Bonacich and Appelbaum, 2000).

What is absent from these regulatory campaigns and projects is any sense of the political inherent in the very notion of social policy or a recognition of the ways in which *power constitutes not only that which activists seek to change but the activists themselves*. Through constitutive politics, decisions must be made by subjects – those objectified by distributive politics – about what is necessary and what must be done to achieve the good and just life. Instead, what we find is liberalism limiting democracy. Returning to the case of Nike, for example, there is a widely-held expectation that, if the company manages to improve conditions in its subcontractors' plants, other corporations, subcontractors, and factory managers will go along in order to remain competitive. Manufacturers will impose standards on their own businesses in order to maintain the good reputation of their brand, to sustain and even increase profit margins, and because it is the 'right thing to do' (Fung *et al.*, 2001). There is only limited evidence, however, to indicate that such outcomes do follow. Moreover, if political conditions in a particular country are generally unfavourable to unions, collective bargaining and other workers' rights – and this is the case even where countries have ratified relevant ILO conventions – improvements in individual plants are not likely to have much impact on labour across the country as a whole (Lipschutz, 2003, forthcoming: Chapter 4).

This observation suggests strongly that social regulation, and the general relationship between politics and economics, should not be left to determination by markets. Regulation of any sort inevitably means that both business and polity will have to pay some costs, and yield back certain property rights to the public and political realm. But the arguments and justifications for redistribution – and to whom and why – must come about through politics and the political, and this must happen not within or through the market but in the *public* sphere, within the communities where such laws are made, implemented, and monitored, where the relations of power embedded in discursive structures can be revealed, and where strategies for resistance and change can emerge (Chaloupka, 2003). The globalization of social regulations is not irrelevant to this point, to be sure. Such rules set normative standards to which states ought to adhere and, having ratified them, citizens can demand that governments observe them (Keck and Sikkink, 1998). But it is only through political action *within* political communities that people and societies will come to recognize and acknowledge the need for social regulation and accept them as necessary.

Resistance and governmentality

How might such action take place? The types of activities described above pursue two goals, one intentional and the other not. The first is to affect corporate behaviour through some kind of influence on consumer preference, corporate profit, and organizational ethics. The evidence seems to suggest that growing numbers of shoppers do pay some attention to the sources and production methods of the things they buy, although it is also clear that the conscientious constitute only a small fraction of all consumers (most of whom have neither the interest nor the resources to be too choosy). Whether such campaigns have any consequent impact on the bottom line of individual companies is much less clear, but many, concerned about maintaining the purity of their brand names, have adopted codes of conduct and social responsibility.

The second, unintended consequence is rather more problematic. Namely, is it within the ambit of corporations to establish their own, individualized ethical codes? From a Hegelian perspective, society's ethics should emerge from civil society and not directly via the sphere of the market. Corporations should act according to the standards set by civil society and instantiated within the legal system of the state. In creating their own codes of social responsibility, however, corporations are, in effect, *privatizing* human rights and other social norms and principles (such as environmental protection or labour's autonomy). The result is that these principles hold, at most, only within the commodity chains associated with the specific corporation, and have no external authority or standing. This is one reason why there is so little effect outside the factory walls (Lipschutz, 2002; forthcoming): yet another portion of the public realm has been privatized and enclosed. All of the 'corporate social responsibility' in the world will not alter this fundamental fact.

The critical point here is that market-based solutions to market-generated problems will not eliminate the problems that such campaigns have set out to address. They only shift costs elsewhere, usually onto those who have less power and wealth and, in this instance, are outside of the factory walls. However, the answer is not necessarily to get rid of markets, to resist and overthrow capitalism, as such. Nor is it to reform certain governmental institutions such as the World Trade Organization or the World Bank. Rather, real and effective resistance must emerge through structural changes generated through reasserting the control of *politics* over markets. But what does this mean, exactly?

In *The Great Transformation*, Karl Polanyi argued that the two World Wars were a direct result of this 'disembedding' of economics from social life, and that attempts to make these two spheres completely distinct could only result in what he called a 'stark utopia' which 'would have physically destroyed man and transformed his surroundings into a wilderness' (Polanyi, 2001: 3). In effect, under a self-regulating system, or even the 'watchman' state of classical liberalism, short-term self interest becomes so dominant that destruction is the norm, rather than the exception (Schumpeter, 1942). The compulsion to short-term thinking is not, however, a tragic flaw in some kind of essentialist human nature. Rather, it is inherent in the very structure of capitalism.

Marxists point out that capitalism is a social system unlike any other in human history, in that it requires the separation of politics and economics in order to function (Wood, 2002). States, as the grantors and guarantors of private property rights, give to the owners of property what is, in effect, a private grant of political authority within a limited domain. In theory, the owner of such property is empowered to do whatever he or she wishes with it, including destroying it to make a profit, even if such destruction has impacts on things vital to life and wellbeing. And the state is enjoined strongly from intervening in those privatized domains, having given up its prerogative to impose rules there. Of course, states find it necessary or desirable to constrain individuals in what they can do, but this is frequently decried as 'political intervention in markets'. Hence, benefits to private parties are counterpoised to costs imposed on others and, because the former are concentrated and the latter usually diffuse, private interests frequently trump any notion of a public good.

The potential of resistance, then, is not to be found in attempts to recapture some pale version of public ethics articulated through and within markets. Rather, as argued above, it is to be found in politics, not as distribution but about constitution: deciding how, and to what ends, power is to be used. Recall that Foucault pointed out that power is productive and not only a mode of oppression or a tool of consensus. As he famously wrote:

> If power were never anything but repressive, if it never did anything but say no, do you really think one would be brought to obey it? What makes power hold good, what makes it accepted, is simply the fact that it doesn't only weigh on us as a force that says no, but that it traverses and produces things, it induces pleasure, forms knowledge, pro-

duces discourse. It needs to be considered as a productive network that runs through the whole social body, much more than as a negative instance whose function is repression.

(1980: 119)

Although Foucault was nowhere very explicit about how power, in his understanding, could be directed against the 'productive network' of governmentality – indeed, some read him as arguing that 'resistance is futile' and castigate him for it (Epstein, 1995) – we might recognize that power can 'traverse and produce things' in more than the way it is captured through the biopolitical webs of neo-liberal governmentality. This does not involve rearranging parts of the web so as to create different arrangements of governmentality (reform), or destroying it so as to create a chaos out of which a new system might arise (revolution). Rather, it is about generating, through politics, new or different webs of power.

In *Justice and the Politics of Difference*, Iris Marion Young argues that:

One important purpose of critical normative theory [and speculation] is to offer an alternative vision of social relations which, in the words of Marcuse, "conceptualizes the stuff of which the experienced world consists ... with a view to its possibilities, in the light of their actual limitation, suppression, and denial". Such a positive normative vision can inspire hope and imagination that motivate action for social change. It also provides some of the reflective distance necessary for the criticism of existing social circumstances.

(Young, 1990: 227, citing Marcuse, 1964: 7)

Young focuses here on domestic politics, striving for a realistic vision of what might be possible from what already exists. She writes that: 'A model of a transformed society must begin from the material structures that are given to us at this time in history' (Young, 1990: 234). We cannot create new societies or even practices out of ideas alone; in other words, we must work with what we have. And when we begin to look around, we discover that there is, in fact, much to work with.

In *Global Civil Society and Global Environmental Governance* (Lipschutz and Mayer, 1996), I wrote in some detail about watershed organizations. While these organizations look very much like standard CSOs, seeking to solve environmental problems through standardized techniques and practices, they are potentially quite subversive. Almost unheard of in 1980, by 2000 they had become ubiquitous. Focused on a single stream or river, they nonetheless share an epistemic vision of the place of watersheds in both the local and global environment. Individual groups hold to the view that their creek, their stream, their river are central to where they live and merit more attention and care than is being given to them, wherever in the world that watershed might be. At the same time, each group recognizes that its creek, stream, or river is different, in terms of political culture, economy, geography, and meaning.

Governments have not been insensitive to local concerns about watersheds, especially insofar as they are required by law to clean them up and keep them clean. Nor have responsible administrative agencies been blind to the role local groups can play in furthering governmental goals. Consequently, in many places 'official' state-sanctioned watershed projects have been launched while, in others, independent groups have been given a role to play as 'stakeholders' in official programs (Lipschutz, 1996). But those state agencies tasked with water-related responsibilities are not entirely comfortable with these independent groups, which often tend to be rather more radical, less manageable, more impulsive, and less systematic than bureaucrats and technocrats would like. They ignore or even trample on private property rights. They have no respect for the legal niceties and procedures of the regulatory process. They do not pay adequate attention to scientific principles and evidence. They are *too political*.

'Too political' is code for a space of appearance in which people can engage in politics and action (Arendt, 1958). In such spaces, people experience what is possible and how action is a form of productive power. Politics and action in the space of appearance – whether focused on the watershed, the urban neighbourhood, toxic wastes, human rights and dignity, global warming, or social disempowerment – is not only about the pursuit of shared interests, as collective action theorists generally describe it, or the mobilization of resources, as social movement theorists would have it. It is also about the power to produce. *People choose. People act.* This is an experience that institutionalized political processes – voting, lobbying, e-mailing representatives – can never offer. It is an experience that illuminates the possibilities of politics in all of its raw, elemental form. It is conflictual, disruptive, aggravating, but in terms of action, productive. It is not a 'solution' to a problem, rather, it is a means of engaging with those things that ought not to be, but are, and attempting to achieve what is not, but ought to be.

Being 'too political' ruptures the web of governmentality. These are small ruptures and not very conspicuous. No one in San José or São Paulo, in Delhi or Davos, cares very much about political actors causing such small ruptures. They have their own problems to worry about. No one fears that political praxis poses a challenge to the stability of the Republic or Kingdom or Union. At most, they might be a nuisance for municipal and civic sensibilities (and who, in the capitals of the world's great nation-states, cares about that?). They are hardly a threat to Western or even world civilization. Or perhaps they are. And therein lies the potential of resistance.

Global civil society and global governmentality

The 'problem' of accounting for GCS in its many variants and alternatives, as well as explaining its relationship to global governance, arises for several reasons. First, many scholars are more interested in fostering the efficiency and transparency of non-governmental participation and process (Tarrow, 1998). Second, they seek to elucidate and develop mechanisms through which the desires, needs and interests of those blocked by powerful actors can be fulfilled (Keck and Sikkink, 1998). They are less interested in the normative implications and consequences of how power is exercised and the results of that exercise (which I take to be the goal of political theory). Both are forms of theorizing aptly suited to a liberal worldview, which eschews foundational questions of politics and power and deals with distribution rather than constitution. Such a focus accepts the deployment of power as a given and begs for dispensations from the powerful.

From this view, global civil society is less a 'problem' for power than a product of power. It is deeply enmeshed with practices of governmentality and biopolitics. It is a means whereby those matters that cannot or will not be addressed by the agents of the state or inter-state institutions will, nonetheless, be dealt with by someone. My view of GCS does not undermine concepts of power, or the importance of GCS to global welfare, so much as it forces us to recognize how particular forms of society and governmentality are constituted and reconstituted, sometimes through the very agency that, at first glance, appears to be a means of opposition and resistance, if not liberation. It also motivates us to ask whether it is possible to (re)create forms of political sovereignty that can function, perhaps, in a counter-hegemonic way to challenge the discourses of neo-liberalism.

I would argue, by contrast, that a sole concern with distributive issues not only leaves the offending discourses intact but also leads to collaboration with those who exercise decision-making power and agenda setting power. What is more important in my view is finding ways of challenging and changing the games of the dominant discourses, and that is something that will never happen if all one seeks to do is to change the rules for scoring in the game. Mixing metaphors, it is not sufficient to focus on the size of the slices of pie alone. It is also critical to act to change the filling, the crust and, indeed, to question whether we really need that pudding. And that is something that global civil society, as much of it is constituted today, cannot and will not do.

Note

1 Other versions of this chapter have appeared as Lipschutz 2004a and 2004b. David Newstone, Angela McCracken, James Rowe and Michael Blackburn provided invaluable assistance in fieldwork and research for this chapter. Funding for the project has been provided by the Institute for Labor and Employment of the University of California, the UC Institute on Global Conflict and Coopera-

tion, the Non-profit Sector Research Fund of the Aspen Institute, the Pacific Basin Research Fund of Sokka University – America, and the Social Sciences Division of the University of California, Santa Cruz. This chapter is based on my forthcoming book, tentatively entitled *Regulation for the Rest of Us? Globalization, Governmentality and Global Politics*.

References

Anheier, H., Glasius, M. and Kaldor, M. (eds) (2001) *Global Civil Society 2001*, Oxford: Oxford University Press.

Arendt, H. (1958) *The Human Condition*, 2nd edn, Chicago: University of Chicago Press.

Beck, U. (2000) *What is Globalization?*, trans. P. Camiller, Cambridge: Polity Press.

Bonacich, E. and Appelbaum, R. (2000) *Behind the Label – Inequality in the Los Angeles Apparel Industry*, Berkeley: University of California Press.

Broad, R. (ed.) (2002) *Global Backlash – Citizen Initiatives for a Just World Economy*, Lanham, Md.: Rowman and Littlefield.

Chaloupka, W. (2003) 'There Must Be Some Way Out of Here: Strategy, Ethics, and Environmental Politics', in W. Magnusson and K. Shaw (eds) *A Political Space – Reading the Global Through Clayoquot Sound*, Minneapolis: University of Minnesota Press: 69–90.

Colás, A. (2002) *International Civil Society*, Cambridge: Polity.

Connor, T. (2001) *Still Waiting for Nike to Do It*, San Francisco: Global Exchange, May, at: http://www.globalexchange.org/economy/corporations/nike/NikeReport. pdf (accessed 30 May 2001).

Dean, M. (1999) *Governmentality – Power and Rule in Modern Society*, London: Sage.

Epstein, B. (1995) 'Why Post-Structuralism is a Dead End for Progressive Thought', *Socialist Review* 25, 2.

Foucault, M. (1991) 'Governmentality', in G. Burchell, C. Gordon and P. Miller (eds) *The Foucault Effect: Studies in Governmentality*, Chicago: University of Chicago Press, 87–104.

Foucault, M. (1980) *Power/Knowledge*, trans. C. Gordon, New York: Pantheon.

Fung, A., O'Rourke, D. and Sabel, C. (2001) 'Realizing Labor Standards – How Transparency, Competition, and Sanctions Could Improve Working Conditions Worldwide', *Boston Review* 26, 1, at: http://bostonreview.mit.edu/BR26.1/ fung.html (accessed 15 July 2002).

Gill, S. (1995) 'The Global Panopticon? The Neoliberal State, Economic Life, and Democratic Surveillance', *Alternatives* 2, 1: 1–50.

Gill, S. (2002) 'Constitutionalizing Inequality and the Clash of Globalizations', *International Studies Review* 4, 2: 47–66.

Jayasuriya, K. (2001) 'Globalization, Sovereignty, and the Rule of Law: From Political to Economic Constitutionalism?', *Constellations* 8, 4: 442–60.

Keck, M. and Sikkink, K. (1998) *Activists Beyond Borders – Advocacy Networks in International Politics*, Ithaca, N.Y.: Cornell University Press.

Lasswell, H. (1936) *Politics: Who Gets What, When, How*, New York: P. Smith.

Lipschutz, R. (1989) *When Nations Clash – Raw Materials, Ideology and Foreign Policy*, New York: Ballinger/Harper & Row.

Lipschutz, R. (1999) 'From Local Knowledge and Practice to Global Governance', in M. Hewson and T. J. Sinclair (eds) *Approaches to Global Governance Theory*, Albany, NY: State University of New York Press: 259–83.

Lipschutz, R. (2000) *After Authority – War, Peace, and Global Politics in the 21st Century*, Albany, NY: State University of New York Press.

Lipschutz, R. (2002a) 'The Clash of Governmentalities: the Fall of the UN Republic and America's Reach for Imperium', *Contemporary Security Policy* 23, 3: 214–31.

Lipschutz, R. (2002b) 'Doing Well by Doing Good? Transnational Regulatory Campaigns, Social Activism, and Impacts on State Sovereignty', in J. Montgomery and N. Glazer (eds) *Challenges to Sovereignty: How Governments Respond*, New Brunswick, NJ: Transaction, 291–320.

Lipschutz, R. (2003) 'Regulation for the Rest of Us? Global Social Activism, Corporate Citizenship, and the Disappearance of the Political', Center for Global, International and Regional Studies, UC-Santa Cruz, CGIRS-2003-1, August, online at: California Digital Library e-Scholarship Repository, http://repositories.cdlib.org/cgirs/CGIRS-2003-1

Lipschutz, R. (2004a) 'Global Civil Society and Global Governmentality', in M. Barnett and R. Duvall (eds) *Power and Global Governance*, Cambridge: Cambridge University Press: 229–48.

Lipschutz, R. (2004b) 'Global Civil Society and Global Governmentality,' in M. Glasius, D. Lewis and H. Seckinelgin (eds) *The Concept and Reality of Civil Society in Different Cultural and Political Contexts*, London: Routledge.

Lipschutz, R. (2004c) 'Sweating It Out: NGO Campaigns and Trade Union Empowerment', *Development in Practice* 14, 1: 197–209.

Lipschutz, R. (forthcoming) *Regulation for the Rest of Us? Globalization, Governmentality, and Global Politics*, London: Routledge.

Lipschutz, R. and Mayer, J. (1996) *Global Civil Society and Global Environmental Governance – The Politics of Nature from Place to Planet*, Albany, N.Y.: State University of New York Press.

Marcuse, H. (1964) *One-Dimensional Man*, 2nd edn, Boston: Beacon.

Mouffe, C. (2000) *The Democratic Paradox*, London: Verso.

Polanyi K. (2001) *The Great Transformation*, Boston: Beacon Press, 2nd edn.

Rosenberg, J. (1994) *The Empire of Civil Society*, London: Verso.

Schumpeter, J. (1942) *Capitalism, Socialism and Democracy*, New York: Harper.

Scientific American (1990) *Managing Planet Earth*, San Francisco: W. H. Freeman.

Sen, A. (1999) *Development as Freedom*, New York: Anchor.

Shaw, M. (2000) *Theory of the Global State – Globality as an Unfinished Revolution*, Cambridge: Cambridge University Press.

Smith, J. and Johnston, H. (2002) *Globalization and Resistance*, Lanham, Md.: Rowman and Littlefield.

Stiglitz, J. E. (2002) *Globalization and Its Discontents*, New York: Norton.

Tarrow, S. (1998) *Power in Movement: Social Movements and Contentious Politics*, 2nd edn, Cambridge: Cambridge University Press.

Wapner, P. (1996) *Environmental Activism and World Civic Politics*, Albany, N.Y.: State University of New York Press.

Wood, E. M. (2002) *The Origin of Capitalism – A Longer View*, London: Verso.

Young, I. M. (1990) *Justice and the Politics of Difference*, Princeton, N.J.: Princeton University Press.

11 Global civil society as politics of faith

Volker Heins

In the beginning, 'global civil society' (GCS) was not so much a discrete idea in search of people putting it into practice but rather a widespread mood in search of a clear idea about itself. 1960s clichés like 'spaceship earth' and 'global village' began to capture the new mood of global inter-connectedness which today has been underpinned by increasingly thick infrastructures linking voluntary organizations, beliefs systems and policy issues on a worldwide scale. These infrastructures are critical for the task of generalizing and creating universal political accountability around human rights standards and other protective rules.

For the past decade or so, GCS has been theorized as something radic-ally new and incapable of being integrated into the standard vocabularies of modern political theory. Prominent forerunners of GCS include Raymond Aron's notion of transnational society (Aron, 1962) and the concept of world society propounded by the political scientists of the English School (Buzan, 2001). GCS theorists blend these concepts with the normative values of the old liberal idea of civil society as a counterbal-ance to the state. All these transnationalist approaches include a common challenge to the classical definition of the concept of 'politics' given by Max Weber: 'For us, politics means: striving for a share of power or for influence over the distribution of power, either *between* states or *within* a state between the groups of people enclosed in it' (Weber, 1976: 822; italics added). The second part of Weber's definition underscores the relevance of nonstate forces in politics. These forces, however, are confined to the imag-inary space of an 'enclosing' state. Trends associated with the globalization of markets and culture have prompted many authors to contest the imagery of states as containers able to impose exclusionary identities upon the citi-zenry. Beyond the well-known inter-state and domestic struggles for power we are now witnessing the politics of civic groups, which virtually free themself from enclosure by state boundaries and engage in close alliances with like-minded groups in other nations. This is the third dimension of modern politics largely ignored by Weber and many of his contemporaries and successors: forms of vying for power and influence by building coali-tions among groups of people from *different* nations.

In this chapter, I argue that although GCS theorists have started to reflect systematically on this third dimension of modern politics, their account of the realities and dilemmas of civic transnationalism is one-sided and largely misleading. GCS theory is ultimately based on a political ontology which both describes and welcomes the primacy of the non-state world over the world of states. This understanding of the modern political universe follows a distinct style of reasoning, which the British philosopher Michael Oakeshott used to call the 'politics of faith'. Contrary to the 'politics of scepticism' which detaches politics and the activity of governing from the quest for human perfection, the politics of faith places an absolute trust in human reason and sees government (backed by non-governmental forces) as the agent that will lead society on the road to perfection (Oakeshott, 1996). By and large, GCS thinking falls under this rubric of the politics of faith. Characteristically enough, even those writers who see the world as a dangerous and uncertain place entertain unjustifiably high hopes about the effectiveness of multilateral 'deliberation' (Kaldor, 2003: 160). In addition, and unlike their sceptical counterparts, most GCS theorists prefer a 'minute' to a 'strong' government (Oakeshott, 1996: 32–3). The activity of governing is supposed both to encompass many new actors, from international to nongovernmental organizations, and also to extend its attention to new fields, including the fine-tuning of personal relationships and communication behaviors (see Keane, 2003: 79).

My main argument against the GCS approach is that it seems to be based on an operation I call 'conceptual overstretch'. This operation proceeds by extending the meaning of the historical concept of civil society by applying it to circumstances very different from those which gave rise to the original concept, while simultaneously obscuring these differences. By overstretching the classical liberal notion of civil society to include completely different constellations of political actors, the new concept mystifies the reality of transnational civic relations. Conceptual overstretch can be seen as a direct expression of the 'politics of faith'. Oakeshott writes:

> The words and expressions of our political vocabulary are each capable of a narrow and an extended meaning (and, of course, a range of meaning between these limits). In the politics of faith, because of its alliance with the enterprise of human perfection, each word and expression will be given its largest and most extended meaning: it goes always to the limit, and (by means of adjectives) sometimes beyond the limit, of what the vocabulary will tolerate without becoming meaningless.
>
> (1996: 28)

Moreover, the praise for the 'globality' of civil society deflects attention from the consequences of the fact that, to a large extent, civic transnationalism is entrenched in international organizations. The paradox here is that international organizations, including United Nations agencies, are seen as possible vehicles for strengthening global democracy whereas in reality these organizations suffer from enormous control deficits which bring them into conflict with basic requirements of liberal democracy.

That said, however, I would also like to emphasize that the conceptual overstretch which shaped the vocabulary of GCS is linked to powerful collective beliefs which have to be analysed in their own right. I shall therefore argue that GCS cannot be reduced to an intellectual construct misrepresenting reality, since the idea of GCS has itself become part and parcel of an emerging reality of transnational civic activism. In other words: the idea or imagination of GCS has begun to *inspire* real groups by entering their self-conceptions and their agendas of social and political change. To a lesser extent, but similar to nations or ethnic communities – entities that do not exist outside the mutual expectations of their members – GCS is real because of belief and the relationships these beliefs inspire. Challenging the ultimately faith-based certainties entertained by GCS theorists, I shall conclude by suggesting a stronger emphasis on what Oakeshott called the 'politics of scepticism', which would share many of the normative concerns of GCS advocates without subscribing to their overall theoretical project.

Demystifying global civil society

Solidarity with strangers is real as are civil societies which nurture such bonds of solidarity through public discourse and voluntary organization (Alexander, 1998). Real civil societies are also spawning transnational associations and networks. However, there is little reason to assume that networks of transnational political and social associations constitute a *global* civil society bearing any resemblance to what used to be called 'civil society' by modern political theorists.

The model of GCS currently in dispute is based on two interconnected propositions derived from the historical study of real civil societies. The first proposition holds that there is an emerging GCS which is as autonomous, self-regulating and independent from state institutions as national civil societies have been. Ken Booth used the much-quoted metaphor of a global community 'omelette' being fried alongside the empty 'shells of sovereignty' (Booth, 1991: 542). John Keane likens GCS to a 'vast, dynamic biosphere' which like the real biosphere is vulnerable to, and should be protected against, 'internal and external interference' (Keane, 2003: 18). Mary Kaldor similarly invokes the image of a pristine space of unrestricted deliberation which is 'subject to invasion' by alien social forces (Kaldor, 2003: 46).

The second proposition suggests that the new global civic sphere is not only *separate* from the world of states, but as a consequence is also *unified* by universally shared moral values like the protection of human rights or the environment. According to Martin Shaw, 'ideas and values ... become increasingly commonly held' (Shaw, 1994: 11). The German sociologist Ulrich Beck even heralds a new moral 'age of homogeneity' (Beck, 1997: 144). Most GCS authors have also been outspoken about the political significance of the emerging global ethic which is meant to prevail over the state-centred world – the principles of non-intervention and sovereignty – as the moral consensus of civil society historically constrained the actions of political rulers in democracies.

In spite of the elegance of this two-tier model, which will certainly continue to attract scholars as well as activists, empirical research has made significant thrusts at both of its aspects. Before I go into some detail regarding this research, it is worth pointing out a persistent logical mystery surrounding GCS thinking. Confusing the 'sovereignty' of the state with its 'autonomy' or 'power', GCS theorists typically (and mistakenly) claim that the sovereign state is 'passing away' (Keane, 2003: 104).[1] However, if this was the case it would be inconsistent to speak of an independent civil society since there would be no political entity left against which to declare and defend independence. GCS would go it alone.

Leaving this problem aside, there can be no doubt about the impact of a multitude of sometimes obstreperously independent civil society actors in today's liberal democracies – actors that are independent from state agencies in terms of funding sources, agenda-setting and mobilization capacity. However, political independence varies according to the degrees and types of modernization in different world regions. In Western societies, where states have consolidated their autonomy vis-à-vis social groups while being at the same time in touch with them, public interest groups and social movements, too, enjoy a considerable degree of autonomy, not least regarding financial matters. In non-Western regions civic activists often have to buy their independence from their *own* state by becoming dependent on *other* states, which typically funnel public funds through specialized donor agencies or foundations. Studying nongovernmental activism in Third-World countries, Benedict Anderson's image of 'lonely, bilingual intelligentsias unattached to sturdy local bourgeoisies' (Anderson 1991: 140) comes to mind. More specifically, Rohrschneider and Dalton observed that the patterns of financial and information flows between environmental NGOs from affluent to less affluent follow the same asymmetries that are generally effective in the global system (Rohrschneider and Dalton, 2002: 529). Even civil society itself – ideas and blueprints for civic self-organization – is now being 'sold' to presumably less civil societies (Henderson, 2002).

These asymmetries lead to a number of pathologies, particularly in those societies where the distinction between social and governmental positions is systematically blurred, to the effect that outsiders (including foreign funders) have a hard time telling 'genuine' from 'mutant' NGOs. Mutant civil society groups emerge when influential power-holders begin to use non-state organizational forms in order to gain a share of the perceived moral goodness and respectability of many international NGOs, thereby hoping to make their voice heeded in international forums (Bryant, 2002). Structures of state-society interaction which are typical for Western societies therefore do not hold across different world regions. In countries like India, where in some states the public administration is on the brink of withering away, civil society organizations have taken over the task of formulating the official position of the government in certain issue areas like, for example, poverty alleviation or climate change policies. Instead of a sovereign state *shedding* some of its powers because of the complexity of the problems, we are confronted with a state which structurally lacks the capacity to produce the knowledge, the legitimacy and the mobilizing power needed for governing vast territories and complex societies. In such a setting, civil society organizations are not independent from the state but rather on the way to partially replacing it (Heins, 2000).

As far as international action is concerned, NGOs from different backgrounds are also wrestling with a level of systematic 'organizational insecurity' (Cooley and Ron, 2002) unknown to voluntary associations in consolidated liberal democracies. Often the expectation, nourished by GCS theorists, that independent civic organizations cooperate on the basis of shared values and convictions is unrealistic. The dependence on outside funding and on renewable contracts that are performance-based and subject to external evaluation procedures leads to enormous institutional pressures. Competition for funds often proves to be working against the noble intentions of many international NGOs. Alexander Cooley and James Ron observed how in wartime Bosnia, competition between aid agencies even helped to empower local warlords and military officers seeking to resist international efforts to protect prisoners of war (Cooley and Ron, 2002: 31–6).

To conclude this brief overview: evidence from empirical political science suggests that independence is indeed a quality of many citizen groups in many countries which however must not be uncritically turned into a quality of GCS. The literature on GCS tends to even out the historical differences between societies and types of modernity, assigning an ontological status of 'independence' to globally-connected citizen groups. As a result, the dynamics of civic transnationalism, in which different groups play differing roles in multiple arenas, including the state itself, have been obfuscated. In reality, what is depicted as an emerging global civic space is both being traversed by domestic struggles as well as mediated by international power relations (Heins, 2001).

Now let us turn to the second proposition. The GCS thesis contends that besides the new space of global citizen action there is also an emerging global ethic animating this space. This ethic is viewed as functionally equivalent to the moral consensus in historical civil societies in supporting new institutional structures of global democratic governance. Historically, a basic consensus on core values was indeed critical for the viability of civil societies providing the armature of democratic states. Here, it is interesting to recall the example of late nineteenth- and early twentieth-century Germany. This country could in no way be characterized as having a weak or underdeveloped associational life outside the state. Quite to the contrary, civil society was flourishing without being backed by any consensus about common values worthy of defending. The lack of a moral consensus eased National Socialism's road to power at a time when the citizens in neighbouring France were able to curb the extreme right and to stop them from taking over the state (at least from within). Historians have demonstrated that the differences between Germany and France cannot be explained in terms of different capacities of national civil societies but are rather due to differing levels of institutionalization of common values and attitudes (see Möller and Kittel, 2002; Berman, 1997).

Bearing these historical examples in mind, I believe that today's global associational scene is closer to the Germany than the France of the 1930s. It seems to me a mild euphemism to say that the emerging global civic space is not populated by like-minded equals – 'with identical norms and goals as is often implied by the global civil society literature' (Rohrschneider and Dalton, 2002: 529). While aggregated figures on associational life are soaring – as a look at the statistics of the Brussels-based Union of International Associations (UIA) shows – there is also ample evidence of the weakness of institutionalization of common values and the extent to which divergent associational scenes are digging themselves in, jealously watching their turfs. With regard to the fundamental values of societal modernization and state sovereignty, citizen groups from different world regions do not even agree to disagree (Heins, 2001: Ch. 5). Only novices to the study of transnational collective action can be surprised at this lack of consensus and the persistence of national interests even within transnational organizations. Some time ago, for example, the Japanese branch of World Wide Fund for Nature (WWF) supported a partial lifting of the international ban on commercial whaling while the British branch called on the United States government to impose economic sanctions against Japan, following reports of its killing of whales.

Much more serious is the institutional weakness of a truly global consensus on *negative* moral universals like the evils of racism or genocidal mass murder, both in world society and in the international NGO community. Here, it is worth listing some recent examples which indicate that the space of GCS is no less traversed by deep moral conflicts as is the world in general.

At the UN World Conference Against Racism in September 2001 (in Durban, South Africa), a number of NGOs openly asked for Israel to be declared an apartheid state to be destroyed while at the same time fighting suggestions to include anti-semitism in the category of racism. This led to the premature departure of a number of Western human rights organizations. In the wake of Durban, the anti-globalization group Attac, which is regularly quoted as a benevolent force in favor of GCS, has made itself unpleasantly conspicuous by a number of anti-Semitic statements (see Jikeli, 2003). Then, three days after September 11, a spokeswoman of the Third World Journalists Network, a quintessential GCS organization, declared over the airwaves of a public radio station in Germany that the massacre in Manhattan in no way ran counter to the 'system of moral values' dear to her organization (see Heins, 2002: 143). Meanwhile, observers at the World Social Forum which took place in 2003 in Porto Alegre, Brazil, described the reception of the official Iraqi delegation as 'frenetic', while Arab feminists demanding human rights got only tired applause (Staud, 2003).

These are random but by no means isolated examples of an impressive lack of moral acuity among some of those meant to 'civilize' global society. They remind us not only of the nasty side of the non-state universe, but also of the fact that the difference between the nice and the nasty within this universe is not always easy to make out. For those who have not already been converted to the belief that GCS is for real, it will be difficult to endorse the view that there is a close affinity between the *space* of non-state actors and *attitudes* of general peace-mindedness (see, for example, Keane, 2003: 13).

There is another serious problem. The opinions of self-defined GCS spokespersons I have just mentioned can be seen as glimpses of a public discourse being voiced across borders. Yet these discourses are not linked to a public space where people can meet and engage in argument continuously. There is no global equivalent of a public sphere of cultural contestation, in which historical civil societies have always been rooted (Delanty, 2001). Apart from specialized issue areas, public discourse remains largely confined by language and national lines. The global voices being heard from United Nations fora are addressing a fictitious global public which has no way to constitute itself by sharing a common language and a common system of mass media or public venues. This point leads us to the problematic relationship between the global associational scene and liberal democratic norms.

Global civil society versus democracy

Goals and attitudes within the non-state world are far from being equal or even compatible. Moral universals, including negative ones, are weak, and cannot be aired and thrashed out in a truly public sphere spanning the globe. What we do find, however, is a new brand of advocacy organizations that operate in similar ways all over the world. It seems that a certain model of non-state political engagement is now spreading even across the north-south divide. To a large extent, successful voluntary organizations in the south and the east struggling for the respect of basic rights are – like their counterparts in the north and the west – virtually memberless, highly professionalized and sometimes remarkably media-savvy. Both share the characteristics of being externally funded by tax-exempt private foundations and run by restricted circles of unelected leaders. The trend towards bypassing broader constituencies in favour of staff-driven, agile 'helicopter organizations'[2] is universal and has obvious strategic advantages in terms of flexibility and networking capacity. Yet these tactical advantages come with a price. As Theda Skocpol has pointed out, the new organizations which are so well-adapted to the environments of international policy deliberations are unable to channel the aspirations of ordinary citizens who want to get involved in public policy. Nonprofessional citizens may sometimes still be able to follow some of the debates being kicked off by advocacy groups, however it is increasingly difficult for them to relate these debates to the problems of their own lives (Skocpol, 2003: 128, 226; Deth, 2000).

Skocpol has also demonstrated how the historical relationship of mutual reinforcement between civic voluntarism and representative democracy has been weakened by the rise of a new type of professional public interest organization (Skocpol 2003: 72–3). My guess is that, on the other hand, we see a different kind of mutual reinforcement between the new organizations – which are celebrated as harbingers of GCS – and international organizations. The parallel growth of NGOs and international organizations over the past decades is only the statistical expression of a deeper affinity. International organizations are attracting global non-state activism in at least four different ways. They provide a public stage for the political concerns voiced by human rights groups and others; they are the addressees of their protests, appeals and blames; they are sources of legitimacy for NGOs; and often they are also indispensable sources of funds. These multiple linkages explain why the idea of GCS is sometimes almost identified with the broader concept of a UN-based 'multilateralism' (Kaldor, 2003: 137–41).

To the extent that the fate of GCS is closely intertwined with the robustness and growth of international organizations we run into the difficulty that these organizations may well be honest brokers in crisis situations or even indispensable problem-solvers; yet they are not democratic nor can they be democratized by simply granting rights of participation to equally unaccountable non-state organizations, however benign their intentions may be. The argument that international organizations are intrinsically at odds with basic requirements of liberal democracy has been made by various scholars. Among others, Robert Dahl has listed a number of factors responsible for the low interest of most citizens in the workings of international organizations including the institutions of the European Union. Some of these factors are: the complexity of many international matters; the absence of a consensus on common goods and bads; the reduced bearing of local knowledge and memories on international fora;

and, of course, the absence of elected representatives exercising some control of international bureaucracies. In combination, these factors result in undermining the readiness of citizens to stay informed about international organizations and, what is more important, to act on the basis of this knowledge (Dahl, 1999).

This dismal situation can also be explicated in terms of the principal-agent problems raised by international organizations. Unfortunately, neither the institutional makeup of the European Union nor other international organizations have followed the model of the constitution of the United States, which is extremely sensitive to the arrogation of power and insists that all those powers not explicitly delegated to the Congress and the President are reserved to the States and to the people. The design of most international organizations today is completely alien to this 'exceptionalist' and profoundly sceptical tradition of systematically impeding the transfer of power to unelected international bureaucracies out of touch with the interests and the knowledge of ordinary citizens (see Ignatieff, 2004). Today, between individual citizens and international organizations there are usually four steps of political delegation, which are increasingly clouded as one moves upward from the parliament to the national government to international boards supposed to exercise some degree of oversight (boards of executive directors, audit offices, international tribunals). With every step the costs of democratic control rise while the incentives to control weaken. Ironically, it is exactly this kind of situation that allows for the increasing political influence of lobby groups including well-intentioned nongovernmental organizations (Vaubel, 2003). As a consequence, many NGOs are not interested in improving their formal rights with regard to international organizations, since they have reasons to assume that by relying on quasi-feudal institutional habits and personal privileges of access they get more out of the political game (Furtak, 2001: 242–3). Against this background it seems fanciful to think, as Mary Kaldor does, that a global civil society based on NGOs can make international organizations more attuned to the concerns of ordinary citizens as opposed to states (Kaldor, 2003: 141).

The unfortunate tendency to look only at the global outreach of international organizations and the 'causes' of NGOs without giving much thought to how these institutions can be integrated into established democratic frameworks, leads to a supreme irony – that GCS discourse, very much against the grain of its liberal-democratic predecessors, is uncritically in favor of *increasing* the power of the states including international bureaucracies and bargaining systems (Baker, 2002). This is a further indication that GCS thinking is more akin to the politics of faith – which historically always welcomed the emergence of new power concentrations in order to promote human perfection (Oakeshott, 1996: 86) – than to the sceptical tradition at the root of democratic constitutionalism.

Global civil society as imagined community

Following Oakeshott, I have so far argued that the adjective 'global' has turned the concept of civil society into a misleading, or even a 'meaningless', term. Yet this is not the whole story. GCS is more than a fantasy or a 'phantasmagoria' conjured up in the 'salons' of international organizations (Drainville, 1998). Rather, it is now an idea many people *live by*. Put differently, GCS is becoming real in the way of an 'imagined community'. Imagination, in the sense of the term as it was introduced into political sociology by Benedict Anderson, is an inexhaustible energy capable of reordering both the reality of social relationships and our feelings toward this reality. Group-forming imaginings have a way of being real that cannot be captured by statistics about the growth of transnational networks or rising attendance figures at international conferences. It is easy to ridicule much of what is going on at big UN conferences and other televised summits, which often do not seem to produce more than container-loads of documents and tons of carbon dioxide created by the international passengers attending the event (Brown, 2002). Yet for those who join the conferences and rallies or who follow them sympathetically, those global gatherings are bristling with moral significance, regardless of their immediate political effects.

From this I conclude that the new politics of faith accounts both for the *meaninglessness* of the concept of GCS from an analytical point of view and for the *abundance of meaning* rendered to the reality of transnational connections, deliberations and gatherings. Whereas I argue that social scientists should not be led astray by a faith-driven way of forming concepts and theories, I am equally critical toward any rationalist analysis trying to account for the formation of political communities without taking into account their collective beliefs (however strange they may appear).

The meaningful aspect of GCS talk can be disclosed by looking at the collective interpretations and representations which shape the actions of those activists who believe in GCS and act accordingly. These interpretations and representations are artificially made but nevertheless very much real in their consequences. To understand how strikingly real fictions can be, briefly recall some earlier key insights on the formation of political communities.

Some important clues about the self-perpetuating role of collective beliefs can be traced back to Max Weber who, in his chapter on ethnic groups in *Economy and Society* (*Wirtschaft and Gesellschaft*), observed that the belief in ethnic or racial affinity, however unfounded and arbitrary it is, can become a powerful source of collective action (Weber, 1976: Ch. 4). Belief in affinity, however, is nothing primary. According to Weber, primary and ubiquitous phenomena are feelings of repulsion and misrecognition among human beings which can be sparked by all kinds of reasons, imaginings and sensations. Only after groups of people discover that they strongly dislike other groups do they tend to believe that they are also deeply akin to those who share their feelings. Weber insists that this artificially generated belief in group affinity, regardless of whether it has any objective foundation, can have important consequences for the formation of political community (Weber, 1976: 237). The belief in affinity is not an illusion which will be dissipated by the forces of rational criticism or social 'progress'. Instead, it is kept alive by the everyday politics of modern states and the experience of sharing liability to the same bordered state institutions. Obviously, the belief in affinity is also fostered by extraordinary events like wars or threats of imminent war.

In addition, three points are worth noting. First, Weber mentioned that the effective belief in group affinities draws on empirical cues (like skin colour or common language) which however are only the '*occasion* for the subjective belief' in real affinities. In order to proceed from the occasion to a fully developed belief in affinity, transformative forces of 'reinterpretation' (Weber, 1976: 237) of reality must intervene. Second, long before Benedict Anderson elaborated on these subjects, Weber was struck by the lack of substance and the inherent 'vagueness' of ethnic or national self-descriptions, as well as by the apparent usefulness of this vagueness for the integration of large collectivities (Weber, 1976: 240). Third, Weber clearly saw the importance of dramatic political events as opposed to perennial structures in shaping or disrupting sentiments of likeness among political communities. Anderson went beyond Weber by stressing the relevance of 'print capitalism' and the modern mass media for any attempt to explain how the imagination of community permeated everyday life, and how people got emotionally attached to the fictions of fateful national togetherness which in premodern times (and non-European spaces) did not stir strong feelings.

These various insights may serve as points of departure for looking afresh at the meaning of GCS talk. Besides questioning GCS as an analytical tool for understanding the post-Cold War world, it is worth pursuing a second path. Along this path, GCS should be treated not only as a questionable intellectual construct but as a belief system with significant, yet under-explored, group-forming powers. GCS theorists should also be seen as active intellectuals reworking the imaginings and self-conceptions of a large number of influential non-state groups trying to change international society. A partial research agenda looking at GCS as an emerging globally-imagined community might include the following issues.

Construction of a self/other dichotomy

In various arenas, we can observe the construction of an Other by those claiming to represent GCS, along with a vaguely defined Self. Whereas moderate globalist forces within the NGO world have always objected to the idea of fighting 'enemies' (see, for example, the 1998 Greenpeace

International Annual Report: 'Greenpeace has no permanent allies or enemies'), the more recent anti-globalization movement goes to endless trouble to construct a symbolic Other in the guises of the Economy or Capitalism. In this connection, the maddening vagueness of GCS talk becomes meaningful since vague self-descriptions against the backdrop of an uncanny Other are proving to be socially integrative, even across borders.

Engineering of a collective memory

The politics of GCS has not only started to construct its Other, it is also keen on encountering the Other – whether at the G8 summits or at the conferences of world trade representatives – as well as its own constituents. The creation of events of togetherness and antagonism are today as critical for the rise of civic transnationalism as motorized travelling 'by huge and variegated crowds' (Anderson 1991: 115) was to the rise of nationalism in the former European colonies. One of the main uses of global meeting events is that they serve as points of reference for the engineering of a collective memory buttressing the imagined Self of GCS. Sometimes those events function as equivalents of common fates similar to the heroic sagas of traditional tribes. Here, the debate on the violent death of a young Italian during demonstrations at the G8 summit in Genoa in 2001 is symptomatic. By transfiguring the victim into a 'first martyr' (Kaldor, 2003: 103) or a 'rebel murdered by a lackey' (Indymedia Germany, 2003), the GCS movement has invented something like the 'Tomb of the Hardly Known Anti-Globalizer' quite similar to the Tomb of the Unknown Soldier famously characterized by Anderson as a major hallmark of the modern imagination of community (Anderson, 1991: 9–10).

Suffusing everyday life with a sense of global simultaneity

In the nationalist era, print media helped to suffuse everyday life with a new sense of belonging and togetherness. Today the Internet is being used in a similar fashion by hundreds of thousands of world 'citizens' exchanging information and opinions across borders. Quite tellingly, NGOs are often counting the 'hits' on their websites, and some donor agencies have made the intensity of web-based communication a benchmark for funding decisions. Allowing for real-time, many-to-many communication, the Internet is even more able to generate a new sense of global simultaneity than newspapers or other media have ever been. Of course, it remains to be seen how the 'imagined linkage' (Anderson, 1991: 33–6) between like-minded activists made possible by the Net will translate into real consequences with regard to the people's sense of belonging. As they struggle to keep abreast of and to anticipate new technological developments, some scholars are sceptical about the possibility of building and maintaining politically effective social relationships via the Net (Tarrow, 1998; Comor, 2001). Still, the way the Net is being celebrated by many GCS activists is in itself interesting and worth studying since it gives us a sense of the ongoing search for new kinds of deterritorialized community.

Politics of scepticism

In a move away from the Weberian conception of politics as something happening either within or between states, GCS thinking is systematically focusing on transborder citizen action. This systematic shift of attention is in itself a strong reason not to dismiss the approach lightheartedly. Yet, whatever its merits in terms of highlighting the importance of neglected issue areas and unconventional actors, the GCS approach has a number of serious flaws. Some of them are linked to the conceptual overstretch of a civil society vocabulary which insinuates that we are in the midst of a worldwide process of narrowing the gap between different value systems, of establishing a relationship of mutual reinforcement between the expansion of civic transnationalism and the establishment of a global democracy, and of setting world society free from the constraints of state sovereignty without leaving it to mafias and terrorists. Put simply, GCS theorists overemphasize the historical parallels between flourishing civil societies in liberal democracies and the global associational landscape which can be studied today. Instead of using the civil society analogy heuristically in order to highlight how today's largely NGO-based associationalism *differs* from civil society – both in terms of its constituencies and in terms of its democratizing effects – the new theory extends the meaning of the old concept to the still fairly uncharted waters of transnational civic communities.

In particular, GCS theorists have so far failed to contribute to our understanding of how the two dimensions of modern politics outlined by Weber (and many others) *interact* with the third dimension of civic transnationalism. The elusive concept of an independent GCS does not shed much light on the multiple ways in which citizen networks stretched across borders are using, amplifying or redistributing state resources, depending on the contexts in which they are struggling. A second, normative question mostly neglected by GCS theory is this one: What exactly do we owe to foreign citizens and the world? GCS theorists avoid asking this question by wrongly believing that state sovereignty is a thing of the past. If, however, sovereignty persists (as I contend), there are differences to be further explored in what we owe to our fellow-citizens, with whom we share the liability of certain state institutions, versus what we owe to the rest of the world.

All in all, GCS looks more like a rhetorical edifice perched on observations and political hopes, rather than a device for generating data and for opening new possibilities for inquiry. To be sure, there may still be excellent pragmatic reasons for continuing to use the term, if, for example, it really 'holds out some promise of being heard' (Kaldor, 2003: 107) by marginalized populations in faraway regions. There may also be ways of transforming the statements of faith characterizing much of GCS discourse into testable hypotheses. The basic hypothesis of GCS theory sounds like this: Rising levels of global interactions have structural, lasting and beneficial consequences for the exercise of state power, the future of democracy and the taming of nationalism (see, for example, Kaldor, 2003: 138). Lurking in the background of such a hypothesis is the kind of Panglossian 'global thinking' first advocated by the American Vice President Henry Wallace, who after the Second World War planned to promote world peace by building airports all over the planet. Still, there is no reason not to pursue similar questions regarding the positive side-effects of globalization empirically.

Indeed, for the empirically-minded authors writing on the prospects of a truly global civil society there may even be a bridge leading from the politics of faith to the politics of scepticism. As Barry Buzan has argued recently, GCS advocates may feel increasingly compelled to ask for a strengthening of the state. With new forms of rampant violence – originating not from states but from the factionalism of warlords and their clienteles – ravaging large regions of the world, there are good reasons to strengthen fragile states against uncivil societies or to side with strong democratic states able to put pressure on, stabilize or change the behavior of weak but dangerous states (Buzan, 2004). As we cannot avoid confronting regions where the most basic government services have collapsed, whether tax collection or policing, we are reminded of the truth that the existence of a minimal political order is nothing to be taken for granted, but 'a great and difficult achievement never beyond the reach of decay and dissolution' (Oakeshott, 1996: 32).

Notes

1 Sovereignty means that the state has a final, not an exclusive say in matters concerning the preservation of the political community. Consider the following examples: Libya takes over formal responsibility for the bombing of PanAm flight 103 over Lockerbie, Scotland. The government of the Czech Republic wants property claims filed by ethnic Germans who were exiled after the Second World War to be handled by the Constitutional Court, the nation's highest judicial authority. Israel decides to hand over two towns, Jericho and Qalqilya, to Palestinian authorities. These three messages taken from a single edition of a daily newspaper illustrate that sovereignty is alive and well (see *Boston Globe*, August 16, 2003: A1, A6, A7).

2 I owe this term to Hope Shand, who once used it to characterize her own organization, the Rural Advancement Foundation International (RAFI).

References

Alexander, J. C. (ed.) (1998) *Real Civil Societies: Dilemmas of Institutionalization*, Thousand Oaks CA: Sage.

Anderson, B. (1991) *Imagined Communities: Reflections on the Origin and Spread of Nationalism* (2nd revised ed.), London/New York: Verso.

Aron, R. (1962) *Paix et guerre entre les nations*, Paris: Calman-Levy.

Baker, G. (2002) 'Problems in the Theorisation of Global Civil Society', *Political Studies* 50: 928–43.

Beck, U. (1997) *Was ist Globalisierung?*, Frankfurt: Suhrkamp.

Berman, S. (1997) 'Civil Society and the Collapse of the Weimar Republic', *World Politics* 49: 401–29.

Booth, K. (1991) 'Security in Anarchy: Utopian Realism in Theory and Practice', *International Affairs* 67: 527–45.

Brown, P. (2002) 'Lobbying galore', *Guardian*, 21 August (online edition).

Bryant, R. L. (2002) 'False Prophets? Mutant NGOs and Philippine Environmentalism', *Society and Natural Resources* 15: 629–39.

Buzan, B. (2001) 'The English School: An Underexploited Resource in IR', *Review of International Studies* 27: 471–88.

Buzan, B. (2004) ' "Civil" and "Uncivil" in World Society', in S. Guzzini and D. Jung (eds) *Contemporary Security Analysis and Copenhagen Peace Research*, London: Routledge.

Comor, E. (2001) 'The Role of Communication in Global Civil Society: Forces, Processes, Prospects', *International Studies Quarterly* 45, 3: 389–408.

Cooley, A. and Ron, J. (2002) 'The NGO Scramble: Organizational Insecurity and the Political Economy of Transnational Action', *International Security* 27, 1: 5–39.

Dahl, R. A. (1999) 'Can International Organizations be Democratic? A Skeptic's View', in I. Shapiro and C. Hacker-Cordon (eds) *Democracy's Edges*, Cambridge: Cambridge University Press: 19–36.

Delanty, G. (2001) 'Cosmopolitanism and Violence: The Limits of Global Civil Society', *European Journal of Social Theory* 4: 41–52.

Deth, J. W. van (2000) 'Interesting, but irrelevant: social capital and the saliency of politics in Western Europe', *European Journal of Political Research* 37: 115–47.

Drainville, A. C. (1998) 'The Fetishism of Global Civil Society: Global Governance, Transnational Urbanism and Sustainable Capitalism in the World Economy', in M. P. Smith and L. E. Guarnizo (eds) *Transnationalism From Below*, New Brunswick, NJ: Transaction: 35–63.

Furtak, F. T. (2001) *Nichtregierungsorganisationen (NGOs) im politischen System der Europäischen Union: Strukturen, Beteiligungsmöglichkeiten, Einfluss*, Munich: Tuduv.

Heins, V. (2000) 'From New Political Organizations to Changing Moral Geographies: Unpacking Global Civil Society', *Geojournal* 52: 37–44.

Heins, V. (2001) *Der Neue Transnationalismus*, Frankfurt: Campus.

Heins, V. (2002) 'Germany's New War: 11 September and Its Aftermath in German Quality Newspapers', *German Politics* 11, 2: 128–45.

Henderson, S. L. (2002) 'Selling Civil Society: Western Aid and the Nongovernmental Sector in Russia', in *Comparative Political Studies* 35, 2: 139–67.

Ignatieff, M. (ed.) (2004) *American Exceptionalism and Human Rights*, Princeton: Princeton University Press.

Indymedia Germany (2003) 'Genua 2001 – Der Kampf um die Wahrheit in den Zeiten der Ohnmacht', http://de.indymedia.org/2003/05/51239.shtml (accessed on 1 August 2003).

Jikeli, J. (2003) 'Attac bietet Antisemiten ein Forum', http://de.indymedia.org/2003/01/39823.shtml (accessed on 1 August 2003).

Kaldor, M. (2003) *Global Civil Society: An Answer to War*, Cambridge: Polity Press.

Keane, J. (2003) *Global Civil Society?*, Cambridge: Cambridge University Press.

Möller, H. and Kittel, M. (eds) (2002) *Demokratie in Deutschland und Frankreich 1918–1933/40*, Munich: Oldenbourg.

Oakeshott, M. (1996) *The Politics of Faith and the Politics of Skepticism* (T. Fuller ed.), New Haven: Yale University Press.

Rohrschneider, R. and Dalton, R. J. (2002) 'A Global Network? Transnational Cooperation among Environmental Groups', *The Journal of Politics* 64, 2: 510–33.

Shaw, M. (1994) *Global Society and International Relations*, Cambridge: Polity Press.

Skocpol, T. (2003) *Diminished Democracy: From Membership to Management in American Civic Life*, Norman: University of Oklahoma Press.

Staud, Toralf (2003) 'Saddam und die Imperialisten', *Die Zeit*, 6/2003 (online edition).

Tarrow, S. (1998) 'Fishnets, Internets and Catnets: Globalization and Transnational Collective Action', in M. P. Hanagan *et al.* (eds) *Challenging Authority: The Historical Study of Contentious Politics*, Minneapolis: University of Minnesota Press: 228–44.

Vaubel, R. (2003) *Principal-Agent-Probleme in internationalen Organizationen*, Discussion Paper No. 219, Hamburg: HWWA.

Weber, M. (1976) *Wirtschaft und Gesellschaft: Grundriss der verstehenden Soziologie* (5th edn), Tübingen: Mohr.

Index

accountable government 48–50, 56, 70, 79, 120, 121, 194
age of empire 23
agency 115–17
Algeria (civil society in) 24
al-Qaeda 76–80, 83
Amnesty International 120
anarchy (international) 150–1
Anderson, Benedict 195–7
anti-apartheid movement 73
anti-globalisation movement 9, 10, 73, 85–98, 108, 111, 139, 142, 192, 197
anti-imperialism 25–6, 32
Arendt, Hannah 131
Aristotle 36, 103
autonomy 106, 119, 123, 135, 189

Baker, Gideon 140–1, 194
balance-of-power politics 37
Beck, Ulrich 175, 189
bio-politics 172–4, 181, 183
Blair, Tony 97
Bolingbroke, Henry St. John 43
'boomerang' theory 158–62
Bosnia 64, 190
British Petroleum (BP) 92–3, 96
Bush, George W. 47, 76–80, 97, 110–11
Buzan, Barry 199

Callinicos, Alex 87
Cammack, Paul 164
capitalism 21, 22, 31, 71, 89–90, 172, 176–8, 180, 197; 'turbo-' 34, 39, 42, 44–5, 47–8
capitalist elites 10, 92–3, 98
Carnival Against Capitalism 94
Carr, E.H. 155
Chandler, David 118
Chandhoke, Neera 108–9, 143–4

Charter 77 40, 42, 100, 161
Chaterjee, Partha 23, 30
citizenship 3, 6, 8, 19–20, 27, 52–3, 56, 62, 82–3, 116–17, 124–5, 135; global/cosmopolitan 2, 6, 65, 116–18, 121, 124–5, 134–5, 137, 140, 197
civic virtue 53, 124–5
Clark, John 3
class-based organisations 10
class conflict 26
Clinton, Bill 93, 97
Club of Rome 90
Colás, Alejandro 69, 165, 171
Cold War, the 2–3, 9, 12, 52, 57, 59, 72–4, 76, 81, 149, 152, 154, 161–2, 166, 174
colonialism 23–30, 133
communism 90, 138
constructivism 11–12, 149–66
cosmocracy 8, 35–7, 50; structural problems of 43–7
cosmopolitanism 11, 49, 54, 103, 116–17, 120, 122, 130–1, 134–8, 140–5
court society 35
Cox, Robert 126–7
critical theory 134, 165

Dahl, Robert 193–4
Dean, Mitchell 172–4
democracy 49–50, 70, 77, 107, 119, 194, 199; cosmopolitan/global 48–50, 70, 110, 114–15, 119, 125, 134–5, 137, 140, 188, 198; direct 94
democratisation 6, 8, 19–20, 22, 72, 107, 155; of global governance 1, 3, 9, 49–50, 70, 81, 115, 190
development 52, 57, 59, 62–4, 133; aid 59–61; sustainable 92
de Witt, J. 48

Duffield, Mark 62–3

Earth Summit (Rio, 1992) 42, 92
ecological movement 88, 90–1
Empire 138–42, 144–5; American 9,
    46–8, 79; British 46; French 27;
    Habsburg 46; Ottoman 24–5; Soviet
    40, 46, 72
'end of history', the 132–3, 135, 141, 145
English School, the 151, 186
Enlightenment, the 81, 105, 131–2, 140;
    reason 135–7, 144
environmental movement 88–91, 95–7,
    164
eurocentrism 122, 132–3, 135
European Court of Human Rights 37
European Court of Justice 39
European Parliament 97
European Union 97, 136, 193, 194

Falk, Richard 4, 6, 114–15, 118–21, 124,
    165
feminist movements 32, 135
Ferguson, Adam 105, 171
Florini, Ann 3, 159
Foucault, Michel 12, 131, 138, 171–4,
    180–1
Friends of the Earth 88–9, 93–4, 96–7
Frost, Mervyn 19–20

G8 summits 85, 197
Germany (civil society in) 191
Ghils, Paul 116
Gill, Stephen 126
Global Compact, the 172
global ethics 2, 119–25, 189–91
Global Forum (1992) 42
globalisation 5–6, 10, 20, 46, 48, 55, 76,
    103, 107, 110–11, 122, 135–6, 138, 155,
    172, 174, 178–9, 186, 199; 'from
    below' 4, 114–28
global polity 36–7, 121
Goldsmith, Edward 90–1
Gorbachev, Mikhail 92, 154
governance: global 2, 6, 8, 10, 36, 45, 52,
    59, 64–5, 69, 75, 80, 82, 103, 108–10,
    114–15, 117, 121–5, 135, 139, 171–2,
    174, 183; technologies of 54;
    'therapeutic' 54
governmentality 12, 171–3; global
    173–83
Gramsci, Antonio 18, 104, 126–7
Gramscianism; neo- 125–6

Greenpeace 94–7, 196–7
Grugel, Jean 2
Guantanamo Bay 79
Gulf War (first) 47

'imagined community' 195–8
Indigenous Forum 38
individualism 53, 58, 105, 109
industrialisation 57, 62–4, 89, 92
institutionalisation 124–7, 140, 149
International Criminal Court 39, 75, 79,
    81, 108
internationalism 133–4
International Labour Organisation
    (ILO) 178
International Monetary Fund (IMF) 73,
    80, 96
international political time 130–1, 134–5
International Relations theory 2, 5,
    11–12, 63, 91, 103, 105, 110–11, 127,
    130, 138, 149–57, 162, 166, 174
International Tribunal for the Former
    Yugoslavia 37
Internet, the 197–8
Islam 27–8

Japan (civil society in) 40
Jubilee 2000 94

Kaldor, Mary 2–7, 119, 136–41, 157,
    161–2, 164, 188, 194
Kantianism 101, 103; neo- 116, 120
Kant, Immanuel 103, 105, 131–4, 138,
    145
Keane, John 19, 141, 162, 188
Keck, Margaret 157–61
Kenny, Michael 124–5
Kingsnorth, Paul 87, 89, 90
Klein, Naomi 5, 34, 87
Köhler, M. 120, 123
Konrad, George 107, 112
KOR (Poland) 40, 106, 161
Koselleck, R. 131–2
Kosovo 47, 61, 75
Kyoto Summit on Climate Change 92

law: global/cosmopolitan 38, 110, 115,
    122, 125, 137; international 49, 61, 75,
    78, 82, 110–11, 119, 125; 'of humanity'
    3, 115
League of Arab States 30
League of Nations 41
Left, the 88–90, 98

liberal democracy 5, 133, 183, 193, 198
liberal imperialism 8
liberalism 52–4, 58, 122, 173, 176, 178, 180, 183
Linklater, Andrew 5, 116–17, 130–1, 134–41, 143, 151
Lipschutz, Ronnie D. 114
Locke, John 18, 171

Machiavelli, Nicolo 48, 131, 134, 145
Maghreb, the (civil society in) 17, 23–30
Mamdani, Mahmood 31, 109
Marx, Karl 18, 89–90, 104, 131–2, 134, 138, 145, 171
Matthews, Jessica 3
Michnik, Adam 106
Mill, J.S. 133, 143
modernism 130, 134, 138, 142–5
modernity 20–2, 23, 62, 131–2, 135–6, 143, 145, 190
Monbiot, George 87, 89–90, 94, 96
Montesquieu 43
Morocco (civil society in) 32
multiculturalism 125, 133, 135
multilateral agreements 37–8, 86

nation state *see* state
neoconservatism 77–9, 80
neoliberalism 4–5, 12, 31, 48, 73, 81–2, 87, 108–9, 115, 119, 123, 126–7, 136, 151,
163, 171–2, 174–7, 181, 183
neo-Marxism 127, 135
network theory 157–8
New Right, the 91
new social movements *see* social movements
Nike Corporation 172, 177–8
non-governmental organisations (NGOs) 3, 9–10, 18, 34–5, 39–42, 44, 57–62, 70–1, 74, 94–8, 108–10, 119, 126, 136, 139–40, 142, 153, 160, 162–5, 173, 187, 189–91, 194, 197–8
non-violence 9, 19, 30, 61, 72, 81–2, 119
norms (in international society) 154–7
North American Free Trade Association (NAFTA) 45
North Atlantic Treaty Organisation (NATO) 49, 75

Oakeshott, Michael 11, 187–8, 195
Offe, Claus 87
Organisation for Economic Cooperation and Development (OECD) 86
Organisation for Security and Cooperation in Europe (OSCE) 161
Oxfam 57–8, 60

participation 2, 50, 70, 82–3
peace movement 10
People's Global Action 87
perfectionism 12, 187, 194
philosophy of history 11, 124, 130–4, 143–5
Pinochet, Augusto 75
Polanyi, Karl 180
political community 1–5, 82, 117, 122, 124–5, 134–5, 141, 179, 195–6
political majorities 8, 56
political parties 23, 25, 29, 44, 72, 88, 91, 94–5, 104, 108
'politics of faith' 12, 186–99
'politics of scepticism' 198–9
populations 173
post-Marxism 11, 130, 131, 140–1, 143–4
postmodernism 11, 109, 130, 140–1
progress 11, 132–5, 137, 139, 143–5
Project for a new America 76
public sphere 64, 120, 136, 179; global 121, 192

Reagan, Ronald 72, 91, 155
realism 11, 35, 54, 70, 111, 130–1, 134, 138, 141, 145, 149–50, 152–4; neo- 150–2, 165
Realpolitik 55
regime change 79
representative government 45, 83, 115, 194
republican tradition 124–5
revolution 104; American 46, 69; Bolshevik 89; French 132; Iranian 72
rights 8–10, 19–20, 23, 26–7, 42, 45, 54–5, 63–4, 79, 104–5, 114, 117, 119–22, 125, 127–8, 135–6, 140; human 1, 3, 8- 9, 41–2, 49, 52, 55–6, 59–62, 65, 70–2, 74, 79–80, 82, 93, 106–7, 110, 115, 117–20, 137, 154–6, 158–61, 179, 186, 188
Risse, Thomas 119–20, 153–6, 159
Rousseau J-J. 18
rule of law 2, 8–9, 20, 30, 32, 35–6, 48, 61, 75, 81–2, 136
Rumsfeld, Donald 45, 76
Rwandan genocide (1994) 37, 59, 60, 74

Salamon, Lester 3
Saul, J.R. 45
Seattle 73, 87–9, 96–7
Second World War 41, 58, 110, 199
Security Council (UN) 49, 61
self-determination 9, 23, 25, 29, 72, 82, 118–19, 133, 135, 141, 143
separation of powers 43
September 11 9–10, 42, 52, 61, 75–6, 78, 79, 103, 110–12, 192
Shaw, Martin 118, 122–3, 160, 171, 189
Sikkink, Kathryn 153, 155, 157–61
Skinner, Quentin 124
Skocpol, Theda 193
Smith, Adam 18
social contract 8, 55–6, 104
social movements 22, 26, 31, 70, 115–16, 126, 136, 189; new 71, 87, 108, 117, 158, 164–5
South Africa (civil society in) 72–3
sovereignty 1–2, 4–5, 10, 37, 52, 56–7, 59, 60–1, 69, 75, 103, 108, 114–18, 121–3, 140, 154, 183, 189, 191, 198; equal between nations 56–7, 63, 118
state 2–5, 9–12, 18, 22, 26, 32, 35–7, 42, 44, 48, 54–5, 69–70, 73, 103–5, 107, 109–10, 114, 116–18, 120–24, 126, 136, 149–57, 166, 173–6, 180, 186, 199; bifurcated 31; colonial 24–5, 30; global/world 35, 109–10, 121–3, 171; liberal 53–4, 175–6; system 1, 3, 21–2, 30–2, 117, 123, 127, 133–5, 154–5, 171, 174, 186–7
statism 70, 72, 120–2, 124–5, 128, 130

Taliban regime 60, 78
terrorism 111–12; *see also* war on
Thatcher, Margaret 92
Thompson, E.P. 21
Tlili, Béchir 23
Tocqueville, Alexis de 171
totalitarianism 106–7, 110
trade unions 26–9, 88, 91, 104, 108, 164, 178

Transparency International 36
Treaty of Westphalia 1; *see also* Westphalian system
Tunisia, civil society in 26

'uncivil' society 24, 26, 31–2, 75, 82, 199
UNESCO 41
United Nations (UN) 30, 35, 37, 39, 41–3, 49, 61, 71, 74–5, 78, 81–2, 92, 112, 118, 123, 172, 177, 188, 191–3, 195
urbanisation 62, 91
utopianism 71, 90

Wapner, Paul 157–8, 165
war: Afghanistan 77–8; crimes 39; humanitarian 61; Iraq 61, 75–9, 103, 110–12, 118; 'on terror' 9–10, 52, 75–7, 110–12
Weber, Max 95, 186, 195–6, 198
Welfare State 64
Wendt, Alexander 150–4
Westphalian model 1, 8, 10, 36–7, 69–70, 75, 77, 81–2, 114, 116–17, 120, 122–3, 128, 134, 139
World Bank 40, 73, 80, 96, 164, 180
World Court Project 38
World Economic Forum 94
world government 8, 37, 49, 150
World Health Organisation (WHO) 41
world political time *see* international political time
world polity *see* global polity
World Social Forum 5, 74, 81, 93–5, 192
World Trade Organisation (WTO) 39, 42, 73, 97, 180
World Wide Fund for Nature (WWF) 191

Young, Iris Marion 181

Zapatistas 87, 123, 141